# FALASTIN

A COOKBOOK

# FALASTIN

SAMI TAMIMI    TARA WIGLEY

Photography by Jenny Zarins

# Contents

# Foreword

I love Palestinian food. I probably love it more than any other cuisine. That's a tricky thing to say, I know, since I am not a Palestinian. As a Jewish boy from the Jerusalem of the 1970s and 80s, though, I probably had enough kubbeh, bamia and ma'amoul for these magnificent foods to insert themselves deep in my young psyche. Not to mention those dishes that were also becoming part of the nascent Israeli cuisine – like falafel, hummus and tabbouleh – either as a direct result of Palestinian influence on our food or through Jewish emigrants from the Arab world settling in the city.

I had been living outside Jerusalem for more than twenty years when I got to revisit all these pleasurable memories while writing *Jerusalem* with Sami Tamimi in 2012. That book was an unashamed celebration of a rather eclectic set of dishes that Sami and I liked to eat growing up, or that we felt were instrumental to understanding the soul of our city. The job was complicated, politically, since we had to put aside the harsh reality of the occupation of the West Bank. But it was a labour of love: love of ingredients, love of our city, love of our families and childhood memories. Through our friendship, helped by a 'healthy' distance of 3,600 kilometres separating London from Jerusalem, we told a story that was pure deliciousness and joy.

Once Sami and I put our proverbial pens down, though, we both knew that there was another story to tell, and that is the wider story of Palestinian cuisine: a tale of a formidable food nation that gave the region and the rest of the world some of its most beloved foods.

In *Falastin*, Tara and Sami have picked up the baton where it was left after *Jerusalem*. Once again, this is a purely delicious affair (you can take my word for it; I was lucky enough to be there when they tested the recipes). It is based on Sami's childhood in Palestine and Tara's journey into the universe of tahini, za'atar and precarious savoury rice cakes (i.e. maqlubeh). Being the two formidable culinary forces that they are, Tara and Sami are the best guides I can possibly think of to take you into this world, to learn, like me, to enjoy it and absolutely love it.

Yotam Ottolenghi

# Introduction

This is a book about Palestine – its food, its produce, its history, its future, its people and their voices. It is a book about the common themes that all these elements share, and how Palestine weaves narrative and cooking into the fabric of its identity. The two go hand-in-hand. Recipes are like stories: events brought to life and shared in the making and telling. They are passed from one person to the next, and in that movement, some details change, others come to the fore, while others will be left by the wayside. And stories are like recipes: a series of individual experiences blended together to create a whole. Where stories and recipes intersect is the nexus, the point, of this book. Rather than telling 'a' story or 'the' story of Palestine, then, we're telling lots of stories. These come in the form of both our recipes and the profiles of some of the people and places we've met along the way.

First, however, an outline of what is at the heart of this book: the story of Falastin, the place and its people; the story of *Falastin*, our book; and the story of Sami and Tara, your host and guide.

# Falastin: the place and people

There is no letter 'p' in the Arabic language so 'Falastin' is, on the one hand, simply the way 'Falastinians' refer to themselves. On the other hand, though – and in the Middle East there is always an 'on the other hand' – the word is a big one, going far beyond a straightforward label. It is about geography, history, language, land, identity and culture. Ask a Palestinian what the word 'Falastin' means to them: the answer will rarely be short and will often end with the word 'home'.

For us, for the purposes of our book, 'Falastin' is about all of these things. Geographically, it refers to a small piece of land at the eastern-most corner of the Mediterranean Sea where Palestinians have been living for many centuries. That this statement is so complicated by the fact that this land is also home to other peoples, Israelis, is something we are very mindful of. Our aim with *Falastin* is to tread the fine line between paying heed to the situation on one hand and remembering, at the same time, that our book is first and foremost a celebration of the food and people of Palestine.

As well as being a geographical label, it's also about identity. For us, it embraces all those who identify as Palestinian, wherever in the world they're now living. The Palestinian story, post 1948 and with the creation of Israel, could be seen as one of relocation. There are as many different stories as to why a Palestinian is now living where they are living as there are Palestinians. And with over 12 million worldwide, that's a lot.

There are those who've chosen to live abroad and those who have had no choice but to live abroad. There are those who have been displaced closer to home and those who are still living where their parents and grandparents lived before them. Some have known nothing but life in a refugee camp and have never seen the nearby coast, and others have travelled the world freely and have now chosen to return. And then there are those who've never actually been to the country itself but who still strongly identify as Palestinian, through the stories and memories passed down from their Palestinian family.

The people of Palestine go by several different names, depending on who you ask. Some favour 'Palestinian', others prefer 'the people of the north', 'Arabs of the Nagev', 'Arab refugees' or '48ers'. 'Arab-Israeli', 'Israeli-Arab' or 'Palestinian-Israeli' are also used. For us, the words 'Falastin' and 'Falastinian' are inclusive, managing to incorporate all these various words at the same time as somehow transcending their often loaded meanings.

# Falastin: our book

*Falastin* is a new kind of Palestinian cookbook: a contemporary collection of over 110 recipes we hope you'll cook, eat, love and make your own. It's the culmination of Sami's lifetime obsession with Middle Eastern food and cooking – born and raised in East Jerusalem, relocated to London in his late twenties, and a founding member of Ottolenghi – and Tara's decade-long obsession with Middle Eastern food and home cooking – raised in London and adopted into the Ottolenghi family.

The recipes come, therefore, from all sorts of places. Some are those Sami grew up with and which will always remind him of home. His father's easy za'atar eggs, for example, or his mother's buttermilk fattoush. Others are those most Palestinians grew up on: classics such as chicken musakhan or the upside-down rice cake, maqlubeh. One recipe – that for hummus – remains untouched from when Sami first published it in his second cookery book, *Jerusalem*. After all, there are some things that can't be played around with or improved upon.

We haven't felt bound by a set list of 'traditional Palestinian dishes', though. We'd rather shine a new light on an old classic than re-create it verbatim. Doing this – 'playing around' – is a risk, we know, because loyalty to the way a dish is cooked is not, of course, just about the dish. It's about tradition and identity and being able to own these things through food. The process has not always been easy for Sami. Like a lot of Palestinian chefs working today, this tension – between a sense of loyalty to the way a dish is traditionally cooked and the desire to move it forward so as to keep it fresh and relevant – is keenly felt.

If *Jerusalem* was Sami and Yotam's joint effort to celebrate the food of their home town and bring it to a wider audience, then *Falastin* is Sami and Tara's focus in on the food of Palestine. Speaking in general terms about 'Middle Eastern' food is rather like saying 'European food', or 'Italian food': it does not pay heed to all the distinct people, produce and dishes which distinguish one country from another within a region. It doesn't allow for the importance of sumac in a dish such as chicken musakhan to shine, for example, or reveal how many Gazan dishes have the trio of dill, garlic and chilli shaping them. It doesn't tell us anything about the red tahini of Gaza or the white salty cheese of Nablus or Akka. Keeping our focus exclusively on Palestine allows us to explore not only the food of this land and people, but the regional differences within.

At the same time as exploring the regions of Palestine, the purpose of *Falastin* is to be full of recipes that work for and delight the home cook today. We really want you to cook from the recipes in our book – to find them practical and doable as well as delicious. This means you'll find fewer recipes for stuffed vegetables in *Falastin* than you would in a 'traditional' Palestinian cookbook, fewer recipes for celebratory dishes which take half a day to prepare, less call for hard-to-find kishek or jameed, the fermented discs of yoghurt and wheat in which to bake a leg of lamb. Loyalty to the Palestinian pantry, though – and a reliance on the ground allspice and cumin, olive oil, pulses, grains, za'atar, sumac, lemons, yoghurt, dill, garlic and green chillies which fill it – is unwavering. Our recipes feel distinctly Palestinian, even when they are presented in a slightly new light. Luckily, for those living outside the Middle East, the Palestinian pantry is also one which can be easily sourced and put together from mainstream shops and sites.

As well as our recipes, another way to get to know the country is through its people. When talking about Palestine in general terms, conversation can quickly become political and difficult. The day-to-day frustrations for a Palestinian trying to go about their business, when heard by those who don't need to carry an ID card with them or require a permit to travel around their country, are easy not to comprehend. For most Palestinians in the West Bank, the reality of checkpoints, a separation wall, and the complicated systems and differing rules surrounding areas A, B and C (see page 130 for more on this) makes, frankly, for a pretty grim picture.

Focus in, though – travel around the country meeting and eating with people – and the picture painted is a different one. The link between the land and the produce and the people who grow, farm and make it is strong. Meet someone who explains how they make their labneh or yoghurt from the milk of their own sheep or goat, for example, or smell the fresh za'atar leaves on a small farm holding on a sunny spring afternoon, and the outlook is clearly brighter. How things are seen depends on who is looking and through what lens. For all the differing points of view, though, the reality of someone's story – the story they live with day in, day out – cannot be denied. This is why we want to tell the story of *Falastin* through profiles as well as recipes. These are not our stories. They're not even always our views. They are, however, stories we've been moved to tell from people that we've met.

Writing these stories – indeed writing a Palestinian cookbook – feels like a big responsibility. All the food and hospitality that a recipe book celebrates must be served, in the case of Palestine, against a very sobering backdrop. We want this backdrop to be properly painted – things cannot be changed until they are fully seen – but, also, our hope is that everyone will come around the table to cook, eat and talk. When *Jerusalem* was published, Sami was asked many times, with varying degrees of irony to seriousness, about the role hummus could play in the Middle Eastern peace process. On the one hand, as Sami used to say, it's only food. It's chickpeas, it's lemons, it's tahini. At the same time, though, food can mean more. Sharing food is not just about sharing food. It's about sharing time, space, ideas and stories.

## Sami Tamimi: your host

Palestinian home cooks tend to be women. Palestinian cookbooks tend to be
written by women sharing the recipes they have, in turn, learnt from the women
in their lives. Stories of wise ums and tetas – mothers and grandmothers – and
aunties pepper the pages of the traditional Palestinian cookbook. This Palestinian
home cook and chef, though, lost his mother when he was young – Sami's mother
died when he was just seven – and he spent much of his childhood being shooed
away from the kitchen by aunties and sisters.

How did this little Palestinian boy from East Jerusalem, then – whose place
was certainly *not* meant to be in the kitchen – end up spending the best part of his
life at the stove?

Sami left the cobbled streets of East Jerusalem when he was seventeen.
Home was full and busy growing up. On top of the seven kids Sami's dad, Hassan,
had with Na'ama, Sami's mother, five more were born after he remarried. Twelve
kids calls for a lot of pita and a really big pot. Hungry for life further afield, Sami
headed first to West Jerusalem, finding work washing dishes in a hotel restaurant,
before moving on to Tel Aviv. He spent twelve years there, learning his trade, the
last five spent at Lilith, which was the restaurant to be at then. Setting sail next
for London, Sami firmly found his feet at Baker & Spice, where he met Yotam
Ottolenghi and soon after they set up Ottolenghi together.

Life then happened and, before Sami knew it, the gap between leaving home
and returning to see his family was seventeen years. Seventeen years is a long
time and a lot had changed. At the same time as Sami was becoming a big name in

cooking, over thirty nieces and nephews had been born, siblings had got divorced and remarried and Sami's father had died. A long time for everything to change but, at the same time, for nothing to change when Sami, after nearly twenty years, went home to reunite with his family.

Sinking into one of the enormous sofas lining the walls of his sister Sawsan's sitting room, Sami knew exactly what would follow. A cold sweet juice first appears, innocently suggesting that, this time, he might be let off the onslaught of food, gossip and teasing to come. Wishful thinking, of course. Next, little bowls of nuts and pickles, saucers of olive oil and za'atar, chopped salad, Arabic salad, monk's salad and tabbouleh salad are shared. Then the magnificent 'upside down' maqlubeh appears, in all its glory, flipped over on to a large platter, ready to be tucked into and served with thick yoghurt.

And finally, of course – this is a family, after all – the teasing. For all the big, probing questions that could follow so much time apart, Sami and his siblings just tease each other instead. About growing old and growing tummies and joking about things they used to do as kids. Everyone thinks everyone else is just a little bit bonkers – everyone is a bit bonkers! – no one really listens but, at the same time, the love in the air is thick enough to bottle. In the absence of words which can do justice to a family's longing to connect, it falls on the food they are sharing to do the job. Bread is torn apart and handed around.

Maybe this scene contains some clues to the question of what got Sami into the kitchen and kept him there for so long. Maybe it was the memory of his mother's food – which played such a big and important part in the first six years of Sami's life – and his desire never to let this connection disappear. Maybe it was his memory of the food of Palestine more generally – carried with him every time he drizzles tahini on his toast or sprinkles a pinch of za'atar on his morning eggs or white cheese. Maybe it was the sheer *lack* of questions being asked when you are in the kitchen, on your feet, working hard and working fast. Sometimes it's enough just to be getting food that makes you happy on the table for people who are hungry in the hope that it, too, will make them happy. Maybe he's just really, really good at chargrilling wedges of aubergines. Maybe it's all these things combined.

*Falastin* is the book which brings things full circle for Sami. It's his love letter to his country and also to his mother. It's also for his Falastinian family more generally, whom he travelled from all those years ago but for whom, really, he still cooks every day.

## Tara Wigley: your guide

Tara has been part of the Ottolenghi family since 2010. She turned up on her bike, fresh out of cookery school in Ireland, where she'd been for three months. She'd gone there with her eighteen-month-old twins and a great big Bosnian dog named Andie. Tara was leaving a decade in publishing. The plan – the answer to the question of why she was trading in words and writing for food and cooking – was not yet clear.

Luckily, though, Tara didn't need to see the light. In the Ottolenghi family, it quickly became clear, you *can* actually have your cake and eat it; you could learn to cook and still work with words. After a few years collaborating with Yotam on both the writing and cooking of his recipes in the test kitchen, Tara focused exclusively on the writing side of things. She remains a passionate home cook and knows very well how to fill a table with a feast.

For all that Tara is, then – food writer, feast-maker, home cook, mum – she is not, clearly, Palestinian. She has travelled the country many times over several years, inadvertently run the Palestine marathon (the plan was to do just the half!) and fully immersed herself in the food but, still, the point needs addressing. When it comes to all things Palestinian, questions about legitimacy, ownership and who gets to tell the story are very close to the surface. It's one of the reasons why we wanted to tell lots of stories – through the profiles – rather than 'a' story or 'the' story (or even 'Sami's' story).

Tara's story, indeed, is more one of growing up in south London, eating lots of pork fillet, smashed thin, dipped in breadcrumbs and pan-fried. When it came to inheriting recipes from grannies, the heights of exoticism came from the packet of Angel Delight tipped out into a bowl and whisked up with milk. With a choice of five flavours and with a sponge finger sticking out of the side, the pinnacle of 1980s sophistication had clearly been reached.

It's all a far cry, indeed, from the world of tahini and olive oil Tara is dripping in today. Pomegranates and za'atar were things she wasn't going to hear of, let alone taste, for another thirty years. The first thing Tara remembers saying to Sami, in fact, was that she thought preserved lemons tasted like soap! Little did she know that, far from tasting of soap, these little bursts of flavour would be the beginning of her culinary epiphany. That her love of food was not going to come in five flavours with a sponge finger sticking out the side; that her home was soon going to be filled with the smell of aubergines charring on the stove and that her fruit bowl was going to be taken over by lemons. Barely a meal now gets made without the chopped skin and flesh of a preserved lemon being added. Tahini sauce is included in every supper, every egg gets sprinkled with za'atar and drizzled in olive oil, and shatta is such an addiction that she and Sami now think of it as 'shat*tara*'. Tara is knee-deep stuck in tahini and, as anyone who has ever been stuck knee-deep in tahini knows, it's wonderfully impossible to get out. This is not Tara's story to tell but it is her adventure. If any of our readers become half as obsessed with tahini or shatta as Tara has become since discovering them, then we'll know that the adventure has been a shared one.

Sahtein! Welcome to *Falastin*: a book of recipes and stories. Sami, wooden spoon in hand, is your host and Tara, pen in hand, is your guide. Our hope with the recipes is that they will bring you lots of great meals, good times and a strong connection with Palestinian cooking. Our hope with the stories is that they make you want to find out more, talk more, question more, ask more. The story of Palestine – its past, present and, crucially, its future – needs to keep being told, heard and celebrated.

BREAKFAST

Breakfast in Palestine is a proper meal. This is no quick bowl of cereal or piece of fruit eaten on the go: it's a spread of dishes, often savoury, served with sweet mint tea or a short black coffee, to really fuel you up for the day. 'Go to work on an egg', indeed. And then some! We have included some quick one-bowl options – fruit and yoghurt with sesame crumble, for example, and easy eggs with za'atar and lemon – but if you want to make a feast of it, then breakfast is a great place to start.

Breakfast, in fact, is where it all started for Sami, whose first job aged sixteen was working as a kitchen porter in a large hotel in West Jerusalem. Seeing Sami pay more attention to what the chefs were doing than to the dirty dishes at hand, head chef Hans saw his potential and soon moved him up to breakfast service. Cracking about 300 eggs every morning to make scrambled eggs for 150 hungry people allowed Sami to perfect the art of cracking eggs – with conviction, in short – to learn how to make scrambled eggs in a pot wider than his sixteen-year-old skinny self and, crucially, to know that he'd found the place he was meant to be.

If either the thought of 300 eggs or, indeed, some of what is included on the breakfast table in Palestine all sounds like a bit too much for the early morning, that's totally fine. One of the many great things about the dishes in this chapter is that they all work as well for lunch and supper (or even pudding, in the case of the yoghurt and fruit bowl) as they do first thing.

On the table there can be bowls of thick, creamy, warm hummus. All sorts of pickles and olives sit alongside, with a bowl of plain yoghurt and a freshly chopped salad. Cubes of white cheese might also be there, sprinkled with za'atar, sumac or little black nigella seeds and drizzled generously with olive oil. Or a thick spread of labneh, hard-boiled eggs and sliced cucumber. Little cubes of halva, maybe, if something sweet is wanted to go with a short black coffee. Whatever the combination of dishes, the holy trinity that is lemon juice, olive oil and za'atar should always be within arm's reach in order to make everything sing. And bread, always bread: warm, fluffy and freshly baked. If you want to bake for the breakfast table, there are a few recipes in the bread and pastries chapter which work particularly well. See page 282 for the Jerusalem sesame bread, for example, or page 287 for sweet tahini rolls.

For those with more time at the weekend, things such as falafel, fritters, labneh and pickles really come into play. These are as good for snacks before supper as they are for breakfast, so have a look through the Snacks, Spreads and Sauces chapter as well, to find these recipes there.

# Hassan's easy eggs with za'atar and lemon

These eggs will always remind Sami of his father, Hassan, who used to make them at the weekend for Sami and his siblings. It's proof, if ever proof were needed, that few things are not improved by the addition of some good-quality olive oil, a squeeze of lemon and a sprinkle of za'atar. Serve with some warm bread or pita to mop up the oil.

*Playing around:* Eggs pair well with all sorts of chilli flakes, so use what you have: Urfa chilli flakes look particularly great, if you have some, and bring a smoky flavour. Sumac can replace the za'atar, and cubes of creamy avocado are also a lovely addition.

---

Bring a medium saucepan of water to the boil and carefully lower in the eggs. Boil for 5–6 minutes, then refresh at once under plenty of cold running water.

Meanwhile, whisk together the lemon juice, olive oil and za'atar and set aside.

Peel and roughly quarter the eggs, by hand so that they're not too neat, and arrange on a serving plate, yolk side up. Sprinkle with ¼ teaspoon of salt and a generous grind of black pepper and drizzle over the lemon juice and olive oil mix. Sprinkle with the spring onions and chilli and serve at once.

**Serves four**

6 eggs
1½ tbsp lemon juice
3 tbsp olive oil
1 tbsp za'atar
2 spring onions, finely sliced (20g)
⅛ tsp Aleppo (or any other) chilli flakes
Salt and black pepper

# Fresh herb omelette with caramelised onions
## *Ijeh*

Palestinian omelettes have a little bit of flour and baking powder added to the mix. This (along with the fact that they are fried in a generous amount of olive oil) makes them something between an omelette, a pancake and a frittata. They're crisp around the edges, puffed up in the middle, and comforting through and through. The fresh herbs and white cheese are traditional, the caramelised onions less so.

Ijeh can be eaten either warm and fresh from the pan, for breakfast or a light supper, or at room temperature later if taken to work or on a picnic. Serve with a chopped (see page 92) or leafy (see page 93) salad and some bread, if you like.

*Getting ahead / batch cooking*: You can double or triple the quantities for the caramelised onions: they keep well in the fridge for up to 5 days and are lovely to have around, to make more omelettes with or to spoon on top of cheese and bread.

*Playing around*: Use whatever soft herbs you have and like – dill, chives, tarragon, basil, coriander – in any combination; they all work well. Just keep the total amount about the same.

**Serves four**

110ml olive oil
30g unsalted butter
3 onions, thinly sliced (450g)
8 eggs, beaten
2½ tbsp plain flour
6 spring onions, trimmed and finely sliced (90g)
20g parsley leaves, half roughly chopped and the remainder left whole
20g mint leaves, half roughly chopped and the remainder left whole
1 green chilli, deseeded and finely chopped
¾ tsp dried mint
125g feta, roughly crumbled
½ tsp baking powder
2½ tsp za'atar
Salt and black pepper

Put 2 tablespoons of oil and all the butter into a medium frying pan and place on a medium-high heat. Add the onions and cook for about 20 minutes, stirring from time to time, until deep brown and caramelised. Set aside for about 10 minutes, to cool.

Put the eggs and flour into a mixing bowl and whisk well to combine, then add the spring onion, chopped parsley, chopped mint, chilli, dried mint, 50g of feta, ¾ teaspoon of salt and a good grind of black pepper. Mix well to combine. Add the baking powder, mix again to combine and set aside.

Combine the caramelised onion with the picked herbs, remaining feta and 1½ teaspoons of za'atar, and set aside.

Put 2 teasoons of oil into a medium frying pan and place on a medium-high heat. Add 4–5 tablespoons of the egg mixture – about 35g if you're weighing out – and cook for about 1½ minutes, until the bottom is golden. Using a spatula, carefully flip the omelette and cook for another 30 seconds or so, until golden brown on both sides. Carefully slide the omelette on to a plate and return the pan to the heat. Repeat the process with the remaining oil and egg mixture, to make eight omelettes in total.

Divide the omelettes between four plates, two per person. Top with the caramelised onion mixture, sprinkle with the remaining teaspoon of za'atar, and serve.

# Fruit and yoghurt with sesame crumble and tahini-date syrup

For those who like yoghurt and fruit in the morning, rather than a more hearty chickpea-based breakfast, this is a great (though not strictly traditional) choice. The crumble is unusually *unsweet*, by a lot of granola standards, which we love, allowing for the tahini-date syrup to really stand out.

*Getting ahead / batch cooking:* Double or triple the recipe for the crumble, if you like, so that you're all set for the next breakfast (or snack). It keeps well in a sealed container for 2 weeks.

---

**Serves four**

600g Greek-style yoghurt
80g strawberries, quartered
40g pomegranate seeds (from
    ½ a pomegranate)
60g pistachio kernels, roughly
    chopped
2 tsp dried rose petals (optional)

**Sesame crumble**
50g white sesame seeds
25g black sesame seeds (or just
    increase total of white sesame
    seeds to 75g)
150g rolled jumbo oats
50g flaked almonds
¼ tsp flaked sea salt
1½ tsp cardamom pods (about 14),
    outer shells crushed, removed
    and discarded; seeds crushed in a
    pestle and mortar (or ¼ tsp ground
    cardamom)
50g smooth unsweetened
    peanut butter
100g honey
1 egg white
1 tbsp rose water
2 tbsp olive oil

**Tahini-date syrup**
70g date syrup
50g tahini
2 tsp orange blossom water

Preheat the oven to 160°C fan.

To make the crumble, stir together all the sesame seeds, the oats, almonds, salt and cardamom in a large mixing bowl. Put the peanut butter, honey, egg white, rose water and oil into a separate bowl and whisk until well combined. Add the wet mixture to the dry ingredients and, using a rubber spatula or your hands, mix until everything is well coated. Spread out on a parchment-lined baking tray and bake for 18–20 minutes, stirring once or twice during baking, until golden brown. Remove from the oven and set aside to cool completely, then transfer to a food processor. Blitz as far as you want to take it: for just a few seconds if you want to keep the crumble rough and granola-like, and for longer if you prefer the texture sandy.

To make the tahini-date syrup, place all the ingredients in a bowl along with 40ml of water. Whisk well to combine and set aside.

To serve, divide the yoghurt between four bowls and drizzle over the tahini-date syrup. Follow this with a generous helping of the crumble – and top with the fruit, pistachios and rose petals, if using.

*Pictured overleaf*

# Scrambled red shakshuka

Shakshuka: the signature breakfast of the Middle East. It's a wonderfully informal dish, brought to the table in the pan it's cooked in and served straight from there. There are so many versions of shakshuka, all variations on the same theme of eggs cooked in a nice thick sauce. The eggs are usually braised, which is what we've done with the green shakshuka opposite. Here they've been gently scrambled.

*Getting ahead:* The base sauce can be made a day or two ahead, up to the point before the eggs are added. The feta can also be marinated up to 3 days in advance. Make more of the feta than you need here, if you like: it's a lovely thing to dot over roasted wedges of sweet potato, or all sorts of salads.

*Playing around:* The shakshuka base can go in all sorts of directions and colours: red here with the tomatoes and red peppers, or green with any leaves and herbs in need of using up. Either way, it's a really versatile and robust dish, so feel free to play around with the spices and toppings. Spice-wise, for example, smoked paprika and roughly crushed caraway seeds work in the red shakshuka instead of the cumin seeds and regular paprika. Toppings-wise, for either of the shakshukas, chunks of tangy feta, black olives or finely chopped preserved lemon skin work well dotted on top. A drizzle of tahini or a spoonful of yoghurt is also great when serving, along with some crusty fresh bread and a crisp green salad.

**Serves two generously**

45g feta, roughly crumbled
5g parsley leaves, roughly chopped
¾ tsp Aleppo chilli (or ½ tsp regular chilli flakes)
75ml olive oil
1½ tsp coriander seeds, lightly toasted and roughly crushed in a pestle and mortar
1 onion, thinly sliced (150g)
1 red pepper, deseeded and cut into long slices, 1cm thick (140g)
3 garlic cloves, crushed
½ tsp cumin seeds, lightly toasted and roughly crushed in a pestle and mortar
1 tsp tomato purée
¼ tsp paprika
5–6 tomatoes, roughly chopped (500g)
75g cherry tomatoes
2 tsp shatta (see page 73) (or rose harissa, as an alternative)
4 eggs, lightly beaten
Salt and black pepper

Place the feta in a bowl with the parsley, ½ teaspoon of chilli flakes, 3 tablespoons of oil and ½ teaspoon of coriander seeds. Mix well and set aside (in the fridge if making in advance) until needed.

Put the remaining 2 tablespoons of oil into a large sauté pan (for which you have a lid) and place on a medium-high heat. Add the onion and cook for 5 minutes, until softened and lightly browned. Add the red pepper, cook for another 5 minutes, then add the garlic, cumin, tomato purée, paprika and the remaining teaspoon of coriander seeds. Cook for another minute, until fragrant, and then add all the tomatoes, the shatta (or harissa), 80ml of water, 1 teaspoon of salt and a generous grind of black pepper. Cook on a medium heat for about 15 minutes, stirring occasionally, until the tomatoes have broken down and the sauce has thickened.

Add a pinch of salt and a good grind of black pepper to the eggs and mix well. Slowly pour this into the tomato mixture, swirling the pan and giving it a couple of gentle folds: you don't want the eggs to be too mixed in. Lower the heat to medium-low, cover the pan and leave to cook for 4 minutes.

Remove the pan from the heat, spoon over the marinated feta, sprinkle with the remaining ¼ teaspoon of Aleppo chilli and serve at once.

*Pictured overleaf*

# Green shakshuka

*Getting ahead:* As with the red shakshuka opposite, the base can be prepared a day or two in advance if you want to get ahead. If you do this, just hold back on adding the lemon juice (as well as the eggs) until you are ready to eat. Adding the lemon juice too early to the leaves will cause them to discolour.

*Playing around:* Chunks of feta dotted on top are a lovely addition here, instead of or as well as the yoghurt. A final sprinkle of za'atar also works really well.

**Serves two**

2½ tbsp olive oil
1 tsp green shatta (see page 73)
  (or 1 tsp green harissa, as an
  alternative)
15g unsalted butter
1 large leek, halved lengthways and
  the white parts sliced 2cm thick
  (180g)
400g Swiss chard, leaves pulled
  off the stems and chopped into
  roughly 2cm pieces; stems cut into
  roughly 2cm dice
3 large spring onions, thinly
  sliced (60g)
½ a green chilli, finely chopped (5g)
1 garlic clove, crushed
¾ tsp ground cumin
¾ tsp ground coriander
20g parsley leaves, roughly chopped
10g dill, roughly chopped
1 tbsp lemon juice
4 eggs
Salt and black pepper
Greek-style yoghurt, to serve
  (optional)

Mix 1½ teaspoons of olive oil with the shatta (or harissa) and set aside.

Put the remaining 2 tablespoons of oil and all the butter into a large sauté pan (for which you have a lid) and place on a medium heat. Once hot, add the leek, then reduce the heat to medium-low and cook for 6 minutes, covered, stirring a few times, until the leek has softened but has not taken on any colour.

Add the chard stems – in batches, if you need to – and spring onions and cook for another 6 minutes, covered, stirring occasionally, until completely softened. Add the chilli, garlic and ground spices and cook, uncovered, for another minute before adding the chard leaves, parsley, dill and ¾ teaspoon of salt. Stir to wilt slightly, then add 100ml of water and cook for 10 minutes, covered, until the leaves cook down and completely wilt. Add the lemon juice, then use a spoon to make four wells in the mix. Crack an egg into each well and sprinkle each one lightly with salt and pepper. Cover the pan and cook for a final 4 minutes or so, until the egg whites are set but the yolks are still runny. Dot the shatta-oil mix over the eggs and serve at once, with a spoonful of yoghurt alongside, if desired.

*Pictured overleaf*

# Ful medames

Ful medames is best known as an Egyptian staple. It's just as popular in Palestine, though, particularly during Ramadan where it's often served for suhur, the pre-fast Ramadan meal. As with all pulses, the dish either sets you up for the day if eaten in the morning or provides comfort at the end of it if eaten for a simple supper. Warm pita, as ever, is a must.

*Playing around:* We've given the directions for some sumac onions, a simple salsa and a soft-boiled egg but, really, you can go in all sorts of directions: fried eggs, a simple sprinkle of parsley, some chopped spring onions, coarsely grated hard-boiled eggs – they all work well.

*Dried vs. tinned fava beans:* We choose to start with tinned beans here because they are easier to find than dried and, also, they cook with much more consistency. Dried beans also require peeling, which rather takes the edge off the quick morning option (see page 340 for more on this).

---

Add a litre of water to a medium saucepan and bring to the boil. Add the beans and simmer on a medium heat for 5 minutes, just to warm through and soften up. Drain, reserving about 50ml of the water, and return the beans to the pan. Add the 50ml of reserved cooking water to the beans, along with 2 tablespoons of lemon juice, the garlic, chilli, cumin and ¾ teaspoon of salt. Using a fork, crush the beans to form a rough mash. Set aside (or keep warm, if eating soon) until needed.

Place the onion in a bowl with ¼ teaspoon of salt. Use your hands to rub the salt in a bit, then set aside for 10 minutes, for the onions to soften. Mix in the sumac and parsley and set aside until needed.

To make the salsa, put the avocado and tomato in a bowl with 2 tablespoons of lemon juice and ¼ teaspoon of salt. Mix to combine and set aside.

When ready to serve, heat through the fava bean mixture, if needed, then transfer it to a large serving platter. Smooth out the surface and make a little well in the centre. Top with the salsa, followed by the onions and a drizzle of oil. Serve as is, with a wedge of lemon to squeeze over, or with a soft-boiled egg on top, if desired, and some warm pita alongside.

**Serves two generously, or four if bulked up with an egg and pita**

3 x 400g tins of cooked fava beans, drained and rinsed (470g)
3 lemons: squeeze 2 to get 60ml juice and cut the third into wedges, to serve
4 garlic cloves, crushed
½ a green chilli, finely chopped
1½ tsp ground cumin
½ small red onion, thinly sliced (60g)
¾ tsp sumac
5g picked parsley leaves
1 large avocado, flesh cut into ½cm dice
1 tomato, cut into ½cm dice (70g)
2 tbsp olive oil
Salt
4 soft-boiled eggs, to serve (optional)
Warm pita bread (shop-bought or see page 278 for homemade), to serve

# Warm hummus with toasted bread and pine nuts
## Fattet hummus

Fatteh roughly translates as 'crushed' or 'crumbled'. It refers to a group of dishes where chunks of flatbread (either stale bread in need of using up, or fresh) are layered in a dish with various toppings. Fattet hummus, where the layers are chickpea, tahini and yoghurt-based, feels like a sort of savoury chickpea 'bread pudding'. It's warm, comforting, hearty and rich and can be eaten for breakfast, lunch or supper.

*Dried vs. tinned chickpeas:* Instructions are given for dried chickpeas. If starting with tinned, drain and rinse the chickpeas and put them into a pan with 600ml of water, 1 teaspoon of ground cumin and the 4 whole garlic cloves. Simmer for just 8–10 minutes, then transfer them to a blender or food processor, as per the recipe instructions, along with the yoghurt, tahini, lemon juice and remaining garlic.

---

Preheat the oven to 160°C fan.

Put the pita pieces into a bowl with 2 tablespoons of olive oil, ½ teaspoon of cumin and ¼ teaspoon of salt. Mix well until coated, then tip out on to a parchment-lined baking tray. Bake for 20–25 minutes, or until the pita is golden and crispy. Transfer two-thirds of the pita to a 30 x 20cm dish with sides which rise up about 8cm (or individual plates with a lip, if making individual portions) and set the remaining third aside.

Combine the parsley, lemon zest, 60ml of olive oil and ⅛ teaspoon of salt in a small bowl and set aside.

Drain the chickpeas and put them into a large saucepan, for which you have a lid, along with the extra ¼ teaspoon of bicarbonate of soda, the 4 whole garlic cloves and the remaining 1 teaspoon of ground cumin. Pour over 1 litre of water and bring to the boil on a high heat. Lower to a simmer, cover loosely with the lid and cook on medium-low for about 30–40 minutes, stirring a few times, removing the scum as you go. Add a bit more water, if you need to, to keep the chickpeas submerged, until they are completely soft and cooked through. Stir through ½ teaspoon of salt, then (without draining the chickpeas, as you need the cooking water later on) transfer just under half the cooked chickpeas (200g) to a blender or food processor along with the yoghurt, tahini, lemon juice, the crushed garlic clove, ¾ teaspoon of salt and 100ml of the hot cooking liquid. Blitz until smooth and set aside. Keep this and the remaining chickpeas in the pan warm.

When ready to serve, top the pita in the baking dish (or individual plates) with half the pine nuts, two-thirds of the whole chickpeas and 100ml of their cooking liquid. Pour over all of the chickpea-tahini sauce and stir together. Top with the remaining pita, the remaining chickpeas (but without any extra cooking liquid at this stage) and the remaining pine nuts. Spoon over the parsley oil, sprinkle with the sumac and paprika and serve at once.

**Serves six for breakfast or as a side for lunch or supper**

3 pitas (shop-bought or see page 278 for homemade), torn into roughly 2–3cm pieces (200g)
90ml olive oil
1½ tsp ground cumin
10g parsley leaves, finely chopped
2 lemons: finely grate the zest of 1 (to get 1 tsp), then squeeze both to get 60ml juice
250g dried chickpeas, soaked overnight in double their volume of water and 1 tsp bicarbonate of soda (or 600g cooked chickpeas – the best part of 3 tins)
¼ tsp bicarbonate of soda (you don't need this if you are starting with tinned chickpeas)
5 garlic cloves, 4 peeled and left whole, 1 crushed
200g Greek-style yoghurt
150g tahini
60g pine nuts, lightly toasted (see page 339)
½ tsp sumac
¼ tsp paprika
Salt

# Hummus: two ways

If anything is going to keep you going until lunch it's a dish of hummus to start the day. It's filling and hearty and pairs with all sorts of things. If meatballs seem a bit too epic for breakfast (though they're no more epic than the bacon or sausage we might not think twice about), try the version with fried aubergine. Cubes of aubergine have a 'meaty' quality which makes them a great substitute for meat, if you're looking for one.

We like to double the quantity for the hummus and make both toppings at the same time so that there is something for everyone (and both things for some!). Either way, serve the hummus with warm pita (see page 278, or shop-bought) for scooping, along with a chopped salad (see page 92) to lighten things up. And if this still all sounds a bit too much for breakfast, that's fine: it works just as well for lunch or supper instead.

*Getting ahead:* Hummus should, ideally, be served freshly made and still warm. For anyone who's grown up on little tubs of hummus bought from the refrigerated section of a supermarket aisle, eating it while still warm, smooth, creamy and 'loose' will be a revelation. If you do want to make it in advance, though, that's fine: just store it in an air-tight container and keep it in the fridge for up to 4 days. If the hummus develops a bit of a 'skin' then just give it a stir before serving. The most important thing if storing in the fridge, is to bring it back to room temperature before serving, to warm and loosen up.

The meatballs can be made, rolled and kept in the fridge for a day before serving, all ready to fry. If doing this, store them in an airtight container but don't pack them too tightly: you want them to keep their round shape. They also freeze well, for up to a month. If you fry them from frozen they will need a couple more minutes in the oven to warm through.

---

To make the hummus, drain the chickpeas and place them in a medium saucepan on a high heat. Add the bicarbonate of soda and cook for about 3 minutes, stirring constantly. Add 1½ litres of water and bring to the boil. Cook for about 30 minutes – timing can vary from 20 to 40 minutes depending on the freshness of the chickpeas – skimming off any foam that appears. The chickpeas are ready when they collapse easily when pressed between thumb and finger: almost but not quite mushy.

Drain the chickpeas and transfer them to a food processor. Process to form a stiff paste and then, with the machine still running, add the tahini, lemon juice, garlic and 1½ teaspoon of salt. Finally, slowly drizzle in the iced water and continue to process for another 5 minutes: this will feel like a long time but it is what is needed to get a very smooth and creamy paste. Transfer to a bowl and set aside at room temperature, until needed. If you are making it in advance then transfer to a sealed container and keep in the fridge. Remove it half an hour before serving, to bring it back to room temperature, and give it a good stir if a 'skin' has formed.

*Continued overleaf*

## Serves six

### Hummus
250g dried chickpeas, soaked overnight in double their volume of water
1 tsp bicarbonate of soda
270g tahini
60ml lemon juice
4 garlic cloves, crushed
100ml ice-cold water
Salt

### Meatballs (for kofta version)
500g beef or veal mince (or a mixture of both)
1 small onion, peeled and coarsely grated (120g)
1 large tomato, coarsely grated and skin discarded (65g)
20g parsley, finely chopped
1 red chilli, deseeded and finely chopped
About 45ml olive oil, to fry
Black pepper

### Topping (for kofta version)
1 tbsp olive oil
25g pine nuts
5g parsley, roughly chopped
½ tsp Aleppo chilli flakes (or ¼ tsp regular chilli flakes)
A few small picked mint leaves (optional)

### Aubergines (for aubergine version)
2 large aubergines, cut into roughly 2cm cubes (500g)
About 300ml sunflower oil, to fry
160g walnut halves, roughly chopped
10g parsley leaves, roughly chopped
10g mint leaves, roughly chopped
2 tbsp lemon juice
2 tbsp olive oil
½ tsp Aleppo chilli flakes

*If making the kofta version:* Place all the ingredients for the meatballs, apart from the olive oil, in a medium bowl with 1 teaspoon of salt and a good grind of black pepper. Using your hands, mix well to combine. With wet hands, roll the mixture into roughly 3cm balls (weighing about 15g each): you should make about 45 balls.

Put the tablespoon of oil for the topping into a large frying pan and place on a medium heat. Add the pine nuts and cook for a minute, stirring constantly, until they are golden brown. Spoon the nuts, along with the oil from the pan, into a little bowl and set aside.

Add a tablespoon of the oil for frying to the same pan and place on a medium heat. Add a third of the meatballs – or as many as you can fit into the pan without overcrowding – and cook for about 3 minutes, turning throughout so that all sides take on colour and the balls are just cooked through. Keep them somewhere warm while you continue with the remaining balls, adding another tablespoon of oil with each batch.

When ready to serve, spoon the hummus into individual shallow bowls, creating a slight hollow in the centre of each. Divide the meatballs between the bowls, placing them in the middle of the hummus, and spoon over the pine nuts and their cooking oil. Sprinkle over the parsley, chilli and mint, if using, and serve with a final drizzle of olive oil.

*If making the aubergine version:* Place the aubergines in a colander placed over a bowl or in the sink and sprinkle over 1 teaspoon of salt. Use your hands to mix well, then set aside for about 45 minutes: this is so that the bitter juices can be released (see page 335 for more). Transfer the aubergines to a tray lined with kitchen paper and pat dry as best you can.

Put the sunflower oil into a medium frying pan and place on a medium-high heat. Once hot, add the aubergines – in two or three batches so as to not overcrowd the pan – and fry for about 8 minutes, until completely softened and golden brown. Using a slotted spoon, transfer the aubergines to another tray lined with kitchen paper (or the same tray lined with fresh kitchen paper) and set aside, for the excess oil to be absorbed, while you continue with the remaining batches. Transfer the aubergines to a bowl, add the walnuts, parsley, mint, lemon, olive oil and Aleppo chilli and mix well to combine.

When ready to serve, spoon the hummus into individual serving bowls, creating a small well in the middle of each portion. Spoon in the aubergine and serve at once.

# Warm chickpeas with green chilli sauce and toasted pita
## *Musabaha*

The word musabaha means 'swimming' or 'floating', here describing the chickpeas floating around in the tahini sauce. It's essentially hummus a step or two before it gets blitzed. The dish should be warm and creamy enough to eat with a spoon or a strip of pita. This is lovely for breakfast, lunch or supper.

*Getting ahead:* The toasted pita can be made up to a day ahead and kept in a sealed container at room temperature. The green chilli sauce can be made a few hours in advance, but hold back on the parsley until just before serving: it will discolour if it sits around. The chickpeas can be made a few hours in advance and just warmed through to serve. Once assembled, the dish needs to be eaten fresh and warm.

---

Drain the soaked chickpeas and put them into a large saucepan. Cover with plenty of cold water and place on a high heat. Bring to the boil, skim the surface of the water, then reduce the heat to medium-low and simmer for 45–60 minutes, adding 1 teaspoon of salt towards the end of the cooking time, until the chickpeas are very soft but still retain their shape. Drain the chickpeas, reserving 100ml of the cooking liquid, and set aside.

If starting with tinned chickpeas, drain them and place in a medium saucepan with enough water just to cover them. Place on a medium heat, bring to a simmer and cook for about 8 minutes, just to soften them up a bit more. Add 1 teaspoon of salt towards the end of the cooking time. Drain the chickpeas, reserving 100ml of the cooking liquid, and set aside.

While the chickpeas are cooking, prepare the other elements of the dish.

*Continued & pictured overleaf*

## Serves four

250g dried chickpeas, soaked overnight in twice their volume of water and 1 tsp bicarbonate of soda (or 2 x 400g tins of cooked chickpeas, as an alternative)
2 tbsp olive oil, plus 1½ tbsp, to serve
4 large garlic cloves, crushed
1 green chilli, finely chopped
1 tbsp ground cumin
100g tahini, plus about 60g, to serve
100g Greek-style yoghurt
2 tbsp lemon juice
Salt

### Toasted pita
2 small pitas (shop-bought or see page 278 for homemade) (about 150g)
1 tbsp olive oil

### Green chilli sauce
1 green chilli, deseeded and finely chopped
3 tbsp lemon juice
1½ tbsp white wine vinegar
1 large garlic clove, crushed
5g parsley, finely chopped

### To serve
½ tsp paprika

Set the oven to a 220°C grill setting.

Pull open the pitas and tear each half in two. Brush the insides of the pitas lightly with oil and place under the grill for about 2 minutes, until crisp and golden brown. Keep a close eye on them while they are under the grill so that they don't burn. Remove from the oven and, once cool enough to handle, break the pitas apart into roughly 4cm pieces. Set aside until ready to use.

Mix together all the ingredients for the green chilli sauce along with ⅛ teaspoon of salt. If you are making this in advance, hold back on the parsley and just mix this through before serving. It will discolour if it sits around for too long.

Once the chickpeas are cooked and drained, put the oil into a medium saucepan and place on a medium heat. Add the garlic and cook for 2 minutes, stirring often, until the garlic is starting to colour. Add the chilli, cook for another minute, then add the chickpeas, reserved cooking liquid, cumin, tahini, yoghurt, lemon juice and ½ teaspoon of salt. Bring to the boil, then reduce the heat to low and simmer for 2–3 minutes, stirring from time to time.

To serve, transfer the warm chickpeas to a large serving platter with a lip or to a wide shallow bowl. Spoon over the green chilli sauce and drizzle over the extra tahini. Sprinkle with the paprika and finish with a drizzle of oil. Dot the toasted pita around and serve.

Breakfast

# SNACKS, SPREADS AND SAUCES

The Palestinian table is only really happy when it's covered with food. Once the empty breakfast dishes get cleared away, the table is ready and waiting for the next array of snacks, spreads and sauces. These are themselves just a prelude to the main meal later on. It's not, however, all about the food. A table constantly covered with all these dishes says a number of things.

The first thing it says is 'Welcome!' Welcome to the table, everyone's invited and please tuck in! Please be hungry and try all sorts of things. It's a way to convey bounty, hospitality and generosity. There will always be more than enough food on the table. If someone turns up unannounced, it's simply a case of pulling up an extra chair or making room on one of the great big sofas.

The secret behind these 'instantly appearing' spreads is, often, the freezer. This way of cooking – of preparing things in batches and getting them into the freezer ready for whenever they are needed – is a big part of the heart and hospitality behind Palestinian cooking. 'Hawader', the name of the practice, translates roughly as 'ready-to-eat'. Open most freezers across the West Bank, for example, and they will be full of things like kubbeh (see page 71), fritters (see pages 66–7), breads and pastries like fatayer (see page 296) or the open-topped flatbread sfiha (see page 226). Groups of women often get together for these big batch cooking sessions, chatting as kubbeh is rolled and packed, fatayer is stuffed and shaped. Freezers and friends: that winning combination behind so much feasting.

The second thing it says is 'let's share'. Maza or mezzeh are the small dishes, sharing plates or appetisers to have with a drink at the beginning of a meal. With a large number of small plates filling the table, no one dish steals the show or acts as centrepiece. Similarly, no one person sits and works their way through a whole plate of m'tabbal (see page 82) or a bowl of labneh balls (see page 49). These are, by their very nature, informal 'family style' dishes which need to be shared and passed around the table. It's a way to say let's eat this together and let's chat while we do.

These dishes can also be a way of both cooking with the season and, on the other hand, being able to still eat something when it is no longer in season. Preserving, pickling, drying and fermenting all play a key part in supplying the Palestinian pantry. It's called 'mooneh'. If hawader roughly translates as filling up the freezer, then mooneh translates as filling up the pantry shelves with things which last in glass jars for months. They're often real little flavour bombs – makdous, for example (see page 56), labneh balls (see page 49) or shatta (see page 73) – there to reach for as a condiment to any meal. A table covered with spreads and dips says so much about the Palestinian way of preparing, cooking and eating food. Welcome, tuck in and pass around. Sahtein! May your health be redoubled!

# Sweet and spicy seeds and nuts

These are everything you want from a pre-supper snack: spicy, sweet, crunchy and very, very moreish.

*Playing around:* The combination of cashews and seeds works really well here: the nuts remain crunchy while the seeds become chewy. A combination of other nuts works just as well, though: macadamias, Brazil nuts, almonds, for example. Use what you have: just keep the total amount of all the nuts and seeds combined the same.

*Keeping notes:* Double or triple the batch, if you like: they keep well in a sealed container for up to 2 weeks. If you do this, only increase the sugar by 50 per cent: the batch will become too syrupy otherwise. If you are going up to 360g of cashews and 40g of each of the seeds, for example, you'll only need to increase to 3 tablespoons/30g of soft brown sugar. All the other ingredients are fine to double.

### Serves four as a snack

2 tbsp light soft brown sugar (20g)
2 tsp flaked sea salt
1 tbsp olive oil
1 tsp mild curry powder
¼ tsp ground turmeric
½ tsp Aleppo chilli flakes (or ¼ tsp regular chilli flakes)
180g raw unsalted cashews
2 tbsp sunflower seeds (20g)
2 tbsp pumpkin seeds (20g)

Preheat the oven to 160°C fan.

Put everything apart from the cashews and seeds into a small saucepan, along with 2 tablespoons of water. Bring to the boil on a medium heat, stirring often, then add the nuts and seeds. Cook for another 3 minutes or so, stirring constantly, until the nuts and seeds are coated in a sticky glaze.

Transfer to a parchment-lined baking tray, then, using a spatula, spread the nuts out so that they're not stuck together. Bake for 14 minutes, stirring once halfway through, until golden. Remove from the oven and set aside to cool completely, then transfer to a bowl to serve or to a sealed container if making in advance.

# Labneh

Labneh is an Arabic cheese made by draining yoghurt so that it loses most of its liquid: the longer it's left to drain, the drier and firmer it becomes. You can either have it as it is, to cook with or just to spread on toast drizzled with olive oil and za'atar, or else you can shape it into balls, for a pre-dinner snack.

Making labneh is one of those things which can feel like a step too far until you actually get around to doing it and realise how simple it is. It honestly takes more effort to hang out your washing than it does to hang up your yoghurt.

*Playing around:* Use either a combination of goat's (or sheep's or ewe's) yoghurt and Greek-style yoghurt or just stick to Greek-style yoghurt. The combination option has a bit more of a tang, which we like, but they both work very well.

*Keeping notes:* Once covered with (and therefore preserved by) oil, labneh keeps in the fridge for up to 2 months. Without the oil it keeps for up to 2 weeks.

**Makes about 500g**

900g Greek-style yoghurt (or a combination of 450g goat's yoghurt and 450g Greek-style yoghurt)
Salt
Olive oil, to seal

---

Line a deep bowl with a piece of cheesecloth or muslin (a clean J-cloth is also fine, as an alternative) and set aside.

In a separate bowl, mix the yoghurt(s) with 1 teaspoon of salt. Pour into the cloth-lined bowl, then bring the edges of the cloth together and wrap tightly to form a bundle. Tie firmly with a piece of string. Hang the bundle over a bowl (or attached to the handle of a tall jug so that the bundle can hang free – and drip – inside the jug) and leave in the fridge for 24–36 hours, until much of the liquid is lost and the yoghurt is thick and fairly dry.

Another method is to put the bundle into a sieve placed over a bowl, with the weight of a plate, for example, or a couple of tins, sitting on top: this weight speeds up the draining process.

Transfer the labneh to an airtight sterilised container or jar (see page 341): just pour over enough olive oil so that the labneh is covered and sealed.

*Pictured overleaf*

# Labneh balls
## *Labneh tabat*

*Keeping notes:* The balls keep for up to 2 months in the fridge. The oil will set in the fridge, so you'll have to bring it back to room temperature before being able to remove the balls and coat them. Save the oil: it can be used again to preserve future batches of labneh.

*Playing around:* Play around with coatings and combinations here: a clash of colours and flavours works really well as part of a larger mezzeh spread. We've given instructions for a combination of chilli flakes and za'atar, but all sorts of coatings work. Nigella seeds, sesame seeds, other chilli flakes (smoky Urfa or sweet Aleppo look great), sumac, chopped pistachios, for example, or a combination of crushed garlic, chopped walnuts and finely diced red chilli. Play around with the size of the balls as well: large balls work well as a snack or as part of a mezzeh spread; smaller balls work well for nibbles with drinks.

**Makes about 20 balls, to serve ten as part of a larger spread**

900g Greek-style yoghurt (or a combination of 450g goat's yoghurt and 450g Greek-style yoghurt)
About 500ml olive oil
3 sprigs of thyme or oregano, or a mixture of both
1½ tbsp chilli flakes (enough to coat 10 balls)
2½ tbsp za'atar (enough to coat 10 balls)
Salt

To make the labneh, follow the instructions in the previous recipe up to the point before it gets transferred to an airtight sterilised container. Then, with lightly oiled hands, spoon a small amount – about 20g – of the labneh into the palm of one hand. Roll it around to shape it into a 3cm-wide ball, and transfer it to a tray lined with a damp (but clean) J-cloth. Continue with the remaining labneh until all the balls are rolled. Transfer to the fridge for a couple of hours (or overnight) to firm up.

Half fill a jar (large enough to fit all the rolled labneh: about 10cm wide and 12cm high) or airtight container with olive oil and drop in the balls. Top with more oil, if necessary – you want the balls to be completely covered with oil – and add the thyme or oregano. Seal the jar and store in the fridge.

When ready to coat – you can do this up to a day before serving – remove the jar from the fridge and bring to room temperature, so that the oil becomes unset. Lift the balls out of the oil and roll them in the chilli flakes or za'atar: an easy way to do this is to spread your chosen coating on a plate, place a few balls at a time on top and shake the plate: the balls will be coated in seconds. If not eating at once, return them to the fridge on a plate (but not in the oil). Bring back to room temperature before serving: you don't want them to be fridge-cold.

*Pictured overleaf*

# The yoghurt-making ladies of Bethlehem

Meeting up with 'the yoghurt-making ladies of Bethlehem' felt a bit like doing a deal. Our friend Vivien Sansour (see page 106), who was in London when we were in Bethlehem, WhatsApped the number of her friend Siham Kalibieh to our friend Raya Manaa, who was driving us around. Siham, we were told, would point us in the right direction. We met Siham by what felt like chance. We were meant to meet on a street corner on the outskirts of Bethlehem, but relying on Waze – our navigational tool of choice – was not always, we quickly found, entirely reliable. Sat nav, it turns out, can get just as confused as the next person trying to get its head around the geography of the area. We might be in what we thought of as Palestine as we drove around Bethlehem. Waze, on the other hand, rather than focusing in on any useful directions, just informed us that we were '*entering an area of high risk*'. The evidence, looking around us, bore no relation to the warning.

Happenstance, however, *was* on our side. After a few left turns, a few right turns and a few going-around-in-circles turns, we spotted the shop we'd been told to keep an eye out for and Siham was standing outside. Happily, in she hopped and, happily, sat nav was turned off in favour of our local in tow and in-the-know! Up a winding hill we went – more lefts and rights and bends – what a view! – before we were 'handed over', package-like, to another lady, Majida Shaalan. She, in turn, led us through the main entrance to a block of flats, up several flights of stairs and into her small flat. It's here, finally, that we met the local crew to see and sample the goods: 'the yoghurt-making ladies of Bethlehem' and their range of white (and yellowy-white) offerings.

From where it was spread out on the easy-wipe plastic tablecloth in her immaculate kitchen, Majida scooped up a tablespoon of butter for us to try straight away. It was incredibly rich and intense: delicious but full-on. Easier to snack on were the balls of labneh, made from yoghurt which has been salted, hung and strained of much of its liquid (see page 337). The yoghurt left behind, after 24 hours or so, is then thick enough to shape into balls. Stored in jars and preserved by being covered in oil, these balls can be rolled in all sorts of things: za'atar, sumac, shatta, chilli flakes, red pepper flakes or nigella seeds before being eaten (see page 49). They're also delicious as they are, without any coating: rich, as with the butter, but with a tartness and saltiness that cuts through to allow for continued snacking.

Much of the tartness of these products comes from the fact that it's generally sheep or goats that are being milked locally, rather than cows with their creamier milk. Kishek (also known as jameed) was also on display for us and offered up for tasting. Kishek are hard discs of sun-dried fermented yoghurt and cracked bulgur wheat. Before refrigeration was available, these discs were a way to conserve and use milk throughout the year. Nowadays, though, they are still widely used: crumbled into stews or savoury pastries or sprinkled over pulses, grains and salads. In Gaza, kishek is flavoured with dill seeds and red pepper flakes. The version we try, on the outskirts of Bethlehem, is plain, allowing the full force of its sharp, sour nature to punch through.

Sitting down on one of the three large velvet sofas which line the otherwise bare walls, little glasses of thick drinking sheep's yoghurt (laban) appear, to continue the dairy theme. It's rich and refreshing at once, smooth and sharp. Slightly yellow versions of all the products sit alongside their white counterparts: they are the same product, just with turmeric or safflower, a spice which is used instead of (but which is not nearly as good as) saffron. Ramallah prefers the white yoghurt, Majida says, Bethlehem prefers the yellow.

Sipping on our laban, Majida tells us about the network of women – the co-operatives – who get together to make the yoghurt, the labneh, the butter and the kishek. The milking is either done by the husband (who then hands the milk over to his wife to carry on the next stages) or else the woman does the milking as well and is in control at every stage: the milking, drying, hanging and shaking. Someone seriously in control of their game is grandma Noura Shaalan, who does it all. Noura has ten sons, five daughters, twenty-five sheep and sixty-five grandchildren, half of whom (the grandchildren, not the sheep) appear at the door as we are sitting around and chatting. Conversation flows as quickly as our plates are replenished when they come close to being emptied. 'Force of nature' is an understatement. 'I've had enough, thank you' is an ignored statement.

Typically, ladies like Noura and Majida sell their produce locally: they have around twenty local customers who buy from them regularly or sell to one or two shops in Bethlehem, Beit Sahour or Ramallah. The operations are small scale but their importance to the community is large. These are women who look out for each other, granddaughters sitting on the laps of their mothers and grandmothers, daughters bonding with their mothers-in-law, aunties, cousins, sisters. When they're not making dairy products, some of the ladies lead women's empowerment groups, who might do a craft activity like embroidery to sell cards, bags, shawls, cushions or tapestries to local tourists. We are all given a little embroidered card to take away with us: an olive tree with the word 'Palestine' sewn below it. Offers of payment are waved away, little glasses of yoghurt are topped up, someone says something to someone else, in Arabic, which makes everyone laugh. Tara misses the meaning of the words but recalls her own 'stitch and bitch' group back in London, smiling to think of the power of women, of connection, of sewing and chatting and making and doing and how much all these things truly mean. We might have lost our way with Waze but sitting there, for that moment, it all feels very much like home.

# Preserved stuffed aubergines
## *Makdous*

Preserves and pickles are a big part of the Palestinian table, adding a real hit of flavour to any meal. They also allow for seasonal vegetables to be eaten year round. The name 'makdous' comes from the Arabic verb 'kadasa', meaning 'to stack'. Stacking the stuffed aubergines on their side and letting them sit for nearly 2 weeks before eating them makes their taste intense. The result is hot, strong, nutty, sharp and garlicky in all the right ways. Start with aubergines as small as you can find: it's nice to be able to eat a whole aubergine at a time, so you don't want to be working your way through a large one.

*Getting ahead / keeping notes:* Once stuffed and covered in oil, these need to be left for 12 days, to ferment. They keep for up to 6 months.

*Kit note:* You'll need a tall sterilised jar – about 19–20cm high and 10cm wide – to store the aubergines in. For notes on how to sterilise your jar, see page 341.

---

Pour about 3 litres of water into a large pot (about 30cm wide and 18cm deep) and add the aubergines and sugar. Place a heatproof plate on top of the aubergines and place a bowl on top of this, so that the aubergines are completely submerged. Bring to the boil, then cook on a medium-high heat for 30 minutes, until the aubergines are soft and have started to pale. Using a slotted spoon, lift the aubergines out of the water and place them in a colander. (You don't need to keep the water, but don't be tempted to pour them through a sieve: the aubergines are soft so they will lose their shape if you do this.) Set aside for about 15 minutes, to cool slightly.

While the aubergines are cooking, place all the ingredients for the stuffing in a medium bowl with ½ teaspoon of salt. Mix well to combine and then keep in the fridge, covered, until needed.

With a small sharp knife, make one slit down the side of each aubergine, about 2½cm long. Spoon between ¼ and ⅛ teaspoon of salt into each aubergine, depending on the size, and spread it inside each cavity. Once they are all salted, return the aubergines to the colander, cut side down, and set the colander over a large bowl. Place a plate on top of the aubergines and place a heavy object on top of that. Leave in the fridge for at least 12 hours for the aubergines to release water: the amount of water released will depend on the aubergines – it can be anywhere between 50 and 150ml.

To assemble, stuff each aubergine with 1–2 teaspoons of the walnut mixture, depending on size, then arrange them, stacked up sideways, in the sterilised jar. Pour over the oil – the aubergines need to be completely covered otherwise they will go mouldy – then seal the jar and turn it upside down. Sit it upside down in a deep saucepan or tray, to catch any oil which might seep out, and leave for 1 hour. Turn it back the right way round and store in a cool, dark place: the kitchen cupboard or pantry. Leave for 12 days before using.

### Serves about eight as part of a larger spread

800g baby aubergines (between 12 and 22, depending on size!), long stems trimmed, leaving the green base
1 tbsp caster sugar
320ml olive oil
Salt

### Stuffing
70g walnut halves, roughly chopped
2 green chillies, finely chopped (30g)
5 garlic cloves, crushed (about 25g)
2 tbsp Aleppo chilli flakes (or 1 tbsp regular chilli flakes)
15g parsley, finely chopped

# Battir: how a little village made a big mark on the map

Battir is a Palestinian farming village in the West Bank. Just over 6 kilometres west of Bethlehem, with a population of around 4,500, it's located on one of the steep sides of the Refaim Valley, just above the modern route of the Jaffa–Jerusalem railway. Farming in Battir is made possible by its stone terraces, which stretch for more than 325 hectares. The village itself is tiny but it's well known for three reasons: 1) its ancient irrigation system and terraces (and the UNESCO world heritage site status gained as a result); 2) its long, thin, sweet Battiri aubergines; and 3) politically, for its bringing together of Palestinian and Israeli activists to successfully resist the building of the separation wall.

First: irrigation. In a region where access to water is often a matter of politics and who has control, Battir shows how much can be achieved on land that has a natural and reliable water source. Supplying the land with all the fresh water it needs is a Roman-era network, fed by seven springs. It's been doing its job for over 2,000 years, and Battir, verdant and fertile, is evidence of its success. Responsibility for making sure that all the terraces are getting all the water they need is shared between the eight main families of the village. These eight clans rotate their roles from one day to the next. The discrepancy between the number of families – eight – and the number of days in the week – seven – is simply worked around: the local saying in the village is that a Battiri week 'lasts eight days, not seven'!

The methods employed to water and farm the land are traditional – timeless, even. The amount the main spring goes down each day is measured, for example, by a simple white stick. It's literally just stuck into the water each morning and night to check the difference in height. In doing so, the amount of water which has been used the previous day can be gleaned. For years, these traditional practices have delivered a resulting bounty of tomatoes, spinach, oranges, figs, apples, peaches, grapes, lemons, olives and, of course, the famous Battiri aubergine.

A Battiri aubergine is smaller, longer and sweeter than a regular aubergine. Its sweetness is attributed to the quality of the spring water that supplies it and helps it grow. Locals use aubergines in all sorts of ways in their cooking, from their maqlubeh (see page 264) to their m'tabbal (see page 82). Their small size and distinct shape, though, make them particularly well suited to being stuffed in dishes like makdous, for example (see page 56), where garlic, crushed walnuts and chillies are piled into them before they are pickled and preserved.

Battir is also on the map for political reasons: for its successful resistance to the building of the separation wall through the village. Had this not been successful, the wall would have cut villagers off from their land and effectively decimated the traditional farming practices. Back in 1949, the railway track that the village looks over served as the armistice line along which the Green Line was drawn up between Israel and Jordan before Israel's decisive victory in the Six-Day War of 1967. Now, the Green Line is the boundary that Israel professes to follow in the building of the separation wall, a massive project that began during the second intifada in 2000, separating Israel on the one side from the West Bank on the other.

The purpose of the wall from the Israeli point of view is to protect its people from Palestinian attacks. The purpose of the wall from the Palestinian point of view is to impede its people's freedom of movement and to destroy the land their houses, olive trees and farms are built on. Perspective on this depends, of course, very much on what side of the line (or wall) you are standing.

For the villagers of Battir, had the wall followed the Green Line, as planned, the terraces and unique farming system of their village would have been destroyed. Both Palestinian and Israeli activists, therefore, came together in 2007 to sue the Israeli Defence Ministry (IDM) to try to change the planned route. The Israeli Nature and Parks Authority, who'd previously agreed to the wall's original route in 2005, was persuaded to change its mind. It was a landmark case and, in 2012, the barrier's route had to be reconfigured. It was the first time that an Israeli government agency permitted a change to the planned construction of a segment of the fence.

The atmosphere in the village today is communal and positive but the day-to-day is still hard. For the villagers, selling their produce requires trips to Bethlehem and beyond, and the village's location, still so close to the Green Line, prevents them from becoming complacent about what the future might hold. Still, it's a real David-and-Goliath story, a testament to the power of the present to preserve the past, about how enough attention, energy and action can move mountains or, in this case, walls.

# Falafel with sumac onion

In Palestine, falafel are more often than not picked up on street corners (rather than made at home), freshly fried and piled into pita bread or paper cones. It's rare to find this street vendor set-up outside the Middle East, though, so for anything resembling the real deal, these need to be made freshly at home. The success of pre-cooked, fridge-cold supermarket falafel is, for Sami – and anyone who grew up eating them in the Middle East – one of life's great mysteries.

A three-part manifesto, therefore, for those who want to eat falafel as they should be eaten:

1. Don't fry them until you want to eat them. They need to be eaten fresh from the fryer.

2. The chickpeas get soaked, overnight, but they do not get cooked. This instruction will not make sense until you have made and eaten your first batch.

3. Pair them with a chopped salad (see page 92), some (warm) hummus or (creamy) tahini sauce (see page 87). Eat them as they are, or else forget about the plate and just pile them into a pita.

Forgive the lesson, but falafel are pretty much part of the DNA of every Palestinian kid walking to or home from school. Queues form around the corner where street vendors set up, shaping their falafel mixture with a large falafel scoop (see page 336). Sami used to take his place in line nearly every day, ready to fill up his pita or paper cone so as to fill up his tummy.

*Getting ahead:* The falafel can be made a day in advance, taken right up to the stage where they are shaped, filled and sprinkled with sesame seeds. At this point they can be kept in the fridge for a day or in the freezer for up to a month. If freezing them, freeze initially on the tray and then, when they are solid, transfer them to a sealable bag. If you are frying them from frozen, just preheat your oven to 180°C fan, fry as per the recipe, then finish them off in the oven for about 5 minutes, until cooked through.

*Shortcut:* The sumac onion is an untraditional addition. It adds a nice bite of tart surprise to the falafel but you can skip this stage, if you like, and just make the falafel without the filling.

---

**Makes 16 falafel, to serve four to six**

250g dried chickpeas
2 garlic cloves, crushed
25g parsley, roughly chopped
25g coriander, roughly chopped
15g mint leaves, roughly chopped
2 medium onions, finely chopped (300g)
1 tsp Aleppo chilli flakes (or ½ tsp regular chilli flakes)
1¼ tsp ground cumin
1¼ tsp coriander seeds, finely crushed in a pestle and mortar
¾ tsp bicarbonate of soda
1 tbsp sumac
About 1 tbsp sesame seeds
About 800ml sunflower oil, to fry
Salt

---

Place the chickpeas in a large bowl and cover with at least twice their volume of cold water. Set aside, overnight, to soak.

The next day, drain the chickpeas (they should weigh 480g now), then combine them with the garlic, parsley, coriander, mint and three-quarters of the chopped onions. Put half the mix into a food processor and blitz for about 2 minutes, scraping down the sides a couple of times if you need to, until the paste is damp and slightly mushy. Transfer to a large bowl and repeat with the remaining half of the mix. Add this to the bowl as well, along with the chilli flakes, cumin, coriander and 1½ teaspoons of salt. Using your hands, mix well to combine. Add the bicarbonate of soda and give the mixture another good mix.

Place the remaining onions in a bowl with the sumac and ¼ teaspoon of salt. Mix well and set aside.

When shaping the falafel, have a small bowl of water nearby so that you can keep your hands wet. This makes it easier to work with the mixture. Spoon 2 tablespoons of the mixture – about 50g) into the palm of your hand and form a ball. Don't press too hard, as this will make the falafel dense. Dip your finger into the bowl of water and make a large hollow in the middle of each ball. Spoon a teaspoon of the sumac onion mixture into the hollow and then shape it again, so that most of the filling is covered. Flatten into a patty – about 6cm wide and 1½cm thick – then, using your little finger, make a small indentation: this will ensure that the inside gets evenly cooked. Place on a parchment-lined tray and continue with the remaining mixture: you should have enough to shape 16 falafel. Sprinkle the tops lightly with the sesame seeds, pressing them in slightly so that they don't fall off when the falafel are fried. At this stage the falafel can be frozen, if you like (see headnote).

When ready to serve, fill a deep, heavy-based medium saucepan – about 20cm wide – with enough of the oil so that it rises about 7cm up the side of the pan. Place on a medium-high heat and bring the oil to a temperature of 180°C if you have a thermometer. If you don't have a thermometer, just add a little bit of the falafel mixture to the pan: if it sizzles at once, you'll know the oil is hot enough.

Carefully lower the falafel in batches into the oil – you should be able to fit 4 in the pan at once – and cook for 5–6 minutes, or until well browned and cooked through. They need to spend this long in the oil to really dry out on the inside, so don't be tempted to take them out too soon. Use a slotted spoon to transfer them to a colander lined with kitchen paper while you continue with the remaining batches. Serve at once.

# Pea, spinach, za'atar and preserved lemon fritters

These work well as either a starter or a snack, or else as a meal in themselves, if bulked out with some smoked salmon or trout or some poached or fried eggs. They can be eaten straight from the oven, all hot and crispy, or at room temperature later on if taken to work or on a picnic. They'll lose their crunch but their flavour will increase.

*Getting ahead:* Both the sauce and the batter can be made up to a day ahead and kept in the fridge, if you like, ready to fry and serve.

Place all the ingredients for the sauce in a bowl, along with ¼ teaspoon of salt. Whisk well to combine and keep in the fridge until ready to serve.

Bring a medium saucepan of salted water to the boil and add the spinach. Stir through, just to wilt, then drain through a sieve. Refresh well under cold running water, to stop the spinach overcooking, and drain well. Transfer to a baking tray lined with kitchen paper, the leaves well spread out, and set aside for 5 minutes to dry. Finely chop the spinach, then place in a large mixing bowl and set aside.

Place the peas in a food processor, pulse a few times until roughly crushed, then add them to the spinach along with all the remaining ingredients (apart from the sunflower oil), 1 teaspoon of salt and a good grind of pepper. Mix until just combined.

Preheat the oven to 180°C fan.

Pour the oil into a large, flat frying pan and place on a medium-high heat. Once hot, use 2 dessertspoons to scoop up the mixture: don't worry about making them uniform in shape, but they should be about 8cm wide and 2cm thick. Carefully spoon about 2 tablespoons of the mixture into the oil – you should be able to do 3 or 4 fritters at a time – and fry for 3–4 minutes, turning once, until they are golden brown. If they are cooking too quickly and taking on too much colour, just reduce the temperature.

Using a slotted spoon, transfer them to a plate lined with kitchen paper while you continue with the remaining fritters. Once they are all fried, lay the fritters out on a baking tray lined with baking parchment and bake for 4–5 minutes, or until cooked through. Serve warm (or at room temperature), with the sauce and a wedge of lemon alongside.

*Pictured overleaf*

**Makes 14–15 fritters, to serve six**

150g baby spinach
300g frozen peas, defrosted
2 preserved lemons, flesh and pips discarded, skin finely chopped (20g)
1 green chilli, deseeded and finely chopped
100g ricotta
3 eggs, beaten
45g cornflour
3 tbsp za'atar
½ tsp Aleppo chilli flakes (or ¼ tsp regular chilli flakes)
¼ tsp baharat (see page 190)
⅓ tsp ground cardamom
¼ tsp ground aniseed
15g mint leaves, finely shredded
15g parsley, roughly chopped
15g dill, roughly chopped
100ml sunflower oil, to fry
Salt and black pepper
1 lemon, cut into wedges, to serve

**Sauce**
300g soured cream
1 tbsp sumac
1 lemon: finely grate the zest to get 1 tsp, then juice to get 1 tbsp
1 tbsp olive oil

# Cauliflower and cumin fritters with mint yoghurt

A version of these fritters featured in Sami's first book, *Ottolenghi: The Cookbook*. We tried to play around with them – adding broccoli to the mix, for example – but kept returning to the classic as something too hard to move far from.

The fritters were something Sami's mother used to make, packing them up for her kids to take to school. They're still a Tamimi favourite, eaten either fresh out of the pan or at room temperature later on. Leftovers are also fine the next day, eaten at room temperature or reheated in the oven for a few minutes. As ever, piling them into flatbread makes for the best kind of quick lunch, but they're also great as they are, to snack on before supper. If you're serving them as a snack, make them half the size so that they can be eaten in a few bites.

*Getting ahead:* The batter keeps for a day in the fridge, if you want to get ahead, ready and waiting to fry.

*Shortcut:* The mint yoghurt is a lovely addition, but there's enough going on, flavour-wise, for the fritters to be eaten as they are, if you like, with just a squeeze of lemon.

**Makes about 10 fritters, to serve four to six**

1 small cauliflower, cut into
  4–5cm-sized florets (300g)
120g plain flour
20g parsley, finely chopped
1 onion, finely chopped (100g)
2 eggs
1½ tsp ground cumin
¾ tsp ground cinnamon
½ tsp ground turmeric
½ tsp Aleppo chilli flakes (or
  ¼ tsp regular chilli flakes)
½ tsp baking powder
250ml sunflower oil, to fry
Salt and black pepper

**Sauce (optional)**
250g Greek-style yoghurt
½ tsp dried mint
2 tbsp lemon juice
1 tbsp olive oil

Place all the ingredients for the sauce, if using, in a bowl with ½ teaspoon of salt. Mix to combine and keep in the fridge until ready to serve.

Bring a medium pan full of salted water to the boil and add the cauliflower. Simmer for 4 minutes, then (making sure to reserve 3–4 tablespoons of the cooking water) drain it into a colander. Using a fork or potato masher, slightly crush the cauliflower, then transfer it to a large bowl along with all the remaining ingredients for the fritters (apart from the sunflower oil), 1¼ teaspoons of salt and a good grind of black pepper. Add 3 tablespoons of the cooking water and mix well, until the mix has the consistency of a slightly runny batter.

Heat the oil in a large sauté pan – about 22cm wide – and, once very hot (120°C if you have a cooking thermometer), carefully spoon 2–3 tablespoons of batter per fritter into the oil. You'll need to do this in batches – 4 or 5 fritters at a time – so as not to overcrowd the pan, and use a fish slice to keep them apart. Fry for about 5 minutes, flipping them over halfway through, until both sides are golden brown. Transfer to a plate lined with kitchen paper and set aside while you continue with the remaining batches. Serve warm or at room temperature, with the yoghurt sauce on the side.

*Pictured overleaf*

# Kubbeh

On every table full of mezzeh, in every kitchen across the Levant, there will be kubbeh. These tightly packed balls of bulgur and minced meat are the king of all snacks, eaten with your hands and dipped in tahini sauce or served as part of a large mezzeh spread, with a freshly chopped salad.

*Getting ahead:* Kubbeh can be made up to a day ahead and kept in the fridge before frying. They can also be frozen once shaped and cooked straight from the freezer. When freezing, lay them first out on a tray (one that fits into your freezer). Once they are frozen, transfer them to a sealable bag or airtight container so that they don't take up all the freezer space. For more on the practice of 'hawader' – getting things into the freezer for whenever they are needed – see page 337.

---

**Makes about 32 kubbeh, to serve twelve as a snack or six as a main**

**Filling**
2½ tbsp olive oil
45g pine nuts
3 onions, finely chopped (450g)
200g beef mince (at least 15% fat)
1 tsp ground cinnamon
1 tsp ground allspice
4 tsp pomegranate molasses
5g parsley leaves, roughly chopped
About 500ml sunflower oil, to fry
Salt and black pepper

**Shell**
1 onion, roughly chopped (150g)
500g beef mince (at least 15% fat)
2 tsp ground cinnamon
1½ tsp ground allspice
270g fine bulgur

**Tahini sauce**
75g tahini
1½ tbsp lemon juice

**To serve**
1 tsp sumac

First make the filling. Put 1½ tablespoons of olive oil into a large sauté pan and place on a medium-high heat. Add the pine nuts and cook for about 3 minutes, stirring continuously, until evenly golden. Drain in a sieve placed over a bowl, to collect the oil, then return the oil to the pan. Add the remaining tablespoon of oil, along with the onions, and cook for about 10 minutes, stirring from time to time, until soft and lightly golden. Add the beef, cinnamon and allspice and cook for another 2 minutes, using a spoon to break up the mince, until the meat is no longer pink. Remove from the heat and stir in the pine nuts, molasses, parsley, 1¼ teaspoons of salt and a good grind of black pepper. Set aside to cool.

To make the shell, put the onion into a food processor and pulse until very finely minced, but not liquidised. Add the beef, cinnamon, allspice, 1 tablespoon of salt (a lot, we know, but it needs it) and a good grind of black pepper. Pulse a few times, for about 15 seconds in total, to form a paste. Transfer to a separate large bowl and set aside.

Put the bulgur into a sieve and place under running water for about 2 minutes, or until the water runs clear. Set aside to drain for a couple of minutes, then add to the raw beef mixture. Knead for about 3 minutes, or until you have a sticky mass that holds together well when pinched.

*Continued overleaf*

To form the kubbeh, have a bowl of water close to hand: you'll need to dip your hands into the water as you shape, to help seal the kubbeh. Begin by rolling out ping-pong-sized balls of the kubbeh shell: they should weigh about 35–40g each. You should make about 32 balls. Working one at a time, hold a ball in your left hand and use the index finger of your right hand to make an indentation in the centre of the ball. (Hands are reversed if you are left-handed.) Gently swivel your finger around, while pushing upwards with your left hand, to form a cavity with sides about ¼cm thick. Fill the cavity with 1½ teaspoons of the kubbeh filling and gently seal the shell around it, so that no filling is exposed. Using both hands, form the kubbeh into an oval shape that is somewhat pointed at one end, making sure no cracks appear and that the kubbeh is completely sealed on all sides. Transfer to a tray lined with baking parchment and continue with the remaining filling and shell mixture.

Put all the ingredients for the tahini sauce into a bowl along with 75ml of water and ¼ teaspoon of salt. Whisk well to combine and set aside.

When ready to fry, put the sunflower oil into a medium saucepan and place on a medium-high heat. When the oil is hot (180°C if you have a thermometer), add the kubbeh in batches of 6 or 7, and fry for about 4 minutes, until deeply browned and crispy on all sides. Transfer to a plate lined with kitchen paper and keep warm while you continue with the remaining kubbeh. Transfer to a serving platter, sprinkle with the sumac, and serve warm, with the tahini sauce to dip into or pour over.

# Spicy olives and roasted red pepper
## *Zaytoun bil shatta*

This is somewhere between a condiment and a salsa, as happy to be spooned alongside some pan-fried fish or meat as it is to be stirred through a simple bowl of rice.

*Keeping notes:* This keeps for about 4 days in the fridge, so make more than you need so that you have it to hand.

**Serves four as a condiment
or as part of a mezzeh spread**

1 large red pepper (150g)
4 tsp olive oil
½ tsp red shatta (see recipe below)
  or rose harissa
170g pitted green olives
2 small preserved lemons, flesh
  and pith discarded, skin finely
  sliced (25g)
10g parsley, finely chopped
2 spring onions, finely sliced (20g)
½ a green chilli, deseeded and
  finely sliced
1½ tbsp lemon juice

Preheat the oven to 220°C fan.

Place the pepper on a tray lined with baking parchment, toss with 1 teaspoon of oil and bake for 35–40 minutes, until soft and charred. Transfer the pepper to a bowl, cover with a clean tea towel or a plate and set aside for 10 minutes or so. Once cool enough to handle, remove the skin, stem and seeds and place the flesh – you should have about 80g – in the small bowl of a food processor. Blitz until smooth, then transfer to a bowl with the shatta or harissa and the remaining tablespoon of oil. Mix well to combine, then add all the remaining ingredients and stir again.

*Pictured overleaf*

# Shatta (red or green)

Sami knew that he had a true partner in culinary crime in Tara when he spotted a jar of this in her bike pannier one day. 'I don't go anywhere without some,' Tara said, as casually as if talking about her house keys. This fiery condiment is as easy to make as it is easy to become addicted to. Shatta(ra!) is there on every Palestinian table, cutting through rich foods or pepping others up. Eggs, fish, meat, vegetables: they all love it. Our recommendation is to keep a jar in your fridge or cupboard at all times. Or your bike pannier, if so inclined.

*Kit note:* As always with anything being left to ferment, the jar you put your chillies into needs to be properly sterilised (see page 341 for instructions). Once made, shatta will keep in the fridge for up to 6 months. The oil will firm up and separate from the chillies once it's in the fridge, so just give it a good stir, for everything to combine, before using.

**Makes 1 medium jar**

250g red or green chillies,
  stems trimmed and then
  very thinly sliced (with seeds)
1 tbsp salt
3 tbsp cider vinegar
1 tbsp lemon juice
Olive oil, to cover and seal

Place the chillies and salt in a medium sterilised jar and mix well. Seal the jar and store in the fridge for 3 days. On the third day, drain the chillies, transfer them to a food processor and blitz: you can either blitz well to form a fine paste or roughly blitz so that some texture remains. Add the vinegar and lemon juice, mix to combine, then return the mixture to the same jar. Pour enough olive oil on top to seal, and keep in the fridge.

*Pictured overleaf*

# Beetroot and sweet potato dip with pistachio bulgur salsa

Beetroot was not something Sami grew up eating. This is a dish, therefore, which shows how the ingredients that bookend Sami's palate – the ground allspice and cinnamon, the tangy feta and labneh, the bulgur and olive oil – can be used in a fresh way. The dip is lovely as it is, as part of a spread, or can be served as a side to an oily fish like salmon or mackerel.

*Shortcut:* The dip works well alone without the salsa, if you are keeping things simple. If you do this, just increase the pistachios to 100g. If you want the salsa to be gluten-free, use cooked quinoa instead of the bulgur.

*Getting ahead:* If you are making your own labneh (see page 48), you'll need to get this going at least 24 hours before serving. The dip keeps well in the fridge for up to 3 days. The salsa can be made up to a day before serving and kept in the fridge. As ever, bring both elements back to room temperature before serving.

---

**Serves four as part of a mezzeh spread**

500g raw beetroots (about 4 medium), unpeeled
1 medium-sized sweet potato (240g)
70g bulgur wheat
75g pistachio kernels, lightly toasted (see page 339) and finely chopped
15g parsley, finely chopped
15g mint, roughly chopped, plus a few extra leaves to serve
1½ tbsp lemon juice
105ml olive oil
4 garlic cloves, crushed
½ tsp ground cinnamon
¼ tsp ground allspice
1 Medjool date (20g), pitted and soaked in 50ml of boiling water for about 20 minutes
2 tbsp cider vinegar
100g labneh (shop-bought, or see page 48 for homemade) or thick Greek-style yoghurt
35g feta, roughly crumbled
Salt

Preheat the oven to 220°C fan.

Tightly wrap the beetroots and sweet potato individually in foil and bake for about 1 hour, or until a knife inserted into the middle of each beetroot and the potato goes in easily. Timings will vary, depending on the size of the beetroots. Remove from the oven and, once cool enough to handle, peel and discard the skins of both vegetables. You should end up with around 180–200g of cooked sweet potato flesh and about 400g of beetroot. Roughly chop the beetroot into large chunks and set aside. The sweet potato can stay as it is. Keep the two separate, until needed.

Put the bulgur into a small saucepan, for which you have a lid, along with 75ml of water and ⅛ teaspoon of salt. Bring to the boil on a high heat, then remove from the heat. Leave to sit, covered, for about 20 minutes, then fluff the bulgur up with a fork. Tip into a bowl and set aside for about 20 minutes, to cool. Stir in the pistachios, parsley, mint, lemon juice, 3 tablespoons of olive oil, ½ teaspoon of salt and a grind of black pepper. Set aside until needed.

Put 3 tablespoons of oil into a small sauté pan and place on a medium-high heat. Once hot, add the garlic and cook for about 2 minutes, or until lightly browned. Add the spices, cook for another couple of seconds, stirring frequently, then remove from the heat. Set aside to slightly cool and then put into the bowl of a food processor. Add the beetroot, 1 teaspoon of salt and a good grind of black pepper. Remove the date from its water, add to the food processor and blitz the mixture for about 1 minute, or until smooth. Add the sweet potato and pulse for another 20 seconds, until just incorporated.

Transfer the mixture to a bowl and add the cider vinegar and 50g of labneh. Fold to combine – you still want to see some streaks of the labneh – then spread out on a large platter or in a shallow bowl. With the back of a spoon, smooth out the surface and make a well in the centre. Top with the remaining 50g of labneh, swirling it gently through the mix without incorporating it too much. Fill the dip with the bulgur salsa, top with the feta and extra mint leaves, drizzle with the remaining tablespoon of oil and serve.

# Nablus

Say 'Nablus' to someone who's not travelled around Israel, the West Bank and the Galilee and, chances are, they won't have heard of it. Destination-wise, other places are clearly on the map. Bethlehem, Nazareth, Jerusalem: these are the cities firmly rooted in the mind of those who want to bear witness to various sites of huge religious importance. The Church of the Nativity, Manger Square, the Basilica of the Annunciation, Temple Mount, the Church of the Holy Sepulchre, the Mount of Olives, the Garden of Gethsemane: this is to name just a few of the landmarks which mean so much to those who want to stand where the birth, life and death of Jesus are said to have taken place. The buses getting everyone from Bethlehem to Nazareth and Jerusalem are big, full and constantly on the move, as are the hotels housing and feeding everyone along the way. The well-trodden path is as smooth as the olive-wood carvings being bought as souvenirs to take back from the Holy Land.

There's something about all the wood, though – to invert the wood-for-trees saying – which can hide the reality of being able to see the everyday 'trees': the day-to-day stuff of life going on in a busy, bustling, functioning city. The selling and buying of fresh food and household goods, for example, the everyday business of moving about, commuting, navigating hooting cars and yellow taxis, chatting over coffee and slices of cake: the highs and lows, the bitter and sweet, the norms of city life.

For all this – and for the sweet things in particular – Nablus is the place to be. Slightly off the tourist track (65 kilometres north of Jerusalem, located between Mount Ebal and Mount Gerizim), the city has always been a key trading point for olive oil, soap and cotton across the Levant. With a population of just under 130,000, it's one of Palestine's largest cities. It's had a tough and troubled past, though, suffering badly during the height of the second intifada in 2002, and continues to be challenged by the Israeli military occupation. The reality of multiple checkpoints interrupting the flow of goods in and out of the city, for example, is a huge problem. Despite all this, the city has a strong sense of resilience about it: defiance, even.

If the sense of resilience is palpable, then so too is the smell. The smell, that is, of warm sugar being poured over mild white cheese in a tray which looks like a giant lily pad turning around, day in and day out, inside one of the many bakeries in town. Nablus is, for those whose pilgrimages are shaped more by their appetites than by their faith, *the* city for pastries and sweets. If you want the best knafeh around – the warm, soft, sugar-syrup-drenched, melt-in-the-mouth cheesy pastry so popular in the region (see page 302) – Nablus is where the compass needs to be pointing. Walking

around the cobbled streets of the bustling market, the smell of melted ghee, baked semolina pastry and sweet white cheese wafts around each corner, pulling people on from the piles of seeds and nuts they've stopped to try or buy. If it's not nuts and seeds it'll be mountains of fresh soft herbs, enormous aubergines, tiny aubergines, plastic buckets full of hallucinogenically-coloured pickles, Jenga-like displays of peaches stacked up into a pyramid, live chickens, not-so-live fish and meat, Adidas trainers, shiny high heels and vast arrays of variously coloured pants.

The market, in short, is a welcome assault on the senses: the colours, the smells, the sounds, the clash of offerings on display. But step into Majdi Abu Hamidi's Al-Aqsa bakery on Al-Naser street, a well-known institution in the city, and time stands still for a moment. Plastic stools are pulled up at Formica tables and portions of knafeh are transferred from metre-wide round trays to the plates they are being served on. Portions are either large or really large – 250g or 500g – and strong, black coffee appears in small cups on big trays. Abu Hamidi, who has been making and serving knafeh from this spot for over forty-five years, hands around the coffee. Coffee is fine – necessary, even, to take the edge off the sweetness – but customers are encouraged (only half-jokingly) not to drink water for half an hour after eating his knafeh, to allow the taste to linger. Memories last for a lot longer than this, though: the sight of groups of friends or family huddled around a table, sharing a sweet moment, or – just as common and as meaningful – locals pulling up a pew by themselves, taking five or ten minutes out from their day to sit and delight in the sheer comfort, simple sweetness and incomparable pleasure that is knafeh Nabulseyeh.

# Burnt aubergine with tahini and herbs
## M'tabbal

If Tara was to take ten things to her desert island, to live off forever, this is what the list would look like: aubergines, tahini, garlic, lemons, olive oil, pomegranate seeds, fresh mint, dried mint, parsley and salt. M'tabbal, then – quite literally a roll-call of this top ten – is one of Tara's favourite dishes. Serve it either as a side to some pan-fried fish or grilled meat or as part of a larger spread. For instructions on how to char your aubergines to smoky perfection see page 335.

*Keeping notes:* This keeps well in the fridge for 4–5 days. As ever, serve it at room temperature rather than fridge-cold.

---

There are various ways to burn the aubergines. These are outlined in the glossary on page 335. Whichever way you choose, once the flesh has been scooped out of the burnt aubergine you should have about 500g. Set this aside in a colander over the sink or over a bowl for at least an hour (or overnight, in the fridge).

Once drained, put the aubergine flesh into a large mixing bowl and, using your hands, start to mash it: you want to create long, thin strands. Add the tahini, garlic, lemon and 1 teaspoon of salt and mix to combine. Spoon the mixture on to a serving plate with a lip (or into a bowl) and sprinkle over the pomegranate seeds, dried mint and fresh herbs. Finally, drizzle over the oil.

*Pictured overleaf*

**Serves four to six as part of a mezzeh spread**

4 large aubergines (1kg)
50g tahini
2 large garlic cloves, crushed
60ml lemon juice
Salt

**To serve**
2 tbsp pomegranate seeds (from ½ a small pomegranate)
¼ tsp dried mint
About 10 picked mint leaves
5g parsley leaves, roughly chopped
About 1 tbsp olive oil

# Roasted red pepper and walnut dip
## *Muhammara*

**Serves four as part of a
mezzeh spread**

110g walnut halves
6–7 red peppers (1kg)
80ml olive oil
1 red onion, finely chopped (120g)
4 garlic cloves, crushed
2 tsp tomato purée
2 tsp ground cumin
2 tsp Aleppo chilli flakes (or 1 tsp
  regular chilli flakes)
35g panko breadcrumbs
1½ tbsp pomegranate molasses
2 tsp lemon juice
1 tbsp parsley leaves, roughly
  chopped
Salt and black pepper

The word 'muhammara' can mean both 'roasted' and 'red' and can also
(though not here) refer to the use of paprika in a dish to bring a smoky depth
of flavour and reddish colour. Muhammara is Syrian in origin, moving freely
to Palestine and Lebanon when the Levant was a single territory. It still moves
freely now, across whichever table it is served at, acting as a dip, spread or
side in all sorts of contexts. Scoop it up with warm toasted pita, for example,
spoon it alongside some cooked butter beans or lentils or any roast meat, pair
it with some creamy hummus or cheese or use it as part of a mezzeh spread.
You can't really go wrong.

*Getting ahead*: This keeps well in the fridge for up to 3 days.

*Gluten-free note*: Adding the panko breadcrumbs makes the mix firm up and
slightly dry, in a good way. For a gluten-free alternative, use an equal quantity
of ground almonds or else increase the quantity of walnuts by about 20g.

Preheat the oven to 160°C fan.

Spread the walnuts out on a parchment-lined tray and roast for about 8
minutes, until lightly toasted. Remove from the oven and set aside.

Increase the oven temperature to 220°C fan. Place the peppers on a
parchment-lined baking tray and toss with 1 teaspoon of oil. Bake for about
40 minutes, or until completely softened and charred. Transfer to a bowl,
cover with a clean tea towel or a plate and set aside to cool for about 20
minutes. Once cool enough to handle, remove and discard the skins, stems
and seeds – the remaining flesh should weigh about 380g.

Put 2 tablespoons of oil into a medium sauté pan and place on a medium-high
heat. Add the onion and cook for about 7 minutes, stirring a few times, until
softened and browned. Add the garlic, tomato purée and spices and cook
for another 30 seconds, stirring constantly. Remove from the heat and tip
into a food processor, along with the roasted pepper, panko breadcrumbs,
pomegranate molasses, lemon juice, 1 tablespoon of olive oil, 1 teaspoon of
salt and a grind of black pepper. Blitz for about 30 seconds, to form a coarse
paste, and then add 90g of the walnuts. Blitz for another 20 seconds or so: not
much longer than this, as you want the walnuts to just break down rather than
form a paste. Transfer to a serving platter and drizzle with the remaining 2
tablespoons of oil. Roughly crush the remaining walnuts with your hands and
sprinkle these over, followed by the parsley.

*Pictured overleaf*

# Butternut squash m'tabbal
## *M'tabbal qarae*

The difference between m'tabbal and baba ganoush is the addition of tahini. For us, if it has tahini in it then it's m'tabbal. Other opinions, as always, are available. Whatever you call this sort of dip, three rules remain absolute: it's all about the smokiness of the aubergines, lemons will be squeezed and there will be garlic. The squash is our own (quite literally) sweet addition.

Serve this as a dip, to scoop up with warm pita, or as a side to all sorts of things: grilled meat or fish, for example, or a range of roasted veg.

*Keeping notes:* Double the batch and make more than you need, if you like: it keeps well in the fridge for up to 3 days. As ever, just bring it back to room temperature rather than serving it fridge-cold.

---

Preheat the oven to 200°C fan.

Cut the squash in half, lengthways, and then scoop out and discard the seeds. Using a knife, make shallow cross-hatch indentations across the flesh and then place cut side up on a baking tray lined with baking parchment. Drizzle each half with 1 teaspoon of olive oil, ⅛ teaspoon of salt and a good grind of black pepper. Bake for 50 minutes, or until the squash is very soft.

While the squash is roasting, slice the top off the head of garlic, horizontally, so that the cloves are exposed. Place in the middle of a square of tin foil and drizzle with ½ teaspoon of olive oil and a sprinkle of salt and pepper. Wrap tightly in the foil and bake for 40 minutes (at the same time as the squash is in the oven), until the cloves are soft and golden brown.

Remove both the squash and the garlic from the oven and set aside to cool. Once cool, scoop out the flesh of the squash and mash it coarsely with a spoon or fork: this should weigh about 500g. Place the flesh in a mixing bowl and set aside. The skin can be discarded. Squeeze out the cooked garlic cloves, roughly chop them and add to the bowl with the squash. The papery skin and the foil can be discarded.

For instructions on how to chargrill the aubergines, see page 335. Once you have the charred flesh, roughly chop it to form a coarse mash: this should weigh around 350g. Add this to the bowl of squash and garlic along with the tahini, lemon juice and 1½ teaspoons of salt. Mix well to combine – we like the texture rough, but use a hand-held blender to blitz and make it a bit smoother, if you prefer – then spread out on a large serving platter or individual plates. Top with the chilli, dried mint, mint leaves and spring onions, drizzle over the remaining olive oil – just over 2 tablespoons – and serve.

*Pictured on previous page*

**Serves eight as a dip or six as part of a spread**

1 small butternut squash (900g)
3 tbsp olive oil
1 large head of garlic (about 70g)
4 aubergines (1kg)
75g tahini
3 tbsp lemon juice
½ red chilli, thinly sliced into rounds
½ tsp dried mint
5g mint leaves, torn
1 spring onion, thinly sliced (10g)
Salt and black pepper

# Tahini sauce

Tahini sauce: the creamy, nutty, rich addition to many a snack, dish or feast. It's there on every table in Palestine, ready to be dipped into or drizzled over all sorts of things: roasted vegetables, fish or meat, and all sorts of leaf, pulse or grain-based salads. It keeps well in the fridge for 3–4 days, so always make the full recipe here, even if what you are cooking only calls for a few tablespoons.

**Makes 1 medium jar**

150g tahini
2 tbsp lemon juice
1 garlic clove, crushed
Salt

Mix together all the ingredients, along with 120ml of water and ¼ teaspoon of salt. If it is too runny, add a bit more tahini. If it is too thick, add a bit more lemon juice or water. You want the consistency to be like that of a smooth, runny nut butter. It will thicken up when left to sit around, so just give it a stir and some more lemon juice or water every time you use it.

# Tahini parsley sauce
## *Baqdunsieh*

Like the tahini sauce above, this keeps well in the fridge, so always make the full quantity even if your recipe asks for less. You'll find it goes with pretty much whatever else you are eating in the next few days.

**Makes 1 small jar**

75g tahini
2 tbsp lemon juice
2 garlic cloves, crushed
20g parsley, finely chopped
Salt

Put the tahini, lemon juice, garlic, 60ml of water and ¼ teaspoon of salt into a small bowl. Whisk well until smooth, then stir in the parsley. Thin it out with an additional tablespoon or so of water or lemon juice, if you need to, if it's been sitting around. You want it to have the consistency of creamy nut butter.

VEGGIE
SIDES
AND
SALADS

No Palestinian table is considered set without vegetable sides and salads. Not one big bowl of salad and a veggie or two, but a great big array of dishes all served in their own little bowls. A simple chopped salad will always be there, of cucumbers, tomatoes, peppers, chillies and fresh herbs. Fattoush as well, using up yesterday's leftover bread, now pulled into chunks and bulking out today's salad. Sides of fried cauliflower and steamed carrots; cubes of roasted aubergine stirred through with bulgur; lentils with tahini and crispy onions: the list goes on and on. For those who like their vegetables, it's a very happy sight.

So ubiquitous is the salad offering that, when eating out in the restaurants of Bethlehem, Haifa, Nazareth, Jenin or East Jerusalem, for example, these dishes will arrive at the table spontaneously, at the beginning of a meal. Whether or not they've been ordered, they appear along with the bread and often won't feature on the bill. On the one hand it's great that all these vegetables are as integral to the meal as bread. There's a downside to this ubiquity, though, and to the fact that the customers don't often expect to pay for these dishes. This is that the offering can, in all honesty, get rather stuck in a rut and be made without a whole lot of 'nafas' (see page 339) – heart and soul – or imagination being put into it.

It's completely understandable and the bind works two ways: customers know what they want and often want what they know, so are not always keen to experiment or suddenly start paying for something that has, previously, turned up by itself at the table. Chefs, therefore, either continue to stick to the status quo, saving their energy and imagination for the main dish, or run the risk of pushback if they try to elevate (and start charging for) a salad. This tension is touched upon in the 'Tale of Two Restaurateurs' profile (see page 164), but it's something we saw time and again on our travels, where a chef's imaginative approach to a salad or veggie side was, more often than not, quietly relegated to the 'chef's special' board.

For our part, then, we have a real mix of dishes here. Some are traditional – the chopped salad three ways (see page 92), braised broad beans with olive oil and lemon (see page 123) or shulbato (see page 140), for example. With others we've taken the traditional but given it a twist: fattoush with a tangy buttermilk dressing, for example (see page 99), tabbouleh three ways (see pages 102–4) or roasted new potatoes with an injection of punchy flavour (see page 137).

Reflecting all the years Sami has spent working, eating and shaping his palate in London, several of the salads will, however, be much more familiar to the Ottolenghi customer than they will be recognisable on the traditional Palestinian table. These are the dishes where Sami has taken the ingredients of his home town, ramped up their boldness and put them on platters and plates so large they'd cast a shadow over all the little bowls they'd otherwise be served in. These are big and bold dishes in all senses, not just the platters. They're big on flavour, big in colour, big in surprise. In salads such as the baby gem lettuce with burnt aubergine yoghurt and shatta, for example (see page 96), or the roasted figs with radicchio and goat's cheese (see page 100), the ingredients are traditional: they're just shown in a deliciously new light.

There are, also, some salads we would have liked to include but which we haven't because the ingredients are hard to source outside Palestine. Green almonds, for example, picked young and fresh from the tree and eaten by the handful, mark the beginning of spring in Palestine. Their taste and texture is distinct: fuzzy-skinned and crunchy like an unripe apricot or peach to eat but without any of the tartness you'd expect. Picked at this stage, green almonds are sold in big bags by the side of the road, ready to be snacked on as they are or cut into thin slivers to add to leafy salads. We tried to experiment with very firm apricots, peaches or plums to make a substitute but nothing really came close. Other ingredients that we would have used if they were more widely available include vegetables like akkoub – a prickly thistle which, when its spines are removed, is one of the most celebrated foods of village cuisine – or yaqteen, a smooth long gourd that is shaped like a bottle with a nozzle on top. Colocasia – a root vegetable with a pink stem poking through – is another, as is molokhieh, the much-loved jute leaves that are widely grown. We came up with a substitute for these in besara (see page 150) – a molokhieh soup – and in our recipe for chicken meatballs in molokhieh (see page 239) but, uncooked, didn't feel happy with any of the alternatives we could have used.

A lot of the salads and sides here are robust enough to be able to handle being played around with, though, with alternatives suggested in each recipe depending on what is in season or what you have around. Likewise with the dressings and the amount of chopping you want to do: play around with alternating a tahini or yoghurt dressing where a lemony one is suggested and vice versa. And so with the chopping: if you don't like the idea of chopping a large bunch of vegetables into 1cm dice, then don't. It will still taste good if everything is roughly chopped. Start with the ripest, sweetest ingredients you can get hold of, cook what's in season and you can't go far wrong. And, if ever in doubt, just add cubes of tangy feta or some chunks of creamy avocado and a great big squeeze of lemon. 'Everything's better with feta!' as Tara says, near-on every day.

# Chopped salad: three ways
## *Salata Arabieh*

Salata mafrumeh, salata na'ameh, salata baladiye, salata fallahi: whatever name this goes by, it's the same fresh chopped Palestinian salad. It's as ubiquitous as it is compulsory alongside every meal. It's there at breakfast, to have with hummus and falafel. It's there at lunch, inside a warm pita stuffed with kofta. It's there at supper, alongside the spread of pickles and olives and a rich meat stew. There are many versions on the theme, we've offered three. One as it is, allowing the ingredients to really sing, one with a nutty tahini dressing and one with a yoghurt dressing. Play around as you like, though: cubes of tangy feta, black olives or creamy avocado are a really nice addition, as is a sprinkle of za'atar. Just two rules: start with vegetables as ripe and sun-kissed as possible and a knife as sharp as you can get it. It's a simple salad but one which requires a lot of chopping.

*Getting ahead:* Do all your chopping a few hours in advance, if you like (it can take a while, particularly if you are scaling up the recipe to feed a crowd), but don't assemble this too long before serving. It'll get watery if it sits around for too long.

---

*To make the original version*, place all the ingredients in a large bowl along with 1¼ teaspoons of salt and a good grind of black pepper. Mix well to combine, then transfer to a serving platter or individual plates.

*To make the tahini version*, add the tahini, 1½ teaspoons of salt and a good grind of black pepper to the bowl with all the other ingredients. Mix well to combine, transfer to a serving platter or individual plates, and sprinkle over the sumac.

*For the yoghurt version*, place the cucumber, tomatoes, pepper, chillies, spring onions, herbs, garlic and ½ teaspoon of salt in a colander and set it over a bowl for 20 minutes, for the water to drain. Put the yoghurt into a separate large bowl along with 2 teaspoons of dried mint, the lemon zest and juice, the olive oil, 1 teaspoon of salt and a good grind of black pepper. Add the drained salad to the yoghurt dressing and mix well to combine. Transfer to a large serving platter, or individual plates, sprinkle over the final teaspoon of dried mint, and serve.

*Pictured overleaf*

**Serves four as a side**

**Original version**
4 small Lebanese cucumbers (or 1 large regular cucumber), quartered lengthways, seeds removed and cut into ½cm dice (300g)
420g ripe tomatoes (either 2 large heirlooms or 6 plum tomatoes), cut into ½cm dice
1 red pepper, cut into ½cm dice (140g)
2 green chillies, deseeded and finely chopped
About 5 spring onions, finely sliced (70g)
3 tbsp olive oil
30g parsley, very finely chopped
15g mint leaves, finely shredded
1 large garlic clove, crushed
2 lemons: finely grate the zest to get 2 tsp, then juice to get 3 tbsp
Salt and black pepper

**Tahini version**
All the ingredients for the original, plus:
80g tahini
1 tbsp sumac

**Yoghurt version**
All the ingredients for the original, plus:
250g Greek-style yoghurt
1 tbsp dried mint

# Spicy herb salad with quick-pickled cucumber

This is a green leafy salad dialled right up to ten. It's packed with flavour, so keep what you're serving it with really simple. Pan-fried salmon or cod, for example, both work really well.

*Getting ahead / batch cooking:* Make more of the seeds than you need: they keep well in an airtight container for a week or so and are lovely sprinkled over all sorts of salads or roasted vegetables.

If you want to get ahead with the salad then you can pick all the herbs and have them prepped. Don't assemble until just before serving, though: the leaves will wilt if they sit around for too long.

---

**Serves four as a side**

2 cucumbers (650g)
60ml cider vinegar
1 tbsp caster sugar
2 lemons: leave one whole, and juice the other to get 1 tbsp
20g picked parsley leaves (with some stem attached)
10g picked tarragon leaves
15g picked dill leaves
15g mint leaves, roughly torn
4 spring onions (60g), thinly sliced at a sharp angle
40g lamb's lettuce
1½ tbsp olive oil
Flaked sea salt and black pepper

**Seeds**

½ tsp white sesame seeds, toasted
½ tsp nigella seeds, toasted
20g pumpkin seeds, toasted
1½ tsp coriander seeds, toasted and roughly crushed in a pestle and mortar
½ tsp Aleppo chilli flakes (or ¼ tsp regular chilli flakes)
½ tsp sumac

Using a vegetable peeler, peel both cucumbers from top to bottom, to make long, wide, thin ribbons. Keep going until you get to the seedy centre, which can be discarded (or eaten). Place the ribbons in a bowl with 1 teaspoon of flaked salt and mix well. Transfer to a sieve placed over a bowl and set aside for 15 minutes, for some of the liquid to drain. Put the vinegar and sugar into a separate bowl and whisk until the sugar dissolves. Add the cucumber, toss to combine, and set aside for 20 minutes, to lightly pickle.

Place all the ingredients for the seeds in a bowl with ¼ teaspoon of flaked sea salt. Mix to combine and set aside.

Using a small, sharp knife, trim the top and tail off the whole lemon. Cut down along its round curves, removing the skin and bitter white pith. Release the segments from the lemon by slicing between the membranes, then roughly chop the lemon flesh. Put these into a large bowl along with the lemon juice, parsley, tarragon, dill, mint, spring onions, lamb's lettuce, oil, 1 teaspoon of flaked sea salt and a good grind of pepper. Mix well to combine. Drain the pickled cucumber, discarding its liquid, and add to the bowl along with half the seed mixture. Mix to combine, then transfer to a serving platter or individual serving plates. Top with the remaining seeds and serve at once.

*Pictured overleaf*

# Baby gem lettuce with burnt aubergine yoghurt, smacked cucumber and shatta

This works well either as a stand-alone starter or as part of a spread or side. It's lovely with some hot smoked salmon or trout. 'Smacked' cucumbers sounds a bit dramatic but, really, it's just a way of bruising them so as to allow all the flavour to seep through to the flesh. Thanks to Craig Tregonning for this salad.

*Getting ahead:* Make all the elements well in advance, here, if you like: up to a day for the cucumber and the aubergine yoghurt, and the shatta needs to be made in advance, so you'll be all set here.

*Playing around:* Some crumbled feta on top works very well, and if you don't have the Urfa chilli flakes, just use a pinch of black nigella seeds or some black sesame seeds.

---

There are two ways to chargrill the aubergines: on an open flame on the stove top, or in a chargrill pan on an induction hob followed by 10 minutes in a hot oven. See page 335 for more detailed instructions. Once cooked, the scooped-out flesh should weigh about 160g. Place this in the bowl of a food processor along with the yoghurt, garlic, lemon juice, tahini and ½ teaspoon of salt. Blitz for about a minute, until completely smooth, then set aside until needed.

Prepare the cucumber by placing each half on a chopping board, cut side facing down. Using the flat side of a large knife, lightly 'smack' them until bruised but still holding their shape. Cut the cucumber into roughly 1cm dice and set aside.

Clean the food processor, then add the parsley, mint, garlic, olive oil and ¼ teaspoon of salt. Blitz for about 2 minutes, scraping down the sides a couple of times if you need to, to form a smooth paste, then add to the cucumber. Set aside for at least 20 minutes (and up to a day in advance if kept in the fridge) for the flavours to infuse.

Slice each head of baby gem lengthways to make 8 long thin wedges (per lettuce). When ready to assemble, arrange the lettuce on a round platter, overlapping the outer and inner circle to look like the petals of a flower. Lightly sprinkle the wedges with salt and a grind of black pepper, then splatter over the aubergine yoghurt. Spoon over the cucumber, drizzle with the shatta, sprinkle over the chilli flakes and serve.

## Serves four generously

5–6 baby gem lettuces (500g), bases trimmed
1½ tbsp shatta (red or green) (see page 73) (or rose harissa, as an alternative)
½ tsp Urfa chilli flakes (or a small pinch of nigella seeds or black sesame seeds, as an alternative)
Salt and black pepper

### Aubergine yoghurt
2 large aubergines (500g)
35g Greek-style yoghurt
½ a garlic clove, roughly chopped
1½ tbsp lemon juice
1½ tbsp tahini (25g)

### Smacked cucumber
1 regular English (i.e. not a small Lebanese) cucumber, peeled, sliced in half lengthways and watery seeds removed (180g)
25g parsley, roughly chopped
25g mint leaves, roughly chopped
½ a garlic clove, roughly chopped
50ml olive oil

# Na'ama's buttermilk fattoush

Very few meals are complete in Palestine without bread. Very few dishes are served in Palestine without a chopped salad. That fattoush is such a staple salad, then – which uses up day-or-two-old bread – makes complete sense. You can use any flatbread – Turkish flatbread, naan, pita bread – torn into bite-size chunks. If you only have fresh flatbread that's also fine: just toast it a bit or grill it for a few minutes to dry it out. It'll soon firm up as it cools down.

The buttermilk is not a traditional addition but it is the version of the salad Sami grew up on. Na'ama was Sami's mum – this was her version of the salad and he would not change it for the world. It can be played around with, though, depending on what you have to hand: chunks of feta are, as ever, a nice addition, as are some black olives or green capers. For a more traditional version of the salad just follow the recipe below, leaving out the buttermilk.

*Getting ahead:* Get all the chopping and prep done for this in advance if you like, and even mix the vegetables and herbs with the buttermilk, but don't assemble it with the bread until you are ready to serve: it's not a salad that likes to sit around for too long.

*Ingredients note:* Start with Lebanese cucumbers (sometimes just called 'mini cucumbers') if you can: they're much less watery than larger English cucumbers, so have a lot more flavour. If you only have English cucumber that's absolutely fine: just slice in half, lengthways, scoop out the watery seed-filled core and just use the firm flesh you're left with.

## Serves six

2 large day-or-two-old naan, Turkish flatbread or pita (shop-bought or see page 278 for homemade), torn into roughly 4cm pieces (250g)
300ml buttermilk
3 large tomatoes, cut into 1½cm dice (380g)
10–11 radishes, thinly sliced (100g)
2–3 Lebanese small cucumbers (or 1 regular English cucumber), peeled and cut into 1cm dice (250g)
20g mint leaves, roughly chopped
20g parsley leaves, roughly chopped
2 tbsp picked thyme leaves
2 garlic cloves, crushed
3 tbsp lemon juice
60ml olive oil, plus extra to serve
2 tbsp cider (or white wine) vinegar
1½ tsp sumac, plus ½ tsp to serve
Salt and black pepper

## Sumac onions

½ an onion, cut in half, then each half thinly sliced (100g)
1½ tsp sumac
1 tbsp olive oil

Place all the ingredients for the sumac onions in a bowl with ¼ teaspoon of salt. Mix well and set aside.

Put all the ingredients for the salad into a large mixing bowl with 1½ teaspoons of salt and a good grind of black pepper. Mix well and set aside for about 10 minutes. Add half the sumac onions, mix to combine, then transfer to a large serving platter or individual plates. Sprinkle over the remaining onions, drizzle with olive oil, finish with a final sprinkle of sumac and serve at once.

# Roasted figs and onions with radicchio and goat's cheese

With figs, the riper the better when it comes to flavour and texture. The joy of roasting them, however, is that the sweetness and softness can be drawn out if the fruit is a little underripe. Here the figs and onions have been set aside to cool for 15 minutes before the salad is assembled, to prevent the cheese melting. Don't build this pause in if you don't want to: the salad is wonderfully luxurious if you toss it straight away and let the goat's cheese slightly melt. Serve this as either a stand-alone starter or a side. It works particularly well with grilled meat or with a nutty grain salad.

*Getting ahead:* The dressing can be made up to 3 days in advance. Make more of it than you need, if you like, to have around for drizzling over other salads or dishes.

---

Preheat the oven to 200°C fan.

First make the dressing. Mix together the vinegar, molasses, honey, garlic, ¼ teaspoon of flaked salt and a good grind of black pepper. Slowly pour in the 75ml of oil, whisking the whole time until combined and smooth.

Place the figs and onions in two separate bowls and add 1½ tablespoons of the dressing to each of them, along with ⅛ teaspoon of salt and ½ teaspoon of oil (to each bowl). Toss well to combine, then transfer to two parchment-lined baking trays, cut side up for the figs. Both trays can go into the oven at the same time: the figs need 20 minutes, or until softened and slightly caramelised, and the onions need 25–30 minutes, tossing once during baking, until they have softened and taken on some colour. Remove from the oven and set aside to cool for about 15 minutes.

Put half the roasted onions into a large bowl along with the radicchio, rocket, mint, walnuts, ½ teaspoon of flaked salt, a good grind of black pepper and half the remaining dressing. Toss well to combine, then transfer half the leaves to a large serving platter (or individual plates). Top with half the goat's cheese and half the figs, cut side up. Repeat with the remaining salad, goat's cheese, figs and reserved onions. Drizzle with the remaining dressing, squeeze over the lemon juice and serve.

## Serves four as a starter or side

12 figs, sliced in half
  lengthways (430g)
2 red onions, peeled, each
  onion sliced into 8 wedges (240g)
1 tsp olive oil
½ a head of radicchio, core removed
  and leaves roughly torn (180g)
60g rocket leaves
10g picked mint leaves
40g walnut halves, toasted (see
  page 339) and roughly broken
120g soft goat's cheese, roughly
  crumbled into large chunks
Flaked sea salt and black pepper
1½ tsp lemon juice, to serve

### Dressing
2½ tbsp balsamic vinegar
1½ tbsp pomegranate molasses
1½ tsp runny honey
2 garlic cloves, crushed
75ml olive oil, plus about
  ½ tsp extra to serve

# Green tabbouleh
## *Tabbouleh khadra*

Tabbouleh is so ubiquitous across the Levant that we didn't feel the need to publish our own traditional take on this well-known salad. Rather than tweaking the bulgur and parsley version, then, we've offered three rather novel versions: a green one with kale, a version which uses rice rather than bulgur (see opposite), and a wintry-citrus-purple version as well (see page 104).

Sami's mother used to make a version of this to take on picnics in Jericho in the summer months. The salad was kept fresh by the addition of a few cubes of ice to the bottom of the basket, wrapped up in newspaper. Picnics were, typically, an elaborate affair. Preparations would start the day before, with everyone coming together to chop and prepare for the movable feast.

This is as nice throughout the year as a side or part of a spread, as it is eaten on a picnic outdoors. The dressing is lemony and sharp, so it works particularly well with oily fish or rich meatballs.

*Getting ahead:* You can prepare the salad in advance but don't add the dressing until serving, and shred (rather than chop) the herbs: this will prevent them from bruising and losing their colour. The difference between chopping and shredding, for us, is the number of times the knife goes through the herb leaf. Chopping sees it getting cut many times – chop, chop, chop – whereas shredding sees the knife just go through once, in a cleaner motion.

*Playing around:* The kale can be replaced by all sorts of other cabbages, depending on what's in season: white cabbage, hispi (aka 'pointed') green cabbage, spring greens and young cauliflower with its tender leaves attached all work very well.

---

Place the bulgur in a small bowl, pour over the water, then set aside for about 20 minutes, or until the water has been absorbed.

Whisk together all the ingredients for the dressing, along with ¾ teaspoon of salt and a grind of black pepper, and set aside.

Transfer the bulgur to a large mixing bowl and add all the remaining ingredients for the salad. Pour over the dressing, toss well and serve.

## Serves four

50g bulgur wheat (regular or
    whole wheat, for extra nuttiness)
70ml boiling water
100g kale leaves (or 180g if starting
    with kale on the stalk, which
    you then need to remove), finely
    shredded
75g parsley (mostly leaves, not
    stalks), finely shredded
35g mint leaves, finely shredded
3 large (or 6 regular) spring onions
    (60g), very thinly sliced
Salt and black pepper

### Dressing
80ml lemon juice (from about
    2 lemons)
35ml olive oil
⅛ tsp ground cinnamon
¼ tsp ground allspice

# Rice tabbouleh
## *Tabboulet ruz*

**Serves four to six**

75g basmati rice (or 190g cooked
  rice, if starting with leftovers)
1½ tsp olive oil
¼ tsp ground turmeric
Salt

**Tabbouleh**
80g parsley leaves, finely chopped
20g mint leaves, thinly shredded
2 medium very ripe tomatoes, finely
  chopped (270g)
2 small Lebanese cucumbers (or
  ½ a regular English cucumber),
  finely chopped (no need to peel or
  deseed) (180g)
4 spring onions, thinly sliced (60g)
2 tbsp lemon juice
3 tbsp olive oil
½ tsp ground allspice
¼ tsp ground cinnamon
1½ tsp sumac, plus ¼ tsp extra
  to serve

This is a great way to use up leftover cooked rice, if you have any (but also delicious enough to start from scratch if you don't!). If you do this you'll need to start with 190g of cooked rice. Eating leftover rice is fine, as long as you chill what you are not going to use soon after it's made, rather than letting it sit around at room temperature for too long. Take it out of the fridge about 20 minutes before you want to eat the tabbouleh, though: you don't want it to be fridge-cold. You won't need the olive oil or turmeric, here: just add the rice to the rest of the salad ingredients as it is along with all the remaining ingredients.

*Getting ahead:* Do all the chopping ahead of time, if you like – up to about 4 hours – and the rice can be made a full day ahead. It can be mixed through an hour or so before serving, but not much more than this.

*Playing around:* The rice can just as well be replaced by other grains, if you want to play around: quinoa is a gluten-free option, like the rice, and couscous, mograbiah and fregola also all work well.

---

Put the rice, oil, turmeric and ⅛ teaspoon of salt into a small saucepan, for which you have a lid. Mix well, until the rice is well coated, then pour over 170ml of water. Bring to the boil on a high heat, then reduce the heat to very low. Cover the pan and cook for about 17 minutes, or until the rice is cooked. Spoon the rice on to a flat plate and set aside until completely cool.

Place all the ingredients for the tabbouleh in a large mixing bowl, along with ¾ teaspoon of salt. Add the cooked rice, mix well, then spoon on to a large serving plate. Sprinkle with the sumac and serve.

# Winter tabbouleh with a blood orange dressing
## *Tabbouleh shatwieh*

Blood oranges have a distinct colour and tartness which makes them really stand out in a salad or dressing. Their season is short, though, so regular oranges are absolutely fine for the rest of the year. As with our other tabbouleh salads (see pages 102 and 103), the bulgur can be replaced by an equal quantity of quinoa, if you like, for a gluten-free alternative. If you do this, then cook quinoa as you normally do – in a pan of boiling water for 9 minutes or so, then refresh under running water. Set it aside to dry, then add the olive oil and spices.

*Getting ahead / keeping notes:* This is a robust salad, so you can make it a good few hours before serving, if you want to get ahead. Leftovers are also lovely the next day.

---

Put the bulgur, cinnamon, allspice, 2 teaspoons of olive oil, the boiling water and ¼ teaspoon of salt into a medium sauté pan for which you have a lid. Bring to the boil on a medium heat, then cover the pan, remove from the heat and set aside for 30 minutes. Remove the lid, fluff the bulgur with a fork and set aside to cool.

Put the cavolo nero into a bowl with the remaining teaspoon of oil and a tiny pinch of salt. Using your hands, mix well, gently massaging the leaves, then set aside.

Put all the ingredients for the dressing, apart from the olive oil, into a bowl with ⅛ teaspoon of salt and a good grind of black pepper. Whisk to combine, then, continuing to whisk as you pour, slowly add the oil until the mix is thick and emulsified.

Tip the cooled bulgur into a very large bowl and add the cabbage, parsley, mint, spring onions, oranges, ¾ teaspoon of salt and a generous grind of black pepper. Mix well to combine, add the cavolo nero and pour over the dressing. Mix just to combine, then transfer to a serving platter or individual plates. Finally, sprinkle over the pomegranate seeds.

**Serves six to eight**

200g bulgur
½ tsp ground cinnamon
½ tsp ground allspice
1 tbsp olive oil
225ml boiling water
250g cavolo nero, stems discarded (or saved to chop up and pan-fry for another dish) and leaves roughly shredded (150g)
½ a small head of red cabbage, core cut out and discarded, then thinly sliced by hand or with a mandoline (550g)
40g parsley leaves, roughly chopped
25g mint leaves, roughly torn
6 spring onions, finely sliced (90g)
4 blood oranges (or 2 regular oranges, as an alternative) (500g), peeled and sliced into ½cm-thick rounds
85g pomegranate seeds (from ½ a pomegranate)
Salt and black pepper

**Blood orange dressing**
1 blood (or regular) orange, juiced to get 50ml
2 tbsp lemon juice
¼ tsp ground cinnamon
¼ tsp ground allspice
2 tsp pomegranate molasses
1 tsp caster sugar
130ml olive oil

# Vivien Sansour and the Palestinian Seed Library

Vivien Sansour is a strong woman. She has made a name for herself as a pioneering agriculturalist, botanist and, perhaps most impressively, founder of the Palestinian Seed Library project. She's forty and feisty and has a vision for her country that she's growing, seed by seed. It's a vision that highlights the vital link between farmers and their land. It's a vision that suggests that the connection between people and place really means something and really matters: that it's not all just about making a quick big buck.

The road to success was not always straightforward for Vivien. Born in Jerusalem and raised in Beit Jala, she moved with her family to North Carolina in the 80s, to make the most of the job opportunities offered in the States. Vivien's family perhaps had some inkling of where her future interests would lie when she enrolled in a PhD programme to study agricultural life sciences. Nonetheless, it came as a surprise to everyone – including Vivien herself – when she decided to drop out part of the way through the course and move back to her home village on the outskirts of Jerusalem. Her family thought she was mad – she had no clear plan, she had not prepared for the move. But Vivien had something more important than a plan – she had a vision, however indistinct in those early days, and she is a woman with the strength to stay true to her vision.

So what had sparked this new direction for Vivien? The journey all started, in fact, with a single seed. Two seeds, actually, and one slide of the herb za'atar, shown to her in a lecture theatre in North Carolina.

First, the slide. Vivien was already slightly uneasy with the thrust of her PhD programme. The emphasis seemed to be more on 'this is what we need to be teaching farmers' rather than 'this is what we should be learning from them'. It was a slide of za'atar, though, pictured clinically alongside its botanical Latin name, that snapped her into realising it was time to go home. Vivien sat on a bench in the park and knew that she wanted to be *smelling* and feeling the za'atar she had grown up with rather than studying it from a distance. She wanted to be working with her hands, not her head. She wanted to be with the farmers, not the academics, of the world.

In Palestine, Vivien quickly landed on her feet, undertaking a two-year project while living in Jenin, in the north of the country. She'd connected with Nasser, the owner of the Canaan co-operative (see page 250), who commissioned her to travel the region meeting, hanging out with and writing about the co-operative's approximately thirty-five farmers.

Time and again, as Vivien travelled the region, she would hear stories about a certain large variety of watermelon called the Jadu'l. Everyone had clear memories of the Jadu'l but it was no longer anywhere to be seen. Stories were told of people hiding in watermelon fields during the war, as the leaves were large enough to provide cover. But when she tried to seek out the seed, Vivien was told that she was 'looking for a dinosaur'.

Look for the dinosaur she did, though, eventually tracking down an elderly farmer-come-odd-job-man in his garage workshop in Jenin. In a drawer full of nails and hammers and behind a mish-mash of screws was a bag of dried-up heirloom Jadu'l watermelon seeds. They were no use to him any more, he said – he was now working with hybrid seeds and fertilisers which were earning him more than these heirloom seeds – so Vivien was welcome to them. She put them in her bag and went on her way, feeling like a detective who'd solved her first case.

Her second 'case' took place closer to home, in her local market in Bethlehem, shopping for vegetables. Vivien was seeking out the purple carrots her mum used to make for her, cooked in a tamarind sauce. Again, this vegetable that she had such fond memories of was nowhere to be found. She scoured the market, speaking to people as though she were trying to do a dodgy deal on the black market. 'If I felt like a detective seeking out the Jadu'l watermelon,' says Vivien, 'I felt like a drug dealer looking for the purple carrots.'

Eventually, though, she found a man who knew a man who eventually lifted up the cloth draped over his table in the market to reveal a sack of the bounty. He couldn't give them all to her – they'd been promised elsewhere – but Vivien was given two carrots which she raced home to plant in the ground, where they would sprout and produce flowers and seeds.

And so, off the back of these two heirloom vegetables, the Palestinian Seed Library was born. 'Seed as metaphor for growth' might seem a bit clichéd, but clichéd it isn't in a place where the very existence of certain heirloom seeds and crops, and the way of life surrounding their farming, is in crisis. For those whose lives, livelihood, identity and connection to the past are so tied up with the land, it all feels very unmetaphorical indeed. Preserving, archiving, protecting and propagating individual heirloom seeds is a very real way to preserve, protect and record the way of life of a people living under occupation. However tough or even hopeless something looks – or shrivelled and dried out in the case of the Jadu'l watermelon seeds Vivien was given – put it in the ground and nurture it and great things will happen: life will start all over again.

The threat and challenges faced by small farmers are many and complex and come from all sides. Accusations are levelled as much at the Palestinian authorities, for example, as they are at the Israeli government, for their setting up of industrial zones for which the main focus is short-term profit. The main challenge is the big incentives given to farmers to abandon their traditional way of farming – using a variety of heirloom crops and working in accordance with the seasons, for example – in favour of a mono-crop approach to farming. The choice between making a living in the short term versus holding out and preserving things for the benefit of the long term is not, for most Palestinian farmers, one they have the freedom to make. The advantages of mono-crop farming – producing strawberries year-round in greenhouses, for example – are obvious from an agri-business and commercial point of view. The disadvantages to the land, though, and the way of life of those who farm in accordance with the seasons, are just as obvious to see, but only by those who want to see them. The outcome, in Vivien's words, is that 'Palestinian farmers are being transformed from agents of their own choice to becoming day labourers on their own farms.'

There are other challenges, as well. Challenges that are controversial to talk about and that incite different opinions depending on who you talk to. Vivien takes it back to 1948, when Israel was created (and even pre-1948), and points to the myth put forward by the Israelis of Palestine being a 'dry area'. Starting from this point, credit for the future fertility of the land – for 'making the desert bloom' – can then be taken by those who are seen to be farming the land, i.e. the Israelis.

Focusing instead on crops that don't need irrigation in the first place – ba'al crops (after the Canaanite fertility deity, worshipped for rain), such as figs, grapes and olives, for example – Vivien has no truck with this narrative. Her passion, instead, is on the genius of her ancestors, those who were clever enough to develop a system of farming which was free, in large part, from the need for irrigation. 'It kept us alive for millennia and gave the world wheat.'

It's a passion she instils in the school kids and visitors who come to look at the seed library, which is now located in Battir, an agricultural village and UNESCO world heritage site just outside Jerusalem (and profiled on page 58). 'So often these kids are taught to think of themselves as a colonised or victimised people: that they need to be white or English-speaking, for example, to succeed.' Vivien tells them, instead, what their ancestors *gave* to the world and sees them puff up with pride. 'It's thanks to us that Italians eat pasta! Why do the kids who come in to see my seed library not know this?'

For such school kids, feeling proud of where you've come from is a great big step towards feeling pride and confidence in where you can go. For the farmers Vivien met during her two years in Jenin, like Khadir Khadir (see page 250), the assistance they receive from the likes of Vivien and Nasser at Canaan enables them to feel supported, as well, in what they can do.

Conditions are tough, no doubt, and 'the reality is true', says Vivien. 'But it's also true that we have the seeds and in these seeds we have our DNA.' In terms of messaging, it's all a long way from a dusty slide pulled up in a lecture theatre that afternoon back in North Carolina. At the time of writing, Vivien was propagating three seeds: the white cucumber, the 'tall dark' Abu Samra wheat and an heirloom tomato. It's exciting to think how much more can be grown.

# Roasted cauliflower and burnt aubergine with tomato salsa

We spent three nights in Haifa on one of our trips and spent two of those eating supper at the same restaurant, Fattoush, in town. The reason we went back two nights in a row was because we ate a version of this salad the first night and then went to bed dreaming about it. We went back the next night and duly ordered a whole portion each. All the elements here are delicious in and of themselves: the combination of all three is positively wonderful.

*Getting ahead*: You can char and marinate the aubergine a day or two ahead, then finish the dish off on the day of serving.

---

There are two ways to char your aubergines: either directly on the flame of your stove top or in a hot oven. The oven takes longer – 55–60 minutes (rather than 15–20 minutes on the stove). For full instructions see page 335.

Once the flesh has been scooped out of the burnt aubergines it should weigh about 500g. Place in a colander set over a bowl and leave for at least an hour (or overnight, in the fridge), to drain. Once drained, put the aubergine flesh into a medium mixing bowl and, using your hands, pull it apart to create long, thin strands. Add the garlic, lemon, vinegar and 1 teaspoon of salt. Mix to combine and set aside (in the fridge if you are making this a day ahead).

Preheat the oven to 200°C fan.

Put the cauliflower into a large bowl along with the olive oil, coriander seeds, turmeric, ¾ teaspoon of salt and a good grind of pepper. Mix well to combine, then spread out on a parchment-lined baking tray. Roast for 30 minutes, until the cauliflower is golden and tender. Remove from the oven and set aside to cool to room temperature.

While the cauliflower is roasting, place all the ingredients for the salsa in a bowl with ½ teaspoon of salt. Mix to combine.

To assemble the dish, spread the aubergine on a serving plate which has a lip and arrange the cauliflower on top. Spoon over the salsa, sprinkle over the mint and parsley and serve.

*Pictured overleaf*

## Serves four generously

4 large aubergines, pricked in a few places with a small, sharp knife (1kg)
1 garlic clove, crushed
1½ tsp lemon juice
2 tbsp cider vinegar
1 large cauliflower (or 2 medium), cut into roughly 3cm florets (800g)
3 tbsp olive oil
1 tsp coriander seeds
¾ tsp ground turmeric
Salt and black pepper

### Tomato salsa
3 large tomatoes, cut into ½cm dice (240g)
10g parsley, roughly chopped
1 tbsp oregano leaves, roughly chopped
2 tbsp olive oil
2 tbsp lemon juice

### To serve
5g picked mint leaves (small ones if you can, or else larger ones, shredded)
5g picked parsley leaves, roughly chopped

# Roasted aubergine, feta yoghurt, Aleppo chilli and pistachio

**Serves four as a starter or side**

4 medium aubergines (1kg)
60ml olive oil
20g pistachio kernels, lightly
   toasted (see page 339) and
   roughly chopped
5g picked mint leaves
5g picked dill leaves
¼ tsp Aleppo chilli flakes
   (or ⅛ tsp regular chilli flakes)
Salt and black pepper

**Feta yoghurt**
10ml whole milk
1 tbsp lemon juice
75g feta, finely crumbled
300g Greek-style yoghurt

There are lots more sheep and goats than there are cows in Palestine as cows are not traditionally reared. Much of the yoghurt and cheese, therefore, is made from sheep's or goat's milk. It's tangy – sour, even – in a way that works particularly well against the rich 'meatiness' of roasted aubergine. The further the yoghurt or cheese is taken – whether that's being hung in the case of labneh (see page 48) or fermented in the case of kishek (see page 54) – the more intense the tanginess. Here – in this dish which often features on the Ottolenghi menu – we use feta. It has a similar tangy-sour flavour profile at the same time as being instantly ready to use.

*Getting ahead:* If you want to get ahead, all the various elements can be made up to a day in advance. Keep the aubergine and the feta yoghurt in the fridge, separately, returning the aubergine to room temperature before serving.

*Playing around:* The feta yoghurt and other toppings work equally well on other roasted vegetables – roast wedges of beetroot or butternut squash, for example – as they do with the aubergine.

Preheat the oven to 220°C fan.

Cut each aubergine, lengthways, into wedges. They should be about 2cm wide at the base. Place them in a large bowl with the olive oil, ¼ teaspoon of salt and a good grind of black pepper. Mix to combine, then spread out on a parchment-lined baking tray. Roast for 30 minutes, until cooked through and golden brown, then remove from the oven and set aside to cool.

To make the feta yoghurt, put the milk, lemon juice, feta, yoghurt and ⅛ teaspoon of salt into a bowl. Whisk well to combine, breaking apart the feta until it almost disintegrates, then keep in the fridge until ready to serve.

Arrange the aubergine wedges on a large platter or individual serving plates and spoon over the feta yoghurt. Top with the pistachios, mint, dill and chilli flakes and serve.

*Pictured overleaf*

# Roasted squash and courgettes with whipped feta and pistachios

This is great as either a starter or as part of a spread. It also works as a side dish, served alongside meatballs or roast chicken. Get hold of yellow courgettes if you can: the clash of colour looks great with the squash.

*Getting ahead:* Roast the squash and courgettes a few hours before serving and mix them with the dressing, if you want to get ahead: they're happy to sit around for 3–4 hours, at room temperature, before serving. The whipped feta and yoghurt mix can also be made up to a day ahead and kept in the fridge until ready to serve.

*Playing around:* You don't need to do both the squash and the courgette, if you'd prefer to have just one or the other. You can also play around with other vegetables: carrots work just as well as the squash, for example.

Preheat the oven to 230°C fan.

Put the squash into a large bowl with 1½ tablespoons of oil, ¾ teaspoon of salt and a good grind of black pepper. Mix well, then spread out flat on a parchment-lined baking tray. Bake for 25 minutes, turning over halfway through so that both sides get some colour. Remove from the oven and set aside to cool. Leave the oven on.

While the squash is cooking, grease a chargrill pan and place on a high heat. Put the courgettes into a large bowl with the remaining tablespoon of oil, ½ teaspoon of salt and a good grind of black pepper. Once the grill pan is smoking hot, add the courgettes, in two batches if you need to, and cook for about 3 minutes, rotating the wedges so that they have chargrill marks on all sides. Transfer to a parchment-lined baking tray and bake for 5 minutes, or until they're cooked through but still retain a bite.

Put the honey, 1 garlic clove, the cider vinegar, tarragon and ⅛ of a teaspoon of salt into a large bowl and mix to combine. Add the squash and courgettes and stir very gently, to coat. Set aside until needed.

Put the ricotta, yoghurt, 60g of feta, the lemon zest and juice, the remaining garlic clove, ⅛ teaspoon of salt and a good grind of black pepper into a bowl. Mix well until smooth, using a whisk to break apart the feta. Spread the mixture out on a large serving platter and top with the courgettes and squash. Scatter over the rest of the feta, followed by the pistachios, coriander seeds and chilli flakes. Top with the mint leaves and serve.

## Serves four

½ a small butternut squash, sliced lengthways (but unpeeled), seeds scooped out, then each half cut widthways into 1½cm-thick slices (550g)
2½ tbsp olive oil
3–4 yellow (or green) courgettes (500g), sliced in half, lengthways and then widthways (to get 4 pieces from each courgette), then each piece cut in half again, lengthways, to make wedges
25g runny honey
2 garlic cloves, crushed
1 tbsp cider vinegar
5g tarragon leaves, roughly chopped
250g ricotta
50g Greek-style yoghurt
100g feta, roughly crumbled
1 lemon: finely grate the zest to get 1 tsp, then juice to get 1½ tbsp
Salt and black pepper

## To garnish

50g pistachio kernels, toasted (see page 339) and roughly chopped
1½ tsp coriander seeds, toasted and roughly crushed in a pestle and mortar
¾ tsp Aleppo chilli flakes (or ⅓ tsp regular chilli flakes)
About 5g small picked mint leaves, to serve

# Yoghurt-roasted cauliflower with quick-pickled chillies, sultanas and red onions

Roasting cauliflower florets in spiced yoghurt makes them feel almost tandoori-like. It creates a lovely crisp crust which works so well against everything else in the dish: the soft sweetness of the sultanas, the creamy crunch of the pine nuts. This works well either as a stand-alone salad or served along with some chicken and rice.

*Getting ahead:* The cauliflower can be roasted ahead of time, but don't mix the salad together until you are ready to serve: the herbs will wilt if they sit around for too long.

Preheat the oven to 230°C fan.

Put the yoghurt, garlic, turmeric, paprika, cumin, 2 tablespoons of oil, 1 tablespoon of lemon juice, 1 teaspoon of salt and a good grind of black pepper into a large bowl. Whisk well to combine, then set aside.

Pull the leaves away from the cauliflower: they'll have different lengths, but keep their shape intact. Slice the larger leaves down the middle, vertically, and place them (along with all the other leaves) in a medium bowl along with 1½ teaspoons of oil, ⅛ of a teaspoon of salt and a good grind of black pepper. Mix to combine, then spread out on a parchment-lined baking tray. Set aside. Remove the stalk from the cauliflower and slice it into roughly ½cm-thick pieces. Cut the cauliflower into large florets, about 6cm, and add these, along with the stalks, to the bowl of yoghurt. Mix until well coated, then transfer to a separate parchment-lined baking tray, spreading the pieces out so that they're not overlapping. Transfer both trays to the oven. Bake the leaves for 15 minutes, until they're softened and charred, and the cauliflower for 30 minutes, or until cooked through and charred in places. Remove from the oven and set both aside to cool completely.

While the cauliflower is roasting, put the sultanas, chilli, onion, vinegar and a tiny pinch of salt into a large bowl (the cauliflower will all be added to this). Mix to combine, then set aside for about 20 minutes, to pickle.

Once the cauliflower is completely cool, add it, with the leaves, to the bowl of pickle along with the pine nuts, herbs, the remaining 2½ tablespoons of oil and the remaining 2 tablespoons of lemon juice. Mix well to combine, then transfer to a serving platter and serve at once.

## Serves four as a side

85g Greek-style yoghurt
2 garlic cloves, crushed
⅓ tsp ground turmeric
1½ tsp paprika
2 tsp ground cumin
75ml olive oil
3 tbsp lemon juice
1 large head of cauliflower, leaves and all (1.2kg)
30g sultanas
½ a red chilli, deseeded and thinly sliced (10g)
½ a red onion, cut into thin rounds (60g)
4 tsp cider vinegar
25g pine nuts, toasted (see page 339)
10g picked parsley leaves
5g picked mint leaves
Salt and black pepper

# Chunky courgette and tomato salad
## *Mafghoussa*

**Serves six**

1kg courgettes (either 10 small
  pale green ones, ideally, or 5 large
  darker green ones), trimmed
  and sliced in half lengthways (or
  quartered lengthways, if large)
5 large very ripe tomatoes (800g),
  cut in half widthways
3 tbsp olive oil
300g Greek-style yoghurt
1 large garlic clove, peeled and
  crushed
1 lemon: finely grate the zest to get
  1 tsp, then juice to get 2 tbsp
1 tbsp date molasses, plus 2 tsp
  extra to serve
2 red chillies, deseeded and finely
  chopped
5g mint leaves, roughly chopped,
  plus 1 tbsp picked small leaves,
  to serve
15g parsley, roughly chopped, plus
  1 tbsp chopped parsley, to serve
Salt and black pepper

Mafghoussa, meaning 'mashed' in Arabic, is more of a spread than a salad.
We've kept our version nice and chunky but, if you want a spread, the
vegetables can be lightly crushed. Either way, it's delicious as it is – spooned
up with some pita – or served alongside all sorts of grilled meats, rice dishes
and other salads. Some lightly toasted and roughly chopped walnuts mixed
through are also a really nice addition.

The vegetables for mafghoussa are traditionally burnt on the embers in
a taboon oven, the clay (and often communal) oven found outdoors in
Palestinian village homes (see page 341 for more on taboon). It's great at a
summer barbecue, when tomatoes and courgettes are at their best and the
barbecue will be out and ready. In the absence of either a taboon oven or the
right weather for a barbecue, a griddle pan set over a high heat on the stove
also, happily, works very well.

*Getting ahead:* The vegetables can be chargrilled, chopped and left to drain
the day before serving, if you want to get ahead. Mix them with the yoghurt
and herbs on the actual day, though.

Preheat the oven to 200°C fan, place a ridged griddle pan on a high heat and
ventilate the kitchen well.

Spread the courgettes and tomatoes on two large parchment-lined baking
trays, cut side up. Brush with 2 tablespoons of olive oil (in total) and season
with ½ teaspoon of salt and plenty of pepper.

By now the griddle pan should be piping hot. Start with the courgettes.
Place a few of them on the pan, cut side down, and cook for 4–5 minutes;
the courgettes should be nicely charred on one side. If you've quartered
your courgettes lengthways, adjust them on the griddle halfway through
so that both exposed sides get charred. Return them to the baking tray,
arranging them all cut side up, and continue with the remaining courgettes
and tomatoes in the same way: the tomatoes just need a minute or so less on
the grill. Transfer the vegetables to the oven and roast for 20 minutes, until
the courgettes are very tender and the tomatoes are cooked through but still
retain their shape. Remove the trays from the oven and allow the vegetables
to cool down slightly. Chop them roughly into 2–3cm pieces and leave to drain
in a colander for 15 minutes.

Meanwhile, whisk the yoghurt, garlic, lemon zest, lemon juice, date molasses
and two-thirds of the chillies in a large mixing bowl. Add the chopped
vegetables, mint, parsley, 1 teaspoon of salt and plenty of pepper. Stir well,
then transfer to a large, shallow serving plate. Spread it all over, then garnish
with the remaining parsley, chilli and little mint leaves. Finally, drizzle over the
extra 2 teaspoons of date molasses and the remaining tablespoon of olive oil.

# Roasted aubergine with tamarind and coriander
## Batinjan bil tamer hindi

Tara's kids are always asking which of them is her favourite child. 'I have a favourite daughter,' she says, to her only daughter, Scarlett. 'And definitely a favourite oldest son,' she says to Scarlett's twin brother, Theo. 'And, of course, my favourite youngest child will always be Casper,' she says to the little one, before he punches the air and runs off to make some noise. When it comes to vegetable 'favourites', though, no such qualifications are needed: it's aubergines all the way. So loved is the mighty aubergine, and in this dish in particular, that they swiftly became Tara's new screensaver for her phone when they were shot for the book. Tara's favourite daughter – who'd previously taken the coveted screensaver spot – was distinctly unimpressed to have been bumped out by a vegetable.

This can be served either as a veggie main, with some rice and yoghurt spooned alongside, or as a side to all sorts of things: some pan-fried tofu, for example, or a lamb chop.

*Getting ahead:* This is a dish which can be made and assembled a good few hours before serving: it's happy to sit around for 4–5 hours. It can even be made the day before, if you like. Keep it in the fridge overnight, and either warm it through for a few minutes (before sprinkling over the fresh coriander) or bring it back to room temperature before serving.

**Serves six as a side or part of a spread, four as a main**

100g tamarind pulp (or 6 tbsp/70g tamarind paste, if starting with ready-made)
120ml boiling water
4 aubergines, sliced in half lengthways (1kg)
90ml olive oil
4 large garlic cloves, crushed
2 lemons: finely grate the zest of both to get 1½ tsp, then juice to get 60ml
2 tsp caster sugar
½ tsp coriander seeds, lightly toasted, then roughly crushed in a pestle and mortar
5g picked coriander leaves
Salt and black pepper

---

Preheat the oven to 200°C fan.

Place the tamarind pulp in a bowl and pour over the boiling water. Set aside for 20 minutes or so, stirring or squeezing the pulp into the water from time to time. If starting with ready-made paste you don't need to do this.

Use a small, sharp knife to make 4–5 deep, parallel incisions in the cut side of each aubergine half. Don't go so far through the flesh that you reach the skin on the other side, though. Repeat at a 45° angle to get a diamond pattern. Place the aubergines on a parchment-lined baking tray, cut side up, and brush evenly with 60ml of oil. Sprinkle with ¾ teaspoon of salt and a good grind of black pepper and roast for about 35 minutes, turning the tray around halfway through, until the aubergines are cooked through, soft and golden brown.

While the aubergines are roasting, pass the tamarind mixture through a fine-mesh sieve into a bowl: it should weigh about 70g. The seeds and pulp left over in the colander can be discarded. Add the remaining 30ml of oil along with the garlic, lemon juice, sugar, ¾ teaspoon of salt and a grind of black pepper. Mix well and then, when the aubergines have been roasting for 35 minutes, spoon the sauce generously over their cut sides. Sprinkle with the coriander seeds and return to the oven for a final 5 minutes. There will be a bit of excess sauce in the tray but that's fine: you can just spoon this over the aubergines when serving.

Remove from the oven and allow to cool for 10 minutes (or longer if serving at room temperature) before transferring to a serving platter or individual plates. Sprinkle over the lemon zest and fresh coriander and serve.

# Marrow and chickpeas cooked in yoghurt
## *Kousa bil laban*

Cooking vegetables in yoghurt is common all over Palestine but particularly characteristic in the north, due to the Syrian and Lebanese influence. Cooking things in a sauce of yoghurt (rather than, say, a tomato sauce) happens due to practical reasons – there is so much yoghurt around that it's a building block of the traditional cuisine – but, also, because it's such a good way to enrich a dish and make it luxurious. Here, for example, two thoroughly humble ingredients – chickpeas and marrows – are totally transformed into something rich and comforting. Don't start with a large marrow here: they can taste bitter and their flesh can be watery. If you can't get hold of a marrow, use an equal weight of courgettes. If you do this they'll just need a couple of minutes less cooking.

Serve this either warm or at room temperature, as a side or as part of a spread.

*Getting ahead:* This is best eaten the day it's made. Leftovers are fine for a couple of days, though. Just bring back to room temperature or gently warm through before eating.

Top and tail the marrow, then quarter the whole marrow lengthways. Using a small knife, cut away and discard the core flesh and seeds. Cut the remaining firmer flesh into 1½cm dice and set aside.

Put 2 tablespoons of olive oil into a large saucepan, about 20cm wide, and place on a medium heat. Add the onion and cook for 5 minutes, stirring a few times. Add the chilli, cook for a minute, then add the marrow. Cook for another 5 minutes, stirring a few times, until the marrow has become slightly greener and is starting to soften.

Put the yoghurt and egg yolk into the small bowl of a food processor (or a free-standing blender) and blend for half a minute, until smooth and runny. Pour into a small saucepan and place on a high heat for about 3 minutes, stirring all the time with a wooden spoon, until the yoghurt starts to bubble. Take care it does not come to the boil, as this will cause the yoghurt to split. Once hot, add this to the pan of marrow, along with the chickpeas, 1½ teaspoons of salt and some black pepper. Cook gently on a low heat, stirring from time to time, for another 5 minutes. Keep an eye on the yoghurt towards the end of cooking: it will split if it gets too hot.

Meanwhile, put the remaining 3 tablespoons of olive oil into a small saucepan and place on a medium heat. Once hot, add the garlic and cook for 1–2 minutes, stirring frequently, until the garlic is a very light golden brown. Add the coriander, stir through for 5 seconds and then set aside.

When ready to serve, spoon the marrow and sauce into a deep bowl (or individual serving bowls) and top with the garlic-coriander mix. Sprinkle over the chilli flakes, if using, and serve either warm or at room temperature.

**Serves four to six**

1 small marrow (800g) (or courgettes, as an alternative)
75ml olive oil
1 onion, roughly chopped (140g)
1 green chilli, finely chopped
400g Greek-style yoghurt
1 egg yolk
1 x 400g tin of cooked chickpeas, drained and rinsed (240g)
2 large garlic cloves, crushed
20g coriander leaves, finely chopped
Salt and black pepper
½ tsp Aleppo chilli flakes (or ¼ tsp regular chilli flakes), to serve (optional)

# Courgettes, garlic and yoghurt
## M'tawameh

M'tawameh is, traditionally, made with the scooped-out flesh of courgettes after they've been hollowed in order to be stuffed. Here, however, we're short-cutting the process by starting with the whole courgette, skin and all. It has a bit more texture as a result, which we love, making it more of a veggie side or condiment than a completely smooth dip. The result is rich, light and comforting all at once.

Serve this either as it is, scooped up with some warm pita for a light lunch with some black olives, or as a side to all sorts of things. Pan-fried fish, grilled chicken or roasted beetroots, for example, all work particularly well.

*Getting ahead / keeping notes:* This keeps well in the fridge for up to 3 days.

Put the oil into a medium sauté pan and place on a medium-high heat. Add the onion and cook for about 5 minutes, stirring from time to time, until it has started to soften. Add the courgettes and ½ teaspoon of salt, and cook for another 10 minutes or so, stirring a few times, until the courgettes are soft. Remove the pan from the heat and set aside to cool.

Put the yoghurt, garlic and ¼ teaspoon of salt into a large bowl and mix to combine. Once the courgettes are cool, add these to the yoghurt and stir to combine. Transfer to either a flat serving platter (with a lip) or a shallow bowl. Sprinkle over the dried mint and peppercorns, drizzle with some olive oil and serve.

**Serves four as a dip or side**

2 tbsp olive oil, plus extra to serve
1 onion, finely chopped (150g)
4 large courgettes, chopped into
    1cm dice (800g)
200g Greek-style yoghurt
3 large garlic cloves, crushed
½ tsp dried mint
1 tsp dried pink peppercorns
    (not the kind in brine), roughly
    crushed in a pestle and mortar
Salt

# Braised broad beans with olive oil and lemon
## Foul akdar

This is a simple dish but, thanks to the generous amount of lemon juice and the even more generous olive oil, wonderfully sharp and rich. It's lovely as it is, warm or at room temperature, with a bowl of rice or some plain yoghurt alongside, or else as a side or as part of a mezzeh spread. Leftovers are also delicious and keep well for a couple of days, so double or triple the batch if you have a glut of beans.

*Ingredients note:* For those used to taking broad beans out of both their pods and their individual fibrous skins, braising them whole will be a little revelation. The younger and more tender the beans that you start with, the more melt-in-the-mouth they will feel.

**Serves four as a side or part of a spread**

90ml olive oil
1 onion, finely chopped (150g)
3 garlic cloves, crushed
600g fresh broad beans, stalks trimmed, stringy part removed, then cut on the diagonal into roughly 4cm-long pieces
200ml chicken (or vegetable) stock
1 lemon: finely grate the zest to get ½ tsp, then juice to get 2 tbsp
¼ tsp dried mint
10g parsley leaves, roughly chopped
10g mint leaves, roughly chopped just before serving
Salt and black pepper

Put the oil into a large sauté pan, for which you have a lid, and place on a medium-high heat. Add the onion and cook for about 7 minutes, stirring occasionally, until soft and golden brown. Add the garlic and cook for another 30 seconds, until fragrant, then add the broad beans, stock, 1½ teaspoons of salt and a good grind of black pepper. Bring to a simmer, then lower the heat to medium-low and cook for about 25 minutes, covered, until the beans are very soft.

Stir in the lemon juice and dried mint and set aside either to cool, if serving at room temperature, or for just 10 minutes if serving warm. Scatter over the parsley, mint and lemon zest and serve.

# Spiced chickpeas
## *Balilah*

**Serves four as a salad or six as part of a spread**

200g dried chickpeas, soaked overnight in twice their volume of water and 1 tsp bicarbonate of soda (or 2 x 400g tins of cooked chickpeas, as an alternative)
2 lemons
1½ tsp cumin seeds, lightly toasted and roughly crushed in a pestle and mortar
1½ tsp coriander seeds, lightly toasted and roughly crushed in a pestle and mortar
75ml olive oil
10g parsley leaves, roughly chopped, plus a few extra leaves to serve
10g mint leaves, roughly torn, plus a few extra leaves to serve
3 spring onions, thinly sliced (30g)
1 tsp Aleppo chilli flakes (or ½ tsp regular chilli flakes)
½ red onion, very finely chopped (70g)
Salt and black pepper

As a kid, Sami used to snack on balilah on the way home from school in East Jerusalem. Traditionally, it's a street-food snack piled into cone-shaped newspaper packages and served warm, but it also works as a salad, served warm or at room temperature. As a salad, it works with all sorts of things: some grilled fish or chicken with a simple green salad or just wedges of roasted butternut squash, for example.

*Getting ahead:* This is served either warm, soon after assembly, or at room temperature: it can happily sit around for a few hours. Leftovers are also great for the lunchbox the next day. Keep in the fridge overnight and bring back to room temperature before eating.

If they've been soaking overnight, drain the chickpeas, place them in a large saucepan and cover with plenty of cold water. Bring to the boil on a high heat, then reduce the heat to medium-low. Simmer for 40–60 minutes (or 5–10 minutes, if starting with tinned), skimming any scum off the surface of the water a few times, until the chickpeas are very soft but still retain their shape. Towards the end of the cooking time – 5–10 minutes before they are ready – add ½ teaspoon (or ¼ teaspoon, if starting with tinned) of salt.

Meanwhile, finely zest one of the lemons to get 2 teaspoons. Set this aside in a large bowl (the chickpeas will end up here). Peel the same lemon, cutting away the bitter white pith. Roughly chop the flesh, removing any pips, and add this, along with all of the juices, to the bowl with the zest. Halve the remaining lemon, lengthways, and squeeze the juice of one half into the bowl. Slice the remaining half into very thin slices, discarding any pips as you go along, and add these to the bowl as well.

Drain the chickpeas once they are cooked and, while they are still hot, add them to the lemon in the bowl. Add the cumin, coriander, olive oil, herbs, spring onions, half the chilli flakes, half the onion, 1½ teaspoons of salt (or just 1 teaspoon if starting with tinned chickpeas) and a good grind of black pepper. Mix well to combine, then transfer to a serving platter. Top with the remaining onion and chilli flakes and the extra parsley and mint leaves. Serve either warm or at room temperature.

# Lentils with tahini and crispy onion
## *Adass bil tahineh w al basal*

This is a really useful and completely addictive side to all sorts of grilled vegetables, meat or fish dishes. It's nutty and creamy from the tahini and almonds, hearty and wholesome from the lentils and, thanks to the crispy fried onions, very hard indeed to stop eating.

*Getting ahead:* You can make the lentils a day ahead, if you like, adding the nuts and crispy onions just before serving. Keep the lentils in the fridge but, as ever, bring them back to room temperature before serving. The onions can also be made a day ahead (and stored separately from the lentils). They need to be kept at room temperature, in an airtight container.

---

Put the lentils into a large saucepan and pour over 1½ litres of water. Set aside for 1 hour, to soak.

To make the crispy onions, put the oil into a large frying or sauté pan: you want it to rise about 2cm up the side of the pan. Place on a medium-high heat. Mix the onions with the cornflour, then, when the oil is hot, add them in two or three batches. Cook for 8–14 minutes (timings vary greatly depending on how hot your oil is), stirring from time to time, until the onions are really golden and crispy. Transfer to a plate lined with kitchen paper – spread them out so that the onion does not get soggy – and sprinkle lightly with salt. Set aside while you continue with the rest of the onions.

Bring the pan of lentils to the boil on a high heat, then reduce the heat to medium-low and cook for about 15 minutes, until the lentils are soft but still retain a bite. Drain the lentils and rinse straight away under cold water, to stop them cooking. Drain well, then tip into a large mixing bowl along with the tahini, garlic, chillies, lemon juice, cumin and 1½ teaspoons of salt. Mix well to combine, then set aside for 10 minutes.

When ready to serve, put half the crispy onions, most of the toasted almonds and a third of the parsley into a wide serving bowl. Mix to combine, then add the lentils. Give everything a gentle stir, and top with the remaining onions, almonds and parsley. Drizzle over the olive oil and finish with a sprinkle of paprika.

### Serves six to eight

350g green lentils
60g tahini
2 large garlic cloves, crushed
2 large green chillies, finely
  chopped
60ml lemon juice (from about
  2 lemons)
2½ tsp ground cumin
60g flaked almonds, toasted (see
  page 339)
15g parsley leaves, roughly chopped
Salt
60ml olive oil, to serve
½ tsp paprika, to serve

### Crispy onions
About 400ml sunflower oil, to fry
2 onions, cut in half, then each
  half thinly sliced (300g)
1½ tbsp cornflour

# Sautéed tomatoes
## *Galayet banadoura*

**Serves four as part of
a mezzeh selection**

800g plum tomatoes (8 or 9)
90ml olive oil
1 green chilli, halved lengthways,
 then roughly chopped, seeds
 and all
8 garlic cloves, 2 crushed and the
 remaining 6 very thinly sliced
 lengthways
½ tsp dried mint
10g pine nuts
5g picked mint leaves, shredded
5g parsley leaves, roughly chopped
Salt and black pepper

This is somewhere between a tomato dip and stewed tomatoes. Either way, it's rich, silky and really versatile. Serve it either as part of a mezzeh, with some crusty white bread to mop it all up, or as a side to all sorts of dishes. Any grilled meat or fish, for example, some pan-fried tofu, and all sorts of grain and pulse dishes work well. It's also really delicious as a pasta sauce.

*Getting ahead:* The tomatoes keep well in the fridge, for 3–4 days. The garlic and pine nuts can also be prepared well ahead (kept at room temperature), ready to be spooned over when assembling the dish.

---

Core the tomatoes and score the base with an 'x': this makes it easier to remove their skins. There are two ways to do this. The first is to bring a medium saucepan of water to a simmer, on a medium-high heat, and lower in the tomatoes. Cook for 1–2 minutes, or until the skins start to shrink back, then remove them with a slotted spoon. While the tomatoes are still warm, peel off and discard the skins. The second way is to place them in a large bowl and cover them with boiling water. Leave for 1–2 minutes, then strain away the water. Again, while the tomatoes are still warm, peel off and discard the skins. Once peeled, slice each tomato into 6 wedges and set aside.

Put 3 tablespoons of oil into a large sauté pan and place on a medium-high heat. Add the tomatoes, chilli, crushed garlic, 1 teaspoon of salt and a good grind of black pepper. Cook for about 18 minutes, stirring occasionally, until the tomatoes have broken down and the sauce has thickened. Stir in the dried mint and transfer to a serving platter. Set aside to cool slightly.

Meanwhile, put the sliced garlic and the remaining 3 tablespoons of oil into a small frying pan and place on a medium heat. Cook for about 4 minutes, or until the garlic starts to become lightly golden. Add the pine nuts and cook for another 3 minutes, or until they have taken on some colour. Pour the mixture, along with the oil, over the tomatoes and garnish with the mint and parsley. Serve warm or at room temperature.

# The Tent of Nations: one family's story of peaceful resistance

Sumud is the Arabic word for 'steadfastness': the stubborn, patient insistence that, despite the odds, things will work out. The Tent of Nations, a small farm 7 kilometres south-west of Bethlehem, is a case study in Palestinian sumud. The story of the farm is one-of-a-kind but only by degree. The issues at the heart of the story – namely the threat Palestinians feel to their autonomy over, ownership of, and freedom within the land of their ancestors – play out for family after family, day after day, all throughout the Occupied Palestinian Territories (see page 339).

The Tent of Nations is home to the Nassar family. Daoud and Amal are husband and wife and they live on the land with their extended family, including Amal's brother Daher and their mother Milada. It's been their home since 1916, when Amal's grandfather bought the land. Amal's father, Bishara, was born in one of the eight caves within the land. The family has been living there, simply, ever since. At the same time, they've been in court since the early 1990s – around thirty years at the time of writing – peacefully and legally defending their right to stay there. Steadfast, they remain.

At the heart of the long-standing case is the question of land ownership. This goes back to the Oslo peace accords, written up in 1993, which stated that the West Bank was to be divided into three distinct areas: A, B and C. On paper, the thinking was simple: dividing the land up this way would make it clear who was allowed to be where, and who was responsible for the upkeep, protection and governance of each particular area. Area A, 18 per cent of the West Bank, remained under Palestinian Authority (PA) control and security authority. Area B, about 22 per cent of the West Bank, was to be shared responsibility, with civil administration under PA control, and exclusive security control under the Israeli jurisdiction (with limited cooperation from Palestinian police). Area C, by far the biggest chunk of land at about 60 per cent of the West Bank, remained under full direct Israeli civil and security control. According to those who drew up the accords, this all made sense and seemed pretty fair, with a plan in place to ensure that full Palestinian governance was achieved by 1999.

Twenty years later, that goal has clearly been missed along the way, and the effects of that missed goal are felt far and wide. Palestinians in Area C feel particularly let down by a system which does little to protect their services and needs. Area C contains most of the West Bank's natural resources and open areas, but the distribution of these resources – most noticeably water and the freedom

to build – is far from equal. If a Palestinian in Area C needs a police car or an ambulance or a rubbish collection, chances are there won't be one rushing to them any time soon.

The Tent of Nations is in Area C. It's surrounded by five Israeli settlements. The nearest is close enough that the Nassar family can hear the voices of the settlers on the farm, carried down the valley. The largest, Beitar Illit, has a population of more than 40,000. The settlements are all deemed illegal under international law, a fact refuted by the Israeli government. If the feeling of being encroached upon was mainly visual for the Nassar family, as the settlements were built and expanded throughout the 80s, it became actual in the early 90s, when the military authorities declared that more than 90 per cent of the farm belonged to the State of Israel. A loophole had been found in the system and was set to be exploited. Unfortunately for the Israelis, however, the Nassars had the faith and, crucially, the paperwork to start their long, determined but peaceable battle. Both their deep faith and robust paperwork were thanks to Amal's grandfather, who'd had the unusual foresight to register the land in 1924.

The loophole was a piece of legislation dating back to the Ottoman Empire which said that if a piece of land is considered 'uncultivated' for over three years (even if this is due to its owners being denied the access to cultivate it) then 'ownership' will revert automatically to the state. The Nassars received their first of many demolition orders. Peacefully, they refused to budge. Peacefully, they have been in court ever since.

This is just one of the cases keeping them in court. Two others are against the military, following the destruction of their fruit trees in 2014 and the hundreds of olive trees which have since been uprooted. Demolishing these trees is an act of destruction in two ways. On the one hand, it's an actual way of preventing the land from being properly cultivated, thus creating 'facts on the ground' which can be used by the Israeli authorities in court. And on the other, in a land where olive trees are so deeply rooted in the identity and livelihood of the people, it's also, symbolically, as well as literally, devastating.

Again, the frustrating irony for a Palestinian trying to take action in Area C is that, because the officials call the shots, the officials can, and do, make it as madly difficult for the family to proceed in court as possible. The situation is Kafkaesque. Amal has lots of stories about attempts that have been made to thwart their legal efforts and progress. After ten years in the military courts, for example, they were told that their Palestinian lawyer was not eligible to contest the case in Israel's Supreme Court because he carried West Bank identity papers. 'Consequently,' Amal says, 'we found an Israeli firm willing to take it on.' On a separate occasion, they were asked to bring witnesses to support the claim that the land had been farmed over three generations. They hired a bus for more than thirty local villagers to go to the military court near Ramallah. After five hours of waiting in the heat of the sun, a single soldier came out and told them: 'We don't want witnesses; go home.'

'At every turn,' says Daoud, 'we are given the option to get violent, to resign or leave. At every turn we choose not to take these options. Nobody can force us to hate. We refuse to be victims and we refuse to be enemies. We want to live in peace and dignity on our own land.' If this all sounds a bit syrupy then we are not doing a good enough job conveying the contrast between the reality Amal and Daoud have to put up with on a daily basis, and the grace, hope and faith with which they do so.

The family have a strong Christian faith, rooted in the 'turn the other cheek' line of thinking rather than the 'eye for an eye' school of thought. Their faith is also strengthened by the steady stream of volunteers and visitors – both international and local – who support their efforts in various ways. Volunteers, for example, can come and stay for a number of days or weeks and provide support with farm work, particularly during times of harvest, after which jams are made, fruit and nuts are dried and olives are pressed. It took twelve years to get their first volunteer to come to the farm in 2011, says Daoud. Now, they get about 8,000 a year. 'No one believed we could withstand the system but we kept going. It's this – something coming from nothing – that gives us hope.'

Some visitors stay for weeks to work while others, just as importantly, come for day trips to see the farm, have a meal cooked for them by Bishara's widow, Milada, and hear from Amal and Daoud about the work being done to fight peacefully for justice. 'COME, SEE, TELL' is written on a sign as you enter the farm. It's a powerful reminder of the importance of visiting, bearing witness to and then telling people who don't know (or aren't listening) about it, to propel them in turn to take action. Local school kids also visit, either for day trips or for longer summer camps.

Donations also help, whether large or small. A solar energy system is thanks to German sponsorship, for example. On a smaller scale, individuals are able to sponsor single or multiple olive trees to replace those that have been destroyed. This all goes an enormous way to restoring not only the land but also the spirits of those that live on it – but of course there is still a long, long way to go.

The Tent of Nations is one-of-a-kind, but, in a land where the number of settlements continues to grow, it's a testament more widely to the power of a Palestinian family's faith, sumud, and desire to stay rooted to the land they feel so part of. It's not just about the actual plot of land and it's certainly not about the money. 'The last cheque we received [from a settler, to buy the land] was blank,' says Daoud. 'We were told by an anonymous caller that we could write out the cheque with any amount we wanted.' It's about the principle, about doing the right thing, about not accepting that the only options open to them are violence or resignation.

Amal's name means 'hope' in Arabic. 'Inshallah hasam: tomorrow will be better,' she says. Their eldest daughter has just graduated from school, studying international human rights law. The next generation stands ready to take on the battle; the battle that the Nassar family call active hope and peaceful resistance.

# Spicy roasted new potatoes with lemon and herbs
## *Batata bil filfil*

Sometimes – oftentimes! – all a dish needs alongside it is some roasted new potatoes. This is the side for the job.

*Getting ahead:* Take this up to the point before the potatoes are ready to go into the oven, if you want to get ahead of yourself: the potatoes and tomatoes can sit around on the tray for a couple of hours. Don't put them into the oven ahead of time, though: they want to be eaten freshly roasted.

**Serves four as a side**

3 tbsp olive oil
1 tsp cumin seeds, lightly crushed in a pestle and mortar
1 tsp coriander seeds, lightly crushed in a pestle and mortar
7 large garlic cloves, thinly sliced (20g)
1 large red chilli, thinly sliced (20g)
200g cherry tomatoes, sliced in half
750g baby new potatoes, quartered
½ tsp caster sugar
1 large lemon: finely grate the zest to get 2 tsp, then juice to get 2 tbsp
10g coriander leaves, roughly chopped
5g dill, roughly chopped
Salt and black pepper

Preheat the oven to 200°C fan.

Put the olive oil into a large sauté pan, and place on a high heat. Add the cumin and coriander seeds and cook for 1 minute, stirring frequently. Add the garlic and cook for another minute, until the garlic starts to colour. Add the chilli and tomatoes and cook for another 2 minutes, stirring from time to time, until the tomatoes have started to soften. Add the potatoes, sugar, 1 teaspoon of salt and a generous grind of black pepper. Give everything a good stir, then transfer the mixture to a large parchment-lined baking tray. Roast for about 40 minutes, tossing once halfway through, until the potatoes are crispy and cooked through and the tomatoes are breaking down.

Remove from the oven and set aside to cool for 5 minutes before adding the lemon zest, lemon juice, coriander and dill. Toss gently and serve at once.

# Turnip mash with greens, caramelised onions and feta

This started off as a way to use up all the turnip and potato flesh we'd generated from recipes in which turnips and potatoes were stuffed. The turnips made the cut (see page 241), the potatoes did not. The resulting mash turned out so good, though, that it soon became a reason to buy the vegetables in the first place! Necessity (not to discard good food) was indeed the mother of great invention here (along with Noor, of course, our crucial right-hand lady on the book, who created the recipe!). If you are making the stuffed turnips, though, and do have all that spare flesh, save it to make this the next day. Just cover it with water until ready to use, to prevent discoloration.

*Playing around:* Don't be too precious with what herbs and greens you add here: try to keep the net weight the same but, if you have more spinach than cavolo nero to use up, for example, or parsley rather than dill, that's absolutely fine. It's meant to be a bit of a fridge-raid-of-leftovers recipe.

---

Put 2½ tablespoons of oil into a large sauté pan and place on a medium heat. Once hot, add the onions and cook for about 35 minutes, stirring only every so often, until deeply browned and caramelised. Scrape the onions into a bowl and return the pan to a medium-high heat. Add 1½ tablespoons of oil, followed by the garlic, and cook for 1 minute, stirring continuously. Add the cumin seeds and cook for another 30 seconds, or until fragrant. Add the cavolo nero, ¼ teaspoon of salt and a good grind of black pepper, and cook for about 5 minutes, stirring often, until softened and lightly charred. Add the spinach and cook for about a minute, until just wilted. Transfer to a bowl and stir in the herbs.

While the onions are cooking, put the turnips, potatoes and 2 teaspoons of salt into a large saucepan for which you have a lid. Fill the pan with water so that the vegetables are covered, and bring to the boil on a medium-high heat. Reduce the heat to medium-low, cover and leave to cook for 15 minutes, or until the vegetables are easily pierced with a knife. Drain through a sieve and return to the pan along with the yoghurt, 2 tablespoons of oil, ½ teaspoon of salt and a good grind of black pepper. Use a potato masher to create a chunky mash, and transfer to a serving platter. Scatter over half of the feta and half the onions. Pile the greens into the centre and top with the remaining onions and feta and the extra herbs. Drizzle all over with the last 2 tablespoons of oil and serve.

## Serves four to six as a side

120ml olive oil
2 onions, thinly sliced (300g)
4 garlic cloves, crushed
1 tbsp cumin seeds, roughly crushed in a pestle and mortar
200g cavolo nero, woody stems discarded and leaves roughly torn (140g)
100g baby spinach
5g parsley leaves, roughly chopped, plus extra to garnish
5g dill, roughly chopped, plus extra to garnish
750g turnips, peeled and cut into roughly 2cm chunks
600g baking potatoes, peeled and cut into roughly 3cm chunks
100g Greek-style yoghurt
120g feta, roughly crumbled into large chunks
Salt and black pepper

# Bulgur, tomato and aubergine pilaf
## *Shulbato*

This makes either a simple lunch, served with some thick Greek yoghurt, or a side to all sorts of things. Grilled chicken, pan-fried tofu, salmon fillet – they all work well.

*Getting ahead:* The aubergine cubes can be roasted ahead of time, if you like, and warmed through with the bulgur before serving.

*Playing around:* Cubes of creamy avocado or tangy feta are a nice addition, dotted on top before serving. Also, if you're looking for an alternative to the aubergine then courgettes can be used. Cut them into roughly 2cm dice and add them to the pan at the same time as the bulgur.

---

Preheat the oven to 220°C fan.

Place the aubergines in a large mixing bowl with 3 tablespoons of olive oil and ½ teaspoon of salt. Mix well, then spread out on a parchment-lined baking tray. Roast for 20 minutes, or until soft and golden brown. Remove from the oven and set aside.

While the aubergines are roasting, put the remaining 2 tablespoons of oil into a large saucepan, for which you have a lid, and place on a medium heat. Add the onions and cook for about 8 minutes, or until the onions have softened and started to colour. Add the garlic and cook for another 2 minutes, then add the tomato purée and sugar. Stir for 30 seconds, then add the tomatoes, chillies and water. Bring to the boil, then add the bulgur, spices, 1¼ teaspoons of salt and a good grind of black pepper. Return to the boil, then reduce the heat to very low. Cook for 15 minutes, covered, then remove the pan from the heat. Keep the lid on and set aside for 10 minutes.

Add the aubergines to the pan and gently stir through. Spoon on to a serving platter or individual plates, sprinkle with the coriander and chilli flakes, and serve with a spoonful of yoghurt, if using.

**Serves four as a light meal or side**

2 medium aubergines, cut into roughly 2cm dice (420g)
75ml olive oil
1 onion, thinly sliced (180g)
1 garlic clove, crushed
1 tbsp tomato purée
1 tbsp caster sugar
3 medium-sized ripe tomatoes, roughly chopped (380g)
2 green chillies, finely chopped, seeds and all
400ml boiling water
350g coarse bulgur
1 tsp ground cumin
¼ tsp ground cinnamon
Salt and black pepper

**To serve**
10g coriander leaves, roughly chopped
About ½ tsp Aleppo chilli flakes (or ¼ tsp regular chilli flakes)
Greek-style yoghurt (optional)

# Buttery rice with toasted vermicelli
## *Ruz bil sh'arieh*

**Serves four as a side**

300g basmati rice
35g unsalted butter
1 cinnamon stick
50g vermicelli wheat noodles or
 spaghetti, as an alternative,
 roughly broken into 3cm pieces
520ml hot water or hot chicken
 stock (optional)
Salt and black pepper

There's an old wives' tale that a woman used to add pasta to rice only if she was an unconfident cook or couldn't cook rice properly. The theory was that adding pasta was a guaranteed way to prevent the rice from sticking together. True or otherwise, it's a guaranteed way to get it seriously fluffy and it's a good few steps up from regular steamed rice. The pasta brings texture, the butter brings comfort and the cinnamon brings a hint of spice.

*Ingredients note:* Don't get the flat Asian rice noodles here: you want the Italian wheat vermicelli nests. They are like spaghetti, but thinner. Regular spaghetti makes a fine alternative.

Place the rice in a bowl and allow tap water to run over it until the water is clear. Set aside to soak for at least an hour (or overnight, if you are getting ahead). Transfer the soaked rice to a sieve placed over a bowl and leave to drain for about 15 minutes.

Put 25g of butter and the cinnamon into a medium saucepan, for which you have a lid, and place on a medium-high heat. Add the vermicelli or spaghetti and cook for 3 minutes, stirring continuously, until deeply golden. Mix in the rice for about 30 seconds, then add the water (or stock), along with 1½ teaspoons of salt (or slightly less – about 1 teaspoon – if using stock and it is salty) and a good grind of black pepper. Cover the pan tightly with foil and put the lid on top of this. Reduce the heat to low and leave to cook for 15 minutes. Turn off the heat and set aside for 15 minutes, covered, to steam.

Remove the lid and foil and dot with the remaining 10g of butter. Set aside for another 10 minutes, covered with the foil and lid, or just the lid, before serving.

# SOUPS

You don't need to grow up eating soup for it always, somehow, to take you straight back home. It's an inherently comforting thing to eat: nurturing and reassuring at the end of the day. For Sami, growing up, what was made into soup at home reflected what was being grown in the fields and sold in the market. Batches made were big and the cost of feeding a large family was kept in check. Spring meant besara, for example, making use of all the broad beans, molokhieh and soft herbs in season. Autumn and winter meant dark green chard and lentil soup or something hearty like freekeh with chicken meatballs.

For all their power to comfort and soothe, soups can also be made to surprise and delight. This can either be from a great big squeeze of lemon (which we've reached for in all but one of our soups in this chapter), or else a texture-giving topping. Fried onions are a frequent addition to lots of soups in Palestine – it makes them quite addictive – but we've only used this winning trick once here, on the chard and lentil soup (see page 157). Layers of texture and topping have been brought about in other ways: with caramelised pistachios, for example, or spicy pumpkin seeds (see pages 153 and 149). A mix of roasted aubergine cubes and chopped walnuts also works well (see page 152), or leaving some broad beans whole to stand out from those which are blitzed in the besara (see page 150). As well as bringing crunch and contrast, these sorts of toppings are also a way to bulk out a soup, making it into a meal in itself, served with, of course, the ubiquitous bread (or rice), olives or pickles.

A clash in colour, as well as texture, can also work really well to bring an element of surprise to a soup: a green herb oil drizzled over an orange butternut squash soup, for example (see page 153), or the addition of finely diced tomatoes to a green cucumber soup (see page 149).

Another great thing about soups is how un-precious they are: as happy to be made ahead of time, waiting in the fridge or freezer to be eaten, as they are to be spooned up there and then. They're also robust enough to be played around with in terms of toppings and garnishes. They can be dressed down for a midweek supper alone, or dressed up for a stand-alone meal or impressive starter with friends. There's a soup for all occasions, a soup for all seasons and a soup for all sorts of reasons. It's the ultimate home-cooked food.

# Chilled cucumber and tahini soup with spicy pumpkin seeds

If you want something to be rich and creamy and vegan all at once, tahini is often the big secret, ingredient-wise. Swirled through a sauce, a dressing or in a soup, as here, tahini is a wonderful way to enrich a dish. With the cucumber, lemon and herbs doing all the work at the other end to freshen and lighten things up, this is a perfect meal for a summer's day.

*Getting ahead:* The soup can be made up to a day in advance: it keeps well and doesn't lose its colour. Just give it a stir before serving, as there'll be a little water separation.

*Playing around:* Double or triple the batch for the pumpkin seeds, if you like: they keep for a week in a sealed container, at room temperature, and are lovely sprinkled over all sorts of salads and roast vegetables.

---

**Serves four**

3 large cucumbers (1kg), peeled
65g tahini
2 tbsp olive oil, plus extra to serve
2 lemons: finely grate the zest to get 2 tsp, then juice to get 60ml
2 large garlic cloves, crushed
10g dill, roughly chopped, plus a few extra fronds to serve
¾ tsp Aleppo chilli flakes (or ⅓ tsp regular chilli flakes)
100g ice cubes
20g mint leaves
20g parsley, roughly chopped
Salt and black pepper
1 tomato, cut into ½cm dice (80g), to serve

**Spicy pumpkin seeds**
3 tbsp olive oil
40g pumpkin seeds
1 tsp ground cumin
¼ tsp chilli flakes

Put all the ingredients for the spicy pumpkin seeds into a small sauté pan, along with ⅛ teaspoon of salt, and place on a medium heat. Cook for about 8 minutes, stirring frequently, until the seeds begin to colour lightly and pop. Transfer to a bowl (or to an airtight container if making a batch) and set aside to cool.

Cut off a roughly 80g chunk of cucumber and slice in half. Scoop out the seedy core (add this to the pile of cucumber to be blended), then finely chop the remainder into 1cm dice. Set this aside, to serve. Roughly chop the remaining cucumber into 2cm chunks and transfer to a free-standing blender (or a deep bowl if you are using a hand-held blender), along with the tahini, oil, lemon zest, lemon juice, garlic, dill, chilli flakes, ice cubes, half the mint, half the parsley, 1 teaspoon of salt and a good grind of black pepper. Blitz for about 2 minutes, until completely smooth, then keep in the fridge until ready to serve.

Divide the soup between four deep bowls and spoon the reserved cucumber and diced tomato on top. Shred the remaining mint and sprinkle this over each portion, along with the remaining parsley, any spare dill fronds, the spicy pumpkin seeds and a final drizzle of oil.

# Molokhieh soup with broad beans
## *Besara*

Besara is somewhere between a soup and a thick, warm dip. Broad beans are the main ingredient, pointing to its Egyptian origins before the dish spread across the Levant. By the time it got to Palestine, the herbs in the Egyptian version – coriander and parsley – were matched by Palestine's flavour-packed green leaf, molokhieh. Wherever it is made across the Levant, the presence of fried onion, chilli, lemon and olive oil are a constant.

Molokhieh is a bit like spinach but its texture is distinct – slimy, almost (without the word putting people off!). It's used a lot in the Middle East but the leaves, fresh or frozen, can be hard to find outside of Middle Eastern stores. We've come up with an alternative of spinach cooked with a bit of okra which is then all blitzed together. Texture-wise, the result comes pretty close (see page 339 for more on this).

*Getting ahead*: This keeps in the fridge and keeps its colour for 2 days, or longer if frozen.

---

To remove the broad beans from their skins, cover them with boiling water for 30 seconds before refreshing them under cold running water and squeezing them out of their skins. They should now weigh about 450g.

*If using just the molokhieh:* put the oil into a large saucepan, about 21cm wide, and place on a medium-high heat. Add the onion and cook for about 8 minutes, stirring from time to time, until the onion is golden brown. Add the garlic and cook for another minute. Take half this mixture out of the pan and set aside: this will be used when serving. Add the molokhieh to the mixture remaining in the pan – it should go in frozen – along with most of the broad beans and all the cumin and coriander seeds. Pour over the stock and bring to a gentle boil on a medium heat, skimming any scum from the surface as you go. Cover the pan and simmer on a low heat for 5 minutes, then add all the herbs, 1½ teaspoons of salt and a good grind of black pepper. Return to the boil, then simmer gently for a final 5 minutes, with the pan covered.

*If using the combination of spinach and okra:* put the oil into a large saucepan and place on a medium-high heat. Once hot, add the onion and cook, stirring occasionally, for about 7 minutes, or until softened and lightly browned. Add the garlic and cook for another minute. Take half this mixture out of the pan and set aside: this will be used when serving. Add the okra to the onion remaining in the pan and cook for 3 minutes more, then add the spinach, spices, stock, 1½ teaspoons of salt and a good grind of black pepper. Bring to the boil, then lower the heat to medium and cook for 20 minutes, or until the okra has completely softened. Add the herbs and most of the broad beans, and cook for another 5 minutes.

Using a blender (hand-held or free-standing), roughly blitz the soup: you don't want to blitz too much, as you still want to see pieces of broad bean.

To serve, ladle the soup into bowls, and top with the reserved fried onions and whole broad beans, followed by a sprinkle of chilli and the extra herbs. Serve with a wedge of lemon alongside and some warm bread, if you like.

## Serves four

700g frozen podded broad
  beans (450g once removed
  from their skins)
2 tbsp olive oil
1 onion, finely chopped (150g)
3 large garlic cloves, crushed
250g chopped frozen molokhieh (or
  400g spinach, stems discarded
  (200g), plus 150g okra, sliced into
  2–3mm rounds)
1 tsp cumin seeds, lightly toasted
  and roughly crushed in a pestle
  and mortar
2 tsp coriander seeds, lightly
  toasted and roughly crushed
  in a pestle and mortar
700ml chicken (or vegetable) stock
15g coriander leaves, roughly
  chopped, plus a few extra chopped
  leaves to serve
15g parsley leaves, roughly
  chopped, plus a few extra chopped
  leaves to serve
15g dill leaves, roughly chopped,
  plus a few extra chopped leaves
  to serve
1 large red chilli (15g), thinly sliced
Salt and black pepper

### To serve
1 lemon, quartered
Warm bread (optional)

# Grilled aubergine and lemon soup

The more you char your aubergines here, the smokier and better the soup will taste. For more on the ways and wonders of charring aubergine, see page 335.

*Getting ahead:* Both elements here – the soup and the fried aubergine topping – can be made a day or two in advance. Keep them both in the fridge, separately, and just warm through before serving.

---

Cut 2 of the aubergines into roughly 2cm cubes. Place them in a sieve set over a bowl or the sink, sprinkle with 1 teaspoon of salt, mix well, leave to drain for 30 minutes, then pat dry with kitchen paper.

Place the remaining 4 aubergines directly over the flames on your stove top (if you have a gas stove) or in a chargrill pan sitting on a very high heat. For instructions on how to chargrill aubergines, see page 335. Once you have your charred, drained flesh, chop it finely: it should weigh about 400g.

Put the aubergine flesh into a large saucepan along with the stock, 60ml of lemon juice, the garlic, cinnamon, cumin, 2 tablespoons of olive oil, 2 teaspoons of salt and a good grind of black pepper. Bring to the boil on a medium-high heat and, once boiling, reduce the heat to medium and simmer for 30 minutes: the liquid will reduce by about a third.

Meanwhile, put the sunflower oil into a medium sauté pan and place on a medium-high heat. Once hot, add the cubes of aubergine (in three or four batches, so as to not overcrowd the pan) and fry for about 5–6 minutes, until they are a deep golden brown. Transfer to a plate lined with kitchen paper while you continue with the remaining batches. Put all the aubergine into a bowl along with the remaining 2 tablespoons of lemon juice and 1 tablespoon of olive oil, the chilli, coriander and walnuts. Mix to combine, then set aside.

Put the yoghurt, egg yolks and cornflour into a medium bowl and whisk well until smooth. Spoon a ladleful of the hot soup into the yoghurt and stir well to combine. Repeat this one more time before stirring the yoghurt mixture into the soup. Doing this prevents the yoghurt splitting when it's added to the hot soup. Cook on a medium-low heat for 2 minutes, stirring continuously, until the soup has come together and slightly thickened.

Divide the soup between four bowls and sprinkle with ½ teaspoon of ground cumin. Top with the fried aubergine and walnut mix and serve at once.

*Pictured overleaf*

## Serves four

6 aubergines (1.5kg)
1 litre chicken (or vegetable) stock
90ml lemon juice (from about 4 lemons)
4 garlic cloves, crushed
1 tsp ground cinnamon
2 tsp ground cumin, plus ½ tsp extra to serve
3 tbsp olive oil
About 300ml sunflower oil, to fry
1 red chilli, finely chopped (10g)
10g coriander leaves, finely chopped
100g walnut halves, roughly chopped
150g Greek-style yoghurt
2 egg yolks
2 tsp cornflour
Salt and black pepper

# Butternut squash and saffron soup with caramelised pistachios and herb salsa

This is the soup to launch your autumn cooking, whether you're looking for a comforting midweek meal or an impressive starter for a feast. Don't make both toppings if you don't want to: the soup works well with either the pistachios or the herb oil alone. The combination of all three, though, is a special one.

*Getting ahead:* All the elements can be made well in advance. The soup keeps well in the fridge for 3 days (or longer in the freezer). The herb oil can also be made a day or two ahead: it keeps its colour well. The pistachios keep well in a sealed container (at room temperature): they'll get less crunchy with time but still taste good. Double the batch for these, if you can: they're lovely sprinkled over salads or just to have around to snack on.

---

**Serves four generously or six as a starter**

2½ tbsp olive oil
2 large onions, roughly chopped (320g)
5 garlic cloves, crushed
1 large butternut squash, peeled, deseeded and cut into roughly 1½cm dice (1kg)
1 large potato, peeled and chopped into roughly 1½cm dice (250g)
1 tsp paprika
¼ tsp saffron threads
1 litre vegetable stock
Salt and black pepper

**Caramelised pistachios**

150g pistachio kernels (or pumpkin seeds, as an alternative)
1 tsp Urfa chilli flakes (or ½ tsp regular chilli flakes)
1 tsp orange blossom water (optional)
2 tsp golden syrup
2 tsp maple syrup
1 tbsp olive oil
¼ tsp flaked sea salt

**Herb salsa**

15g parsley leaves, finely chopped
10g oregano leaves, finely chopped
1 banana shallot, finely chopped (50g)
½ tsp chilli flakes
120ml olive oil
1 tbsp cider vinegar

Preheat the oven to 150°C fan.

Put the oil into a large saucepan, for which you have a lid, and place on a medium heat. Add the onions and cook for about 12 minutes, stirring often, until soft and golden brown. Add the garlic and cook for 30 seconds, until fragrant, then add the squash, potato, paprika, saffron, vegetable stock, 2 teaspoons of salt and a good grind of black pepper. Bring to the boil on a medium-high heat, then reduce the heat to medium-low and simmer for about 25 minutes, covered, or until the vegetables are completely soft and cooked through. If you like your soup smooth, use a blender (hand-held or free-standing) to blitz it as much as you want. We like to half-blitz it so that some texture remains: if using a free-standing blender, transfer half the soup to this, blitz until smooth, then return this to the un-blitzed soup in the pan. Keep warm until ready to serve.

While the soup is cooking, put all the ingredients for the caramelised pistachios into a bowl and mix well to combine. Tip out on to a parchment-lined baking tray and bake for about 15 minutes, stirring halfway though, until the nuts are golden and bubbling. Remove from the oven, set aside until completely cool, then roughly chop the nuts. Set aside (or keep in an airtight container if making in advance) until needed.

Put all the ingredients for the herb salsa into a bowl with ¼ teaspoon of salt and a grind of black pepper. Keep aside until ready to serve.

When ready to serve, ladle out the soup and top with a generous spoonful of the pistachios. Drizzle over the herb salsa and serve at once.

*Pictured overleaf*

# Freekeh soup with chicken meatballs
## *Shorbet freekeh*

It's hard to talk about any form of chicken soup without talking about comfort. Pulling this back from the brink of slippers and Sunday night, though (not that anyone ever needs to resist), is the freekeh (see page 336 for more). Adding this smoked cracked wheat, with its nutty bite, to this soup makes it the best of all worlds: comforting *and* classy.

*Getting ahead:* The meatballs can be made and pan-fried a day in advance. The soup also keeps well, once cooked, for up to 3 days in the fridge.

---

If mincing your own chicken thighs, either pop them into the freezer for half an hour, to firm up, or if you don't have time, put them straight into the bowl of a food processor. Firming them up in the freezer helps them to mince cleanly, but skipping this stage is also fine. Either way, blitz until finely minced.

Put the bread and buttermilk into a large bowl. Set aside for about 5 minutes, then use your hands to squish the mixture into fine crumbs. Add the minced chicken and all the remaining ingredients for the meatballs, apart from the sunflower oil, along with ⅔ teaspoon of salt and a generous grind of black pepper. Mix to combine, then form the mixture into small balls, each weighing about 10–15g: you should make about 30.

Put the oil into a large frying pan and place on a high heat. Once hot, add the meatballs and fry for about 3 minutes, turning throughout, so that they are nicely browned on all sides but not cooked through. Remove from the pan and set aside on a plate lined with kitchen paper until needed.

Put 2 tablespoons of olive oil into a large saucepan, for which you have a lid, and place on a medium heat. Add the leek and celery and cook for about 12 minutes, stirring from time to time, until the vegetables are soft but not taking on any colour. Add the spices, garlic and tomato purée and cook for another minute, until fragrant. Add the freekeh, 20g of coriander, the parsley, stock, 2 teaspoons of salt and a good grind of black pepper. Simmer for about 40 minutes, with the pan half covered, or until the freekeh is soft and the liquid has reduced by a third. Lower in the meatballs and simmer for another 10 minutes, with the pan covered, until they are cooked through. Stir through two-thirds of the spring onions, the remaining 10g of coriander and 50ml of lemon juice, and keep warm until ready to serve.

Combine the buttermilk with the dried mint, the remaining 2 teaspoons of lemon juice and ¼ teaspoon of salt.

Divide the soup between four bowls, drizzle with the buttermilk mixture, sprinkle over the remaining spring onions and serve at once.

## Serves four

### Chicken meatballs
300g minced chicken thighs (either ask your butcher to mince them or follow the instructions in the recipe) (or minced turkey thighs, as an alternative)
1 large slice of sourdough, crusts removed, cut into roughly 1cm dice (55g)
45ml buttermilk
2 spring onions, finely sliced (30g)
5g parsley, finely chopped
10g mint, finely chopped
1 green chilli, deseeded and finely chopped
½ tsp ground cinnamon
½ tsp ground allspice
2 tbsp sunflower oil, to fry the meatballs
Salt and black pepper

### Soup
2 tbsp olive oil
1 large leek, trimmed, cut in half lengthways and finely sliced (200g)
3 sticks of celery, trimmed and finely sliced (150g)
1 tsp cumin seeds, roughly ground in a pestle and mortar
1 tsp ground cinnamon
½ tsp ground allspice
4 garlic cloves, crushed
1 tbsp tomato purée
170g freekeh
30g coriander, roughly chopped
20g parsley, roughly chopped
1½ litres chicken stock
3 spring onions, finely sliced (45g)
60ml lemon juice (from about 2 lemons)
120ml buttermilk
¼ tsp dried mint

# Chard, lentil and preserved lemon soup
## *Shorbet adass w sliq*

### Serves four

200g green or brown lentils
2 tbsp olive oil
1 onion, finely chopped (150g)
3 garlic cloves, crushed
1½ tsp cumin seeds
1 tsp coriander seeds, roughly
   crushed in a pestle and mortar
½ tsp ground turmeric
¼ tsp chilli flakes
250g Swiss chard, stalks removed
   and finely chopped, leaves roughly
   torn
750ml chicken (or vegetable) stock
1 preserved lemon, pips discarded,
   skin and flesh finely chopped (20g)
Salt and black pepper
1 lemon, quartered into wedges, to
   serve (optional)

### Crispy onions

200ml sunflower oil
1 onion, cut in half, then thinly
   sliced (150g)
2½ tsp cornflour

If something is verging on the holier-than-thou in the kitchen, top with some crispy fried onions, we say. They work particularly well when paired with that most virtuous of all things – the lentil! – in something like mjaddarat el burgul (see page 178), rummaniyya (see page 176) or, as here, this soup. For those happy feeling holy, though, the soup also works well as it is, without the onions. If you still want a crunch, then some toasted pumpkin seeds (see either page 93 for herb salad ones or page 149 for chilled cucumber ones), caramelised pistachios (see page 153) or croutons all go really well.

*Getting ahead:* The soup can be made well ahead – up to 3 days if keeping in the fridge, or longer if you are going to freeze it – and the onions also keep well in a sealed container at room temperature for a couple of days. Make more of the onions than you need, if you like – they are lovely to have to sprinkle over all sorts of things: lentils and rice, for example, oven-roasted veg or grilled meat.

---

Wash the lentils in plenty of cold water and place them in a medium saucepan. Cover with 1 litre of water and bring to the boil on a high heat. Reduce the heat to low and simmer for 30 minutes, or until the lentils are just soft. Drain and set aside.

Put the oil into a medium saucepan – about 22cm wide – and place on a medium heat. Once hot, add the onion and cook for 10 minutes, stirring occasionally, until soft and golden brown. Add the garlic, cumin and coriander and cook for another minute, then add the turmeric, chilli, chard stalks, 1½ teaspoons of salt and a good grind of black pepper. Mix well to combine, then add the lentils and stock. Bring to the boil, then reduce the heat to medium-low and simmer for 10 minutes before adding the chard leaves and preserved lemon. Cook for another 4 minutes, then remove from the heat.

Transfer about half the soup to a blender (or to a separate bowl, if using a hand-held blender) and blitz until smooth. Return the blitzed soup to the un-blitzed soup in the pan and set aside until ready to serve.

To make the crispy onions, put the oil into a large, shallow frying pan and place on a medium heat. Once hot, reduce the heat to medium-low. Mix the onions with the cornflour and add them to the oil in two or three batches. Cook for 10–15 minutes, until the onions are really golden and crispy. Transfer them to a plate lined with kitchen paper – spread out so that the onions do not get soggy – then sprinkle lightly with salt and set aside while you continue with the remaining batches.

To serve, warm the soup through and divide between four bowls. Top with the crispy onions and a squeeze of lemon, if you like.

# VEGGIE MAINS

How food is cooked at home in Palestine is very different from the way that it is cooked in restaurants. In restaurants the emphasis is on food which can be cooked fast: marinated and skewered meat, for example, ready to be quickly grilled. Ground meat shaped into kofta, ready to be fried or baked. This sort of cooking – quick-on-and-off-the-heat – is called 'mashawi'. It's something that restaurants in Palestine are really good at. All the work can be done in advance, ready to be quickly whipped up when the order comes through. These are the kebabs and shawarma joints, the falafel, kofta and pita stands, seen on many a street corner in the cities (and in chapters 2, 6 and 7 in this book).

Restaurants are also good at mazzeh, or mezzeh, the spread of little bowls and dishes which take over the table (and much of chapters 2 and 3) at the beginning of a meal. These, again, are all dishes which can be prepared, in bulk if needed, in advance: carrots can be chopped and steamed, cucumbers and tomatoes can be diced, aubergines can be charred and drained for baba ganoush. Lemons are squeezed, bread is made and ready to be warmed through, olives are pickled and ready to be portioned up, labneh is hung. This is all food which is as happy to appear at the table, at the click of a finger, as it is to sit around for a day or so if service is slow and the food needs to go back into the fridge overnight. No time, money or food is wasted. It's an efficient, delicious, often grilled or fried business.

Home cooking, on the other hand, is different. Home cooking is about traybakes or stews, about stuffed vegetables or meats, about roasts and things which take a bit more time to make. This sort of cooking – 'tabeekh' – is the opposite of the 'grab-and-eat' style of restaurant cooking: it's slower and more comforting. This can be the stuffed dishes – 'mahashi' – vegetables which need coring and hollowing out before being stuffed and cooked. Or it can be the category of cooking known as 'sawani' – the roasts, braises and traybakes: dishes which use up the vegetables and herbs you have in the fridge and which, when served from the tray they are baked in, are often described as 'rustic'. These are the dishes which start with the ingredients often called 'humble': pasta, chickpeas, wilted spinach and rice. These are the recipes for easy, comforting, everyday cooking and are what this chapter – and so much Palestinian home cooking – is all about.

# Pan-fried okra with tomato, olives and haloumi
## *Bamia bil siniyhe*

Having noted the difference between home and restaurant cooking (see page 160), this is a dish which blurs any such distinction. Although it feels 'rustic' and 'homely', it's one we first ate and were inspired to re-create after a meal at Daher Zeidani's Alreda restaurant in Nazareth. The fact that the dish blurs the restaurant–home distinction says a lot about Daher himself (see page 166 for more), as much a seasoned chef as he is host, focal point and bringer together of community. People spend time at Alreda not just to eat (though eat very well they do): they come to the restaurant also to meet with their neighbours, to talk, drink, listen to music and debate. This is a dish with bold flavours, which is quick and easy to make. It works as well as a main – served with bread or rice – as it does as a side or as part of a spread.

*Getting ahead:* This is a quick and easy dish but you can make it a few hours in advance, if you like, up to the point before it goes under the grill. That way you can just finish it off in the oven for 10 minutes grilling before serving.

*Ingredients note / playing around:* If you see bags of small frozen okra in a Middle Eastern supermarket, do get hold of these. Not needing to be trimmed, smaller okra don't run the risk of their seeds being exposed (which is what gives okra its reputation for being 'slimy'). Starting with regular okra is absolutely fine, though: trim the tips but not so far that you can see the seeds.

---

Preheat the oven to a 250°C grill setting.

Put the olive oil into a large ovenproof frying or sauté pan, about 28cm wide, and place on a medium heat. Add the garlic and cook for just under a minute, or until it starts to colour. Add the cumin, paprika and shatta and cook for 30 seconds, then add the vinegar, sugar, 60ml of water and 1 teaspoon of salt. Bring to the boil, then add the okra and cook on a medium heat for 5 minutes, stirring once or twice. Add the tomatoes, olives and haloumi to the pan and cook for another 2–3 minutes, shaking the pan from time to time so that things don't get stuck to the base.

Place the pan directly under the grill for 10 minutes: you want the cheese and okra to take on lots of colour and even blister in parts. Remove from the oven and set aside to cool for 5 minutes before serving, with the chilli, parsley and a good drizzle of oil on top and the wedges of lemon alongside.

**Serves two as a main or four as a side**

3 tbsp olive oil, plus extra to serve
4 garlic cloves, thinly sliced
¾ tsp ground cumin
½ tsp paprika
1 tbsp shatta (see page 73) (or rose harissa, as an alternative)
1 tbsp cider vinegar
1 tsp caster sugar
400g okra, trimmed (but not so far so that you expose the seeds, see headnote), or frozen baby okra, defrosted
180g cherry tomatoes (about 15), sliced in half
70g pitted Kalamata olives
120g haloumi cheese (or feta, as an alternative), broken into roughly 1cm chunks
Salt

**To serve**
1 green chilli, thinly sliced
5g parsley, roughly chopped
1 lemon, cut into wedges

# A tale of two restaurateurs:
# the politics (or not) of food

We ate one night in Haifa, up north from Tel Aviv, on the coast. The next night we were in nearby Nazareth, eating again. The same central activity, but the two evenings could not have been more different. Both chef-owners were Palestinian and they both served us great food. What made the two experiences so polar opposite, though, was the chef-owners' relationships to their food and customers, and what they saw as the purpose of having a restaurant in northern Israel.

Contrasting the two shows how different opinions can be about the role of food in the region and how strongly held these opinions are. After sitting at their respective tables, over the course of two nights, we walked away thinking two things. One was that both ways of seeing food in northern Israel, from a restaurateur's point of view, are entirely valid; that we, as guests at their table, should restrict any judgements we might have to their food. The second was that we were getting to eat very, very well. This is the tale of two restaurateurs, then: one in Haifa and the other in Nazareth.

First: 'hip' Haifa. Haifa is a port city, rising steeply up from the Mediterranean Sea on the slope of Mount Carmel. It's home to a lot of start-ups and has the feel of a real technological hub. Through the city stretches a long, wide main road. It reaches from the coast right up to the incongruously coiffed, vibrant green terraces of the Bahá'í Gardens, backdrop to many a selfie.

In Haifa we had supper at the then newly opened Lux restaurant. Located on the port road in Haifa's lower city, Lux is as bustling as the Independence Road it looks out on to. It was Sami's partner Jeremy's birthday the night we were there, and we feasted to celebrate. The open kitchen was in full swing, the music was playing, the bar stools were high, and all the food that came our way was excitingly tasty and something fresh. Chef-owner Alla Musa (pictured opposite) was creating a stir locally, taking the ingredients of the area – the fish, spices, yoghurt and nuts, for example – and giving them to his customers in a sexy, different and very delicious way. Standouts, for us, were pan-fried seafood on a spread of herbed labneh, and a fillet of sea bass with charred aubergine and baby okra. We'd gone to Haifa in search of something new and noteworthy being done with fish, and this was the night we found it.

We'd chatted with Alla the day before in El Marsa, the other restaurant he owns and runs in Akka. Akka is a really pretty fishing port close to Haifa. With a steady flow of tourists and locals on their days off, El Marsa – a seafood restaurant

– caters to what his customers want. In the early days, Alla tried to push the boat out and experiment with the menu, but there was no point. People wanted seafood linguine and a kids' menu, not the foams and finishes Alla had learnt while working in a Michelin-starred restaurant in Sweden. 'People just didn't want it,' he said. With rent and salaries to pay and plans to expand both his family and his business, Alla's goal is to make great food that makes enough money to allow him to carry on making great food. Giving the market what it wants and letting the food speak for itself is not any sort of cop-out, says Alla: it's just plain good business sense.

Alla Musa couldn't have been more generous with his time, beer fridge and bottle of arak. He was happy as anything to sit around and chew the food-related cud, and the conversation flowed as steadily as the drinks, until one topic came up that was evidently out of bounds: politics. Tara asked whether the local Palestinian fishermen were affected by restrictions on the water they could fish in and was met by an affable diversion. Sami asked the seemingly impartial question whether Alla's business partner at Lux, Ahmad Asadi, was an Israeli or a Palestinian Arab. 'He's local,' said Alla. 'How would you describe yourself?' followed up Sami. 'I don't want to talk politics, and saying whether someone is an Arab or Palestinian or Israeli just turns everything into politics.'

Alla's determination not to talk about politics does not mean he doesn't know the lie of the political land. He's politically savvy enough, for example, to know that when there is tension at the Gaza border it affects who his customer base will be for the next few days and weeks. His Israeli regulars, who normally sit side by side with Haifa's Arabs, just don't turn up. Alla is young, ambitious and completely nuts about his food. If he upped the politics of it – if he made it into a question of identity and struggle and connection to the land – he'd be reducing the flow of customers who come through the door. Israeli, Palestinian, Palestinian-Israeli, Arab-Israeli, Arab of the Negev, the people of the north, people of the West Bank, 48ers, Inside Arab, the Shamenet Arab, Arab al beseder: whatever his customers call themselves, Alla just wants them to come and eat, drink and be merry. No politics, no tension, no problem: let's party! With that, Alla finds out that it's Jeremy's birthday the evening we are in, and the shot glasses appear.

The following night we are in Nazareth, pulling up our chairs at the Alreda restaurant, opened by Daher Zeidani in 2003. After the previous night's celebrations, we'd resolved to have a night off booze. Chef-owner Daher pulled up a chair to talk with us before we ordered our food. 'Don't you think it's so rude,' he opened with, 'when customers go to a restaurant and don't have a drink? Who are these people who think it's okay to just ask for water all night? I am the host and I want my guests to sit back and eat what I give them and have a drink.' Cripes, we thought, that'll be three beers then. It was just one of Daher's very many strong opinions.

If Alla Musa's food was all about the food, then Daher's food was food being served with a very large side order of politics. This was food with a strong Arabic identity, served in a restaurant which felt like an old Arabic house made by a chef-owner who didn't give two hoots about whose feathers he might be ruffling. The Germans! The English! The Japanese! Israelis! Never let it be said that national stereotypes don't live on! Having ruled out half of Europe, Asia and the Middle East, Daher clarifies his position, unashamedly: 'This is not a superficial place. This is a place for enlightened liberals.' The very irony of his position – having such a fixed (i.e. illiberal) view on what constitutes being a liberal customer – hangs, with the cigarette smoke, in the air.

The customers Daher is interested in and keen to serve and please are his local, Arabic, regulars, about 80 per cent of whom he knows by name. The restaurant feels as much like a social club as it does a formal restaurant, with lots of hand-shaking and back-patting as Daher pulls up a chair at one of the tables whenever he feels like it. 'I am the host. Why is it odd for me to pull up a chair, tell my guests what they should be eating and then later sit down and ask them if they like the food and what they think?'

Do-as-we-were-told we duly did, then, welcoming the food Daher made for us. A salad of 'flowers and fruit' was followed by a spread of dishes, including the okra baked in tomatoes which inspired us to make our own version once back home (see page 162). We also tried Daher's famous Nazareth salsiccia, long thin beef or pork sausages which have been soaked in white wine and are then cooked in a tangy red pepper sauce flavoured with cloves, allspice, garlic, slices of lemon, pine nuts and parsley. It was all packed full of flavour and wonderful to eat.

Daher explained how difficult it is to please his Israeli customers, using the flowers and fruit salad as an example. If he was to make a traditional 'Arabic salad', with chopped vegetables, white cheese and a lemony dressing, people visiting from Tel Aviv would say, 'Why have we come all the way for this? We could have had this at home: show us something new.' Adding his twists – the flowers and raisins – to traditional dishes, though, means that the next table of Israelis to sit down might baulk at the idea that this is 'allowed' to be called an Arabic salad. We'd seen this tension time and again on our travels: certain salads and dishes stuck in a traditional rut, on the one hand, but then on the other hand not 'allowed' to be played around with or moved forward if they were still to be called, for example, an 'Arabic salad'. Trying to open the point up more generally – suggesting that this tension is as likely to be observed by local Arabs as it is by visiting Israelis and acknowledging all the reasons why this might be the case – does not generate much conversation at the table.

For all his talk, though, you get the impression that Daher is really not too bothered what anyone, apart from his regular locals, might think. Unlike Alla Musa in Haifa, Daher has been in the restaurant game for several decades and his priorities have changed. Unlike Musa, when asked about the day-to-day logistics of running a restaurant and whether life is made inconvenient for him, Daher takes a deep breath, pulls in his chair and pours out a drink. We hear about the Israeli health minister who forced Daher to cancel so many of his dishes due to ingredients which weren't 'allowed' to be used. We hear about his sister's freshly picked olives and olive oil, for example, needing to be replaced by can-bought olives from an Israeli factory. The traditional unpasteurised Arabic cheese he loved had to be replaced by a more industrially made version. The chicken wing pastilla for which he was known had to be taken off the menu, as the three days it takes to actually make a pastilla was too long. And on it goes: the obstacles put in the way of running his restaurant are part of Daher's every day. 'They only come every four years, though,' Daher says, referring back to the visits of the health minister, 'so we can hide.'

This is a guy who is not afraid to air his opinions, no matter who might hear them or whose toes he might be treading on. 'Did you hear about the Palestinian chef who sold out and set up shop in London with an Israeli chef?' he remarks. 'That was me!' says Sami, before they burst into shared laughter and raise hands for a high-five. And for just a moment, around that table of shared food and time, not a single opinion in the world matters.

# Aubergine, chickpea and tomato bake
## *Musaqa'a*

Echoes of the Greek dish moussaka are correctly heard here, both in the name and the feel of the dish. It's a vegetarian take on the hearty, humble, healthy and completely delicious traybake. It works well either as a veggie main or as a side with all sorts of things: piled into a jacket potato, for example, or served alongside some grilled meat, fish or tofu. It's just the sort of dish you want to have in the fridge ready to greet you after a day out at work. It's also lovely at room temperature, so it's great to pile into the Tupperware for an on-the-go lunch.

*Getting ahead:* You can make and bake this in advance: it keeps in the fridge for up to 3 days, ready to be warmed through when needed.

**Serves four as a main or six as a side**

5 medium aubergines (1.25kg)
120ml olive oil
1 onion, finely chopped (160g)
6 garlic cloves, crushed
1 tsp chilli flakes
1 tsp ground cumin
½ tsp ground cinnamon
1½ tsp tomato purée
2 green peppers, deseeded and
  cut into 3cm chunks (200g)
1 x 400g tin of chickpeas,
  drained and rinsed (240g)
1 x 400g tin of chopped tomatoes
1½ tsp caster sugar
15g coriander, roughly chopped,
  plus 5g extra to serve
4 plum tomatoes, trimmed
  and sliced into 1½cm-thick
  rounds (350g)
Salt and black pepper

Preheat the oven to 220°C fan.

Use a vegetable peeler to peel away strips of aubergine skin from top to bottom, leaving the aubergines with alternating strips of black skin and white flesh, like a zebra. Cut widthways into round slices, 2cm thick, and place in a large bowl. Mix well with 75ml of oil, 1 teaspoon of salt and plenty of black pepper and spread out on two large parchment-lined baking trays. Roast for about 30 minutes, or until completely softened and lightly browned. Remove from the oven and set aside.

Reduce the oven temperature to 180°C fan.

While the aubergines are roasting, make the sauce. Put 2 tablespoons of oil into a large sauté pan and place on a medium-high heat. Add the onion and cook for about 7 minutes, until softened and lightly browned. Add the garlic, chilli, cumin, cinnamon and tomato purée and cook for another minute, or until fragrant. Add the peppers, chickpeas, tinned tomatoes, sugar, 200ml of water, 1¼ teaspoons of salt and a good grind of black pepper. Reduce the heat to medium and cook for 18 minutes, or until the peppers have cooked through. Stir in the coriander and remove from the heat.

Spread out half the plum tomatoes and half the roasted aubergines on the base of a large baking dish, about 20 x 30cm. Top with the chickpea mixture, then layer with the remaining tomatoes and aubergines. Drizzle with the remaining tablespoon of oil, then cover with foil and bake for 30 minutes. Remove the foil and bake for another 20 minutes, or until the sauce is bubbling and the tomatoes have completely softened. Remove from the oven and leave to cool for about 20 minutes. Top with the remaining coriander and serve either warm or at room temperature.

# Beetroot and feta galette with za'atar and honey

Beetroot, feta, ricotta, honey and thyme: some flavour combinations are just a match made in heaven. All wrapped up in some short, flaky, golden pastry and you're welcome: our work here is done. Serve this with a green salad (the spicy herb salad on page 93, for example) alongside.

*Getting ahead:* There are lots of ways to get ahead here: the beetroot can be baked and sliced a day in advance, the onions can be prepared in full a day ahead and the pie crust also keeps well in the fridge for up to 3 days (or frozen for longer). Once assembled, the pie can wait in the fridge for a good few hours – at least 6 – before going into the oven. Once baked, the pie is best eaten the same day, either slightly warm or at room temperature.

*Ingredients note:* A mix of purple and golden beetroots looks great here, but don't worry if you can't find golden. Just increase the purple beetroot to 300g.

---

### Serves four

2–3 small purple beetroots (200g)
1 medium golden beetroot (100g) (or just 300g total of purple beetroots, if you can't find golden)
15g unsalted butter
2 tbsp olive oil
1 large red onion, cut into ½cm-thick slices (170g)
2 tsp caster sugar
2 tbsp cider vinegar
1 tbsp za'atar
5g parsley leaves, finely chopped
5g oregano leaves, finely chopped
60g ricotta
2 garlic cloves, crushed
90g feta, crumbled into roughly 2cm chunks
1 egg, beaten
15g runny honey
½ tsp picked thyme leaves, to garnish
Salt and black pepper

### Pie crust

80g plain flour, plus extra for dusting
35g wholemeal flour
1½ tsp caster sugar
½ tsp flaked sea salt
1 tbsp oregano leaves, finely chopped
1½ tsp thyme leaves, finely chopped
115g unsalted butter, fridge-cold and cut into 1½cm cubes
60ml ice-cold water

Preheat the oven to 220°C fan.

Wrap the beetroots individually in foil and bake for 1–1½ hours, or until completely soft and cooked through: timing can vary quite a lot, depending on the size of your beetroots. Remove from the oven and set aside to cool for 10 minutes, then use an old tea towel or clean J-cloth to gently rub away the skins. Slice each beetroot into 2–3mm slices and (if you are starting with a mix of purple and golden) place in two separate bowls. Combine the golden beetroot with ⅛ teaspoon of salt, a good grind of black pepper and ½ teaspoon of oil. Combine the purple beetroot with a good grind of black pepper, ¼ teaspoon of salt and 1 teaspoon of oil. Set both aside until needed. The next time the oven is used it will be 200°C fan, but turn it off for now.

To make the pie crust, put both flours into a large bowl along with the sugar, salt and herbs. Add the butter and use your fingers to rub it into the flour. Don't overwork the butter – you want chunks of it throughout the dough. Add the water and use your hands to gather the dough together into a shaggy ball. Transfer to a well-floured surface and roll out into a rough rectangle, about 28 x 18cm. The dough here is fairly wet and sticky, so you'll need to flour your hands, rolling pin and work surface often. This is the way it is meant to be, though (and it makes for a wonderfully short and flaky pastry).

Fold the shorter ends in towards each other so that they meet at the centre, then fold the dough in half, like a book. Roll out the dough once with a rolling pin and then just fold once in half again, like a book. Cover with cling film (see page 342) and refrigerate for 1 hour (or overnight).

Continue with the filling by putting the butter and 1 tablespoon of oil into a medium sauté pan and placing on a medium-high heat. Add the onions and cook for about 10 minutes, stirring occasionally, until softened and browned. Add the sugar, vinegar and ⅛ teaspoon of salt and cook for another minute, or until most of the liquid has evaporated. Set aside to cool for about 15 minutes, then stir in 1 teaspoon of za'atar, the parsley and the oregano.

*Continued overleaf*

Put the ricotta, garlic, ⅛ teaspoon of salt and a good grind of black pepper into a bowl and set aside.

Transfer the dough to a well-floured sheet of baking parchment (about 30cm square) and roll out to form a rough circle. It will have uneven edges but should be about 28cm wide. Lifting up both the baking parchment and the dough, transfer to a baking tray: you don't want to be lifting it on to the tray once filled.

Spread the ricotta mixture over the base of the dough, leaving a 1cm rim clear around the edges. Top with half the feta, then the onions. Next, and this time leaving a 3½cm rim clear around the outside, top with the beetroot, alternating between purple and golden, with a little overlap between each piece. Wash your hands well (so that the feta does not turn red!), then scatter the remaining feta on top.

Using a knife, make incisions around the edge of the galette: you want these to be about 8cm apart and 2cm deep. Creating these 'strips' will allow for the beetroot and cheese to be encased. Taking one strip at a time, fold it over the beetroot, in towards the centre of the galette. Repeat with the next strip, pulling gently to slightly overlap and seal the last fold. Continue this way with the rest of the strips, then refrigerate the galette for 30 minutes (or up to about 6 hours, if you are getting ahead).

Preheat the oven (or lower, if it's been on since the beetroots were roasting) to 200°C fan.

Brush the edges of the pastry with the beaten egg and bake for 30 minutes, or until deeply golden and cooked through. Drizzle with the honey and the remaining 1½ teaspoons of oil, then scatter over the remaining 2 teaspoons of za'atar.

Transfer to a wire rack so that the bottom remains crisp and leave to cool for about 15 minutes. Garnish with the picked thyme leaves and serve.

# Pomegranate-cooked lentils and aubergines
## *Rummaniyya*

Rummaniyya means 'pomegranatey' in Arabic. It can refer to a dish either garnished lightly with pomegranate seeds or, as here, made rich and tart from an abundant use of pomegranate molasses in the cooking sauce. This is great as a main, served with lots of bread to dip into the juices, or as part of a mezzeh spread. Leftovers are also lovely for breakfast, with a poached or fried egg on top.

*Getting ahead:* This keeps well in the fridge, for up to 3 days, ready to be warmed through or eaten at room temperature. If you are making it ahead, just hold back on the onions: these can be stirred through as you warm up the dish.

---

Preheat the oven to 220°C fan.

In a large bowl, mix the aubergines with 2 tablespoons of oil, ½ teaspoon salt and a good grind of black pepper. Tip them on to a large parchment-lined baking tray (about 35 x 40cm), so that the aubergines are spaced well apart. Roast for 25 minutes, stirring once or twice throughout. Remove from the oven and set aside.

Rinse the lentils and put them into a medium saucepan with 1 litre of water. Bring to the boil on a high heat. Once boiling, reduce the heat to medium and simmer for 20 minutes, until the lentils are almost cooked. Drain the lentils over a bowl – you want to keep 350ml of the cooking liquid – and set both the lentils and liquid aside.

To fry the onions, pour enough vegetable oil into a large sauté pan so it rises 3cm up the sides of the pan. Mix the onions with the cornflour and, once the oil is hot, carefully add the onions in batches. Fry for 6–7 minutes, stirring frequently to stop the onions sticking together, or until golden brown and crisp (timing can vary quite a lot here, depending on the size of your batch and the temperature of the oil). Using a slotted spoon, transfer the onions to a wire rack lined with kitchen paper and sprinkle with a pinch of salt. Continue with the remaining onions in the same way, then set aside.

Wipe clean the pan (the oil can be reused for future frying) and add the remaining 2 tablespoons of olive oil. Place on a medium-high heat and add the garlic and chilli. Fry for 2 minutes, stirring frequently until the garlic is a light golden brown. Add the cumin, fennel and coriander and stir continuously for 30 seconds. Stir in the cornflour for a minute, then add the lentils, the 350ml of reserved cooking liquid, ¾ teaspoon of salt and plenty of pepper. Bring to the boil and cook for 5–6 minutes, stirring frequently until the liquid has thickened to the consistency of a thick porridge. Add the pomegranate molasses, lemon juice, tahini, all the aubergines and half the fried onions. Stir through, then remove from the heat.

Either serve from the pan or transfer to a large shallow bowl. Sprinkle with the remaining onions, the parsley, pomegranate seeds and sliced chillies, and finish with a drizzle of olive oil.

**Serves four as a main (along with some rice or bread) or six as a mezzeh or side**

2 aubergines, cut into 3cm dice (500g)
60ml olive oil, plus 1½ tbsp extra to serve
150g green or brown lentils
4 garlic cloves, crushed
1 green chilli, deseeded and finely chopped
1 tbsp ground cumin
1½ tsp fennel seeds (or dill seeds, if you have them), roughly crushed in a pestle and mortar
1 tsp ground coriander
1 tbsp cornflour
4 tbsp pomegranate molasses (80g)
2 tbsp lemon juice
1 tbsp tahini
Salt and black pepper

**Fried onions**
About 400ml vegetable oil, to fry
2 large onions, thinly sliced (300g)
2 tbsp cornflour

**To serve**
5g parsley, roughly chopped
40g pomegranate seeds
2 red chillies, thinly sliced, with seeds

# Bulgur mejadra
## *Mjaddarat el burgul*

For many Palestinians and Arabs around the world, the answer to the question 'What is your ultimate comfort food?' is mejadra. It's the food a lot of kids grow up on and, for Sami, it will always take him straight back home. Like so many comfort foods, it's a humble dish: lentils, spices, and then a grain in the form of rice, most typically, or the bulgur or freekeh we've suggested here. In terms of what makes it so addictive, though, the fried onions are the secret weapon.

Serve this warm or at room temperature with some yoghurt (either plain or with some diced cucumber and shredded mint stirred through) alongside. If you have some pomegranate seeds, these look lovely sprinkled on top.

*Getting ahead:* The bulgur and lentils keep well in the fridge for a couple of days, ready to be warmed through or brought back to room temperature before eating. The onions can also be prepared ahead of time – stored in a sealed container at room temperature – but keep these apart from the rest of the dish until ready to serve.

---

Place the lentils in a medium saucepan, cover with plenty of water and set aside to soak for 30 minutes.

Meanwhile, fry the onions. Put the onions, cornflour and 1 teaspoon of salt into a large bowl and mix well with your hands. Put the oil into a large heavy-based saucepan and place on a medium-high heat. Once the oil is very hot, add a third of the onions and fry for about 3–4 minutes, stirring occasionally with a slotted spoon, until they are golden brown and crispy. Use the slotted spoon to transfer the onions to a colander lined with kitchen paper and continue in the same way with the remaining two batches.

Place the saucepan with the lentils and their soaking liquid on a high heat and bring to the boil. Reduce the heat to medium and cook for 10–12 minutes, or until the lentils have softened but still retain a bite. Drain in a colander and set aside.

Wipe clean the pan (the pan used to cook the lentils, not the onions) and add the cumin and coriander seeds. Place on a medium heat and toast for a minute or two, until fragrant. Add the bulgur, olive oil, turmeric, allspice, cinnamon, a teaspoon of salt and plenty of black pepper. Stir so that everything is coated, then add the cooked lentils and the hot water. Bring to the boil, then reduce the heat to very low. Cover with a lid and simmer on a low heat for 15 minutes.

Remove from the heat, lift off the lid and quickly cover the pan with a clean tea towel. Seal tightly with the lid and set aside for 10 minutes, to steam.

Finally, add half the fried onions to the bulgur and lentils and stir gently with a fork. Pile up in a shallow serving bowl, or individual serving plates, top with the rest of the onions and serve.

### Serves six

300g green lentils
1½ tsp cumin seeds
1½ tbsp coriander seeds
300g coarse bulgur or freekeh
  (or basmati rice – see headnote)
3 tbsp olive oil
½ tsp ground turmeric
1 tsp ground allspice
½ tsp ground cinnamon
750ml just-boiled water
Salt and black pepper

### Fried onions
3 medium onions, cut in half, then
  each half thinly sliced (500g)
2 tsp cornflour
About 250ml sunflower oil, to fry

# Rice with yoghurt, roasted cauliflower and fried garlic
## *Labaniet alzahar*

**Serves four as a main or
six as a side**

1 large cauliflower, cut into roughly
   6cm florets (650g)
2 tbsp olive oil
400g Greek-style yoghurt
1 egg yolk
1½ tsp cornflour
700ml whole milk
200g pudding (or risotto) rice,
   washed and drained
About 5g picked parsley leaves,
   to garnish (optional)
Salt and white pepper

**Adha**
5 large garlic cloves, thinly sliced
60ml olive oil
2 tsp coriander seeds, lightly
   crushed in a pestle and mortar

This feels like a rich risotto or even, if you play around with the toppings
as suggested below, a thick congee. Either way, it's the most comforting
of dishes, to be eaten either as a main, as Sami used to with his family, from
a bowl with a spoon, or as a side to slow-cooked lamb, beef or some roasted
root veg.

*Getting ahead:* Ideally you want to cook the cauliflower, rice and adha all at the
same time (rather than waiting for one element to be finished before going on
to the next), so that everything is warm and ready at once.

*Playing around:* Instead of (or in addition to) the cauliflower, try roasting some
little turnips or wedges of squash. In addition, for the congee theme, put all
sorts of toppings into lots of different bowls: some thinly sliced spring onions,
for example, a drizzle of shatta, a spoonful of pan-fried minced lamb, charred
cherry tomatoes, thin slivers of garlic fried until golden in oil. People can then
make up their own bowl as they like.

---

Preheat the oven to 200°C fan.

Put the cauliflower into a large bowl with the oil and ½ teaspoon of salt. Mix
well to combine, then spread out on a large parchment-lined baking tray.
Roast for 25–27 minutes, until golden brown and tender.

While the cauliflower is cooking, place the yoghurt, egg yolk and cornflour in
a free-standing blender and work on a medium speed for a minute, until the
mixture is smooth and runny. You can also do this by hand but, if you do,
mix it really well to prevent the sauce splitting when cooked. Set aside.

Put the milk and rice into a large saucepan, for which you have a lid, along
with 1 teaspoon of salt and a pinch of white pepper. Bring to the boil on a high
heat, then reduce the heat to medium-low. Cook for 20 minutes, covered,
stirring from time to time, until the rice is almost cooked. Add the yoghurt
mixture and cook for another 7 minutes, until the rice is tender.

Put all the ingredients for the adha into a small saucepan and place on a
medium-low heat. Cook for 2 minutes, until the garlic is golden, then remove
from the heat and set aside.

When ready to serve, spoon the rice into a shallow serving dish or individual
bowls. Arrange the cauliflower pieces randomly on top and spoon over the
adha. Garnish with the parsley, if using, and serve at once.

# Spinach and toasted orzo, with dill and green chilli salsa

This is a quick, easy and satisfying dish to make for a midweek supper. It works either as a veggie main or as a side to something like grilled salmon or chicken.

*Playing around:* Some cubes of feta or black olives also work well, dotted over the orzo, either along with or instead of the yoghurt.

Place a large sauté pan, for which you have a lid, on a high heat. Add the orzo and toast for 10 minutes, stirring very frequently. Tip the toasted orzo into a bowl and set aside.

Return the same pan to a medium heat and add the olive oil and onions. Cook for about 8 minutes, stirring a few times, until the onions start to turn golden. Add the spinach, in batches, stirring each batch until wilted. Add 2 teaspoons of salt and a good grind of black pepper, then pour over 500ml of water. Bring to a gentle boil, then add the orzo to the pan, stirring it in and pushing it down with the back of a spoon. Reduce the heat to low and cook, covered, for 10 minutes, until the orzo is just cooked but still retains a bite.

Meanwhile, mix together all the ingredients for the dill yoghurt, along with ¼ teaspoon of salt, and set aside.

Just before serving, stir the coriander into the orzo. Divide it between four bowls and top with the dill yoghurt. Sprinkle over the nigella seeds and serve, with a final drizzle of oil and a wedge of lemon alongside.

**Serves four**

250g orzo
70ml olive oil, plus extra to serve
2 onions, roughly chopped (300g)
500g baby spinach
30g coriander, finely chopped
Salt and black pepper

**Dill yoghurt**
200g Greek-style yoghurt
1 green chilli, deseeded and
  finely chopped
1 garlic clove, crushed
10g dill, finely chopped
1 tbsp lemon juice
1½ tbsp olive oil

**To serve**
1 tsp nigella seeds
1 lemon, quartered into wedges

# Pasta with yoghurt and parsley breadcrumbs
## Ma'caroneh bil laban

Pasta was a favourite of Sami and his older brother Azam when they were kids. Na'ama used to make it two ways. The first was ma'caroneh bil foroun, a kind of Palestinian pasta al forno – juicy thick macaroni soaked in a meaty tomato sauce. Azam and Sami used to tussle over who got to the crispy bits on top first, then race to see who could slurp the tubes of pasta the fastest. Na'ama's second pasta staple was lighter and more refreshing, baked this time with yoghurt and nuts. This is our take on that. It can be served warm or at room temperature.

*Getting ahead:* The parsley breadcrumbs can be made a day ahead and kept in a sealed container at room temperature. Everything else should be freshly cooked. It's a quick dish to make, though, perfect for a comforting midweek supper.

---

Put 1 tablespoon of oil into a medium sauté pan along with 15g of butter. Place on a medium heat and, once bubbling, add the panko breadcrumbs, ⅛ teaspoon of salt and a good grind of black pepper. Cook for about 8 minutes, stirring often, or until lightly golden. Add 5g of the parsley and the chilli flakes and continue to cook for another 5 minutes, or until deeply crisp and golden. Transfer to a plate lined with kitchen paper (or a sealed container, if making in advance) and set aside.

Wipe the pan clean and add the remaining 50g of butter. Place on a medium heat and, once bubbling, add the pine nuts. Cook for 3 minutes, stirring often, then add the paprika. Cook for another 3 minutes, continuing to stir, until the pine nuts are deeply golden. Pour the mixture into a bowl and set aside.

Put the yoghurt into a large bowl (large enough to hold the pasta once it's cooked) with the garlic, cumin, egg yolks and the remaining 60ml of olive oil. Whisk until smooth and set aside.

Bring a pan of salted water to the boil and add the pasta. Cook for about 10 minutes (or according to the packet instructions), until al dente. Reserve 60ml of the cooking liquid, then drain the pasta into a sieve. Add the hot pasta to the bowl of yoghurt, along with the 60ml of reserved cooking liquid and the remaining 10g of parsley. Stir well to combine, then divide between four shallow bowls. Spoon over the pine nut butter, sprinkle over the breadcrumbs, top with the basil and serve at once.

## Serves four

75ml olive oil
65g unsalted butter
40g panko breadcrumbs
15g parsley, roughly chopped
½ tsp chilli flakes
60g pine nuts
½ tsp smoked paprika
500g Greek-style yoghurt
3 garlic cloves, crushed
1 tsp ground cumin
2 egg yolks
500g orecchiette (or penne or conchiglie) pasta
Salt and black pepper
5g basil leaves, roughly torn, to garnish

FISH

Growing up in East Jerusalem, on the verge of the Judean desert, Sami didn't encounter many fishmongers in his day-to-day. There was one fishmonger his family would go to, in contrast to the dozens of butchers around. Fish feasts were saved for family trips up north in the summer months, to the coastal towns of Haifa and Akka. When we were travelling and eating our way around Palestine for *Falastin*, it was, still, really only in Haifa and Akka that we found fresh fish. The West Bank is land-locked, obviously, and entry to Gaza, with its once thriving fishing community, is barred (see page 196).

Still, that didn't stop us pushing the boat out and coming home with all sorts of catches.

One of the reasons fish is so great and so easy to cook is that it takes very little time. With just a little bit of preparation – making a batch of the fish spice mix, for example (see page 190), or making the salsa or sauce in advance – many of the dishes in this chapter can be on the table less than ten minutes after you've started making them: the spiced za'atar squid, for example, the roasted cod with a coriander crust, the baked fish in tahini sauce (see pages 191, 204 and 208).

At the same time, fish always carries with it a sense of occasion. From little stuffed sardines (see page 194) to whole mackerel baked in vine leaves (see page 211), bringing fish to the table will always be accompanied by a little 'ta da!' It's not all five-minute fast-food snacks and suppers, though: there are some real show-stoppers here as well: the prawn stew with coriander pesto, for example (see page 212), or sayyadieh – 'the fisherman's dish' (see page 215) – showcasing what the fisherman has brought home that day.

In terms of sauces, we've gone two ways. White firm fish often likes to be paired with a rich tahini sauce. Cod, haddock, pollack and so forth: these are all made comforting and hearty when baked in tahini or finished with a drizzle of this wonderful nutty, creamy paste. Oily fish or seafood, on the other hand, is often best paired with a sharp tomato sauce. A fresh tomato dagga or sharp spicy tomato sauce, for example (see page 194), can cut through the oily richness of sardines or mackerel. Most fish, though – so long as it is fresh and firm– is very often happy to be served as it is, packed with herbs or lightly spiced, quickly cooked and dressed with little more than just a great big squeeze of lemon.

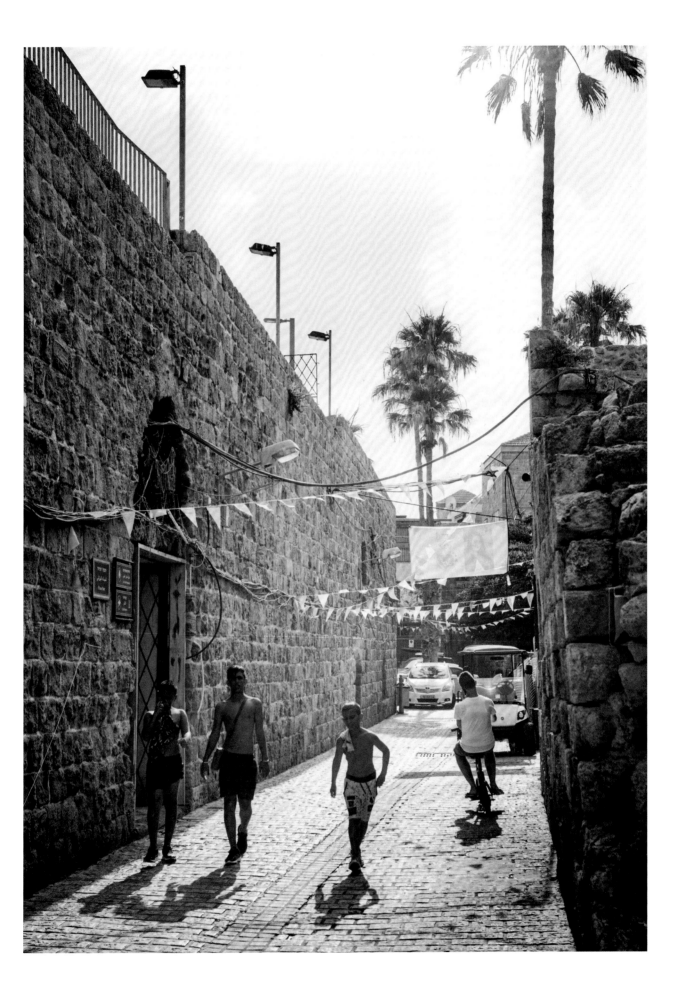

# Fish spice mix
## *Baharat samak*

This is used throughout the chapter – in dishes such as the fish kofta, roasted cod, spiced fish and baked mackerel – so double or triple the batch, if you like. It keeps well in an airtight container at room temperature for up to a month, and much longer in the freezer. It's also great to use as a marinade for all sorts of things: cubes of chicken or tofu, for example, prawns for the barbecue or roasted mixed vegetables.

**Makes just over 2 tbsp**

2 tsp ground cardamom
2 tsp ground cumin
1 tsp paprika
2 tsp ground turmeric

Place all of the spices in a bowl and mix well to combine. If making more than you need, transfer to a sealed container where it will keep for a month.

# Spiced za'atar squid with tomato salsa
## *Habar bil za'atar*

This works well either as a punchy starter or snack, or as a light meal in itself, served with a crisp green salad. If having it as a snack and eating it with your hands, the salsa can happily be replaced with just a squeeze of lemon.

*Getting ahead:* You don't really need to get ahead here – this is such a quick meal – but there are still steps you can take if you want to. The salsa can be made up to a day ahead and be kept in the fridge, the fish can be scored and the two bowls with the various spices can be prepared in advance. With this all done you're then looking at a less-than-five-minute meal.

---

**Serves four as a starter or two as a light meal**

500g medium squid, cleaned
50g cornflour
2 tsp ground coriander
2 tsp ground cumin
1 tsp ground allspice
3 tbsp za'atar
1 tsp flaked sea salt
About 250ml sunflower oil, to fry
Salt and black pepper
1 lemon, quartered, to serve

**Tomato salsa (optional)**
2 tomatoes, roughly chopped (200g)
1 green chilli, deseeded, if you
   don't want the heat, and roughly
   chopped
5g coriander, roughly chopped
1½ tbsp lemon juice
1 tbsp olive oil

Put all the ingredients for the salsa into a food processor with ⅛ teaspoon of salt and a good grind of black pepper. Blitz for just 10 seconds: don't take it too far, as you still want it to be chunky. Transfer to a bowl and set aside until ready to serve.

To prepare the squid, slice through each tube lengthways to create two rectangular halves. With the lines spaced about ½cm apart, lightly score the outside of each half to make a criss-cross pattern. Once scored, cut the squid into long vertical strips, each about 2cm wide, and place in a bowl. Cut the tentacles in half, or leave them whole if they're not too large, and add them to the bowl as well. Pat the squid dry with paper towels, removing as much moisture as possible.

Put the cornflour, coriander, cumin and allspice into a large bowl. Mix to combine, then set aside.

In a separate large bowl (big enough to hold all the squid once cooked), combine the za'atar and flaked sea salt.

Just before serving, put the oil into a large sauté pan and place on a medium-high heat. While the oil is heating up, add half the squid to the cornflour mixture and toss well to combine. Shake off the excess and, once the oil is hot, carefully lower in the squid and cook for 1–2 minutes, or until golden brown and just cooked through. Using a slotted spoon, transfer to a plate lined with kitchen paper and set aside while you continue with the remaining batch.

Once all the squid is cooked, put it into the bowl of za'atar salt and toss well to coat. Serve at once, with a wedge of lemon and the tomato salsa alongside.

# Fish kofta with yoghurt, sumac and chilli
## *Koftet samak*

These herb-and-spice-packed kofta make a lovely starter, or a light meal in themselves, packed into a pita and served with a chopped salad. They're a winner with kids as well: you might just want to leave out the chilli. Play around with the herbs that you add: coriander, parsley and mint (in any combination) also work well. Just keep the total amount of herbs about the same.

*Getting ahead:* These can be made in advance – up to a day, if you like – up to the point where they are about to go into the oven. Once cooked they can be eaten the next day – the flavours actually improve – either at room temperature or warmed through.

---

Preheat the oven to 220°C fan.

Put 3 tablespoons of oil into a large sauté pan and place on a medium-high heat. Once hot, add the onions and cook for 12–14 minutes, stirring occasionally, or until softened and golden. Add the garlic and cook for another 3 minutes. Remove from the heat and set aside until completely cool.

Put the fish into a food processor and pulse a few times until finely chopped but not a complete paste. Transfer to a large bowl and add the cooled onion mixture, chopped chilli, herbs, lemon zest, egg, fish spice mix, 2 teaspoons of sumac, 1 teaspoon of salt and a good grind of black pepper. Mix well to combine, then, using your hands, shape the mixture into about 15 kofta: they should each be about 5cm wide and weigh about 65g.

Put 2 tablespoons of oil into a large frying pan and place on a medium-high heat. Once hot, add the kofta in batches of two or three and fry for about 4 minutes, turning halfway through so that both sides are golden brown. Transfer to a parchment-lined baking tray and bake for 4 or 5 minutes, until just cooked through. Remove from the oven and set aside for 5 minutes or so, to slightly cool.

To serve, spread the yoghurt evenly between four serving plates and top each with 3 fish kofta, saving any extra for seconds. Sprinkle the kofta with the remaining teaspoon of sumac, the picked dill and sliced chilli. Drizzle over the last tablespoon of oil and serve, with a lemon wedge alongside.

### Serves four

90ml olive oil
2 large onions, finely chopped (360g)
6 garlic cloves, crushed
700g cod fillet or loin, skinless and boneless, chopped into 3cm chunks
2 red chillies, one finely chopped and one finely sliced, to serve
15g parsley leaves, roughly chopped
15g dill, roughly chopped, plus a few extra picked leaves to serve
1 lemon: finely grate the zest to get 2 tsp, then cut into 4 wedges, to serve
1 egg
2 tsp fish spice mix (see page 190)
1 tbsp sumac
200g Greek-style yoghurt
Salt and black pepper

# Stuffed sardines with spicy tomato dagga
## *Sardine ma' daggit banadora*

Green chilli, garlic, dill seeds, sardines: this is a roll-call of ingredients which typify Gazan cuisine. As well as being the general term for all pounded dressings or sauces, dagga is, also, the name of Gaza's famous spicy tomato salad. It's traditionally paired with oily fish – sardines, mackerel, salmon – to offset their richness, but really, it can be eaten in abundance alongside anything. It's wonderful with the baked fish in tahini sauce, for example (see page 208), the kofta with tahini and potatoes (see page 234), or the chicken shawarma pie (see page 260).

*Getting ahead:* You can prepare the stuffing a couple of days ahead and even stuff the sardines in advance: they'll keep well in the fridge for a day. The dagga can also be made up to a day in advance and kept in the fridge until serving.

---

Place all the ingredients for the stuffing in a small bowl along with ¾ teaspoon of salt and a good grind of black pepper. Mix well to combine and set aside.

Wash the sardines and pat dry, then lay 9 of the fillets flat on a large tray or chopping board, skin side down. Season lightly with salt, then divide the stuffing equally between the fillets, spreading it all over the fish. Lightly season the other 9 fillets and arrange them on top of the stuffed fillets, to sandwich them together.

Place all the ingredients for the tomato dagga in a medium bowl with ½ teaspoon of salt and a good grind of black pepper. Mix to combine and set aside.

When ready to fry, spread the flour out on one plate or wide shallow bowl and put the eggs into another.

Put the oil into a large frying pan and place on a medium-high heat. Working with one fish at a time, carefully lift one of the fish 'sandwiches' and dip it lightly into the flour, turning so that both sides get covered, then dip it into the egg. Put it into the pan and fry for about 5 minutes, turning once so that both sides are crisp. Transfer to a plate lined with kitchen paper while you continue with the remaining sardines. Serve warm or at room temperature, with the dagga spooned on top or served alongside.

## Serves six

18 large sardines, cleaned and butterflied (ask your fishmonger to do this) (about 730g)
3 tbsp plain flour
2 eggs, lightly beaten
3 tbsp olive oil
Salt and black pepper

### Stuffing
20g parsley leaves, finely chopped
15g coriander leaves, finely chopped
20g pistachio kernels, finely chopped
3 garlic cloves, crushed
1 large green chilli, finely chopped (25g)
3 tbsp lemon juice
1½ tsp ground cumin
¾ tsp ground allspice
1½ tbsp sumac

### Tomato dagga
4 large tomatoes, cut into ½cm dice (450g)
2 green chillies, deseeded and finely chopped (10g)
20g coriander leaves, roughly chopped
2 tsp dill seeds or celery seeds
1 tsp ground coriander
60ml lemon juice (from 2 lemons)
70ml olive oil

# Fishing in Gaza: the catch-22 of the sea

Writing *Falastin*, we've tried to strike a balance between telling it like it is in Palestine (which is not, clearly, always great) and conveying the upbeat spirit and ambition of the people we've met (which *is*, generally, always great). Looking at Gaza, though, it's hard to be upbeat. We say 'looking' but, actually, we haven't been able to look for ourselves. Getting in and out of the city is, for the vast majority, a process totally frustrated by barriers and bureaucracy. The barriers are concrete – the city is surrounded by a large military wall – and the bureaucracy is complex. Apart from journalists and those associated with certain international organisations, the process of obtaining a travel permit to Gaza from either Israel or Egypt is frequently thwarted from beginning to end.

If getting in and out of Gaza is hard, then life inside the wall is even harder. Gaza is a very small strip of land on the eastern coast of the Mediterranean Sea. It's about twenty-five miles long, and between about three and seven miles wide. It borders Egypt in the south-west and Israel for about thirty miles on its eastern and northern border. With a population of around 2 million, about 80 per cent of whom are refugees, the Gaza Strip is one of the world's most densely populated places. It's often described as the world's 'largest open-air prison'.

It's not just the people of Gaza who, since 2000 and the closing of borders during the second intifada, haven't been able to move freely to the West Bank or Israel for their daily work. It's the free movement of goods and produce that also face severe restrictions. Although Israel physically withdrew from Gaza in 2005, its control over the Strip, border and commerce has been maintained. The results of this – of people not being able to get in and out of the city to work and barriers to the movement of goods being so many – are dire.

There are, in short, just not enough resources to go around the massively overcrowded city. Jobs, money, electricity, food, effective sewage maintenance: these are just some of the crucial things in short supply. Long power cuts are part of the Gazan people's every day, as are inflated prices for diesel and food, a dependence on food rations, and high unemployment. Industries which were once thriving are now under threat. The economies of many families and businesses have collapsed, malnutrition has become widespread. What was once a fertile, productive and sustainable territory has turned into a territory with no autonomy, a dependence on aid and, frankly, very little hope for the future.

From a culinary point of view, fishing is the main business caught up in the great big knotty net that has entangled Gaza since 2005, when Israel, which had conquered the Strip in 1967, withdrew unilaterally. In 2006, Hamas, a declared enemy of Israel, took control of Gaza, and cross-border attacks on Israel escalated. In retaliation, Israel imposed restrictions on movement at the border, starting what is in effect a blockade of the Gaza Strip that still continues today. In the eyes of the UN and Britain, though, Israel's occupation and legal responsibility for Gaza and its people still continues.

Just some of the casualties of this political game are the fishermen, whose fathers and fathers before them sourced the sea to support their families. As Laila El-Haddad and Maggie Schmitt detail in their book *The Gaza Kitchen: A Palestinian Culinary Journey*, Gaza was once famous for its fish. Just nine nautical miles off its shores there is a deep channel used by large schools of fish as they migrate between The Nile Delta and the Aegean Sea. The channel supplied Palestinian fishermen with more than they needed to make a wage. This was crucial to both the nutrition of the 1.7 million people of the Gaza Strip and, of course, for the income brought in through exporting much of the catch to Israel, the West Bank and Jordan. The income generated by these exports supported over 30,000 people. Being in a fishing boat was a good, prosperous and safe place to be.

The big issue for fishermen today, by contrast, is the many restrictions placed on how far out to sea they are allowed to sail. Before any such restrictions were in place, a fisherman was able to sail as far as he wanted to get a good catch. It was the Oslo Accords which, in 1993, set up a fishing zone of twenty miles. This was under the guise of detailing Palestinian autonomy and was meant to be an interim agreement. Twenty miles was the line drawn, as this was the point where sardines could be caught as they migrated from The Nile Delta up towards Turkey during the spring. The designated zone was deemed to be enough to support a fishing industry of some 4,000 boat-owning families.

There had not previously, however, been any sort of zone or border, so the very fact of one being imposed only set a precedent which could then be squeezed in the years to follow. Since 1993, the border has shrunk from twenty to twelve to ten to six to three miles. This is a result of Israeli naval ships imposing their own limits as part of the tightening pressure on Gaza that came after the election victory of the Hamas Islamist movement in early 2006. With so much of the fishing grounds cut off, those sardines are now a good few miles out of reach.

Reducing the fishing space but sharing it among the same original number of boats means, furthermore, that the reserves of fish there continue to dwindle. In a horrible catch-22, today's fishermen are often forced to cull from the shallow waters close to the shore. Here they catch the small and young fish which, if left alone as nature dictates they should be, would ensure future prosperity. A day on the sea, then, can yield barely enough fish to feed a family, let alone take to market to sell. Once the pot is shared between all those on board, and the fuel to power the boat in the first place has been factored in, many fishermen are barely breaking even.

It's not even always about making a living, though: it can just be about staying safe. If fishermen from Gaza sail over the appointed border line, the understanding is that they might be approached, targeted, arrested or shot at by patrolling Israeli military boats, coming from the Israeli city of Ashkelon, ten miles away. What is even less understood is how these approaches and attacks can still take place when a fisherman is clearly within the appointed zone. On board with very few things which would be needed to pass the most basic of health and safety tests – a VHS radio, lifejackets, safety equipment – such goings-on make for a very uncertain livelihood.

There are other things, too, all challenging the sustainability of this once-thriving Gazan industry. The sewage system in the city – built to serve just 400,000 people and which collapsed because of war damage and lack of maintenance – has failed, and millions of litres of only partially treated waste water go straight into the sea every day. This, obviously, affects the quality of the fish being caught. Furthermore, export restrictions are firmly in place, dictating what can and cannot leave the city walls with a view to being sold.

It's all, in short, a great big mess. Israel is under constant threat from Hamas attack so it then retaliates in response. It's hard to see what good targeting the Gazan fisherman does, though. For a city dependent in large part on international aid organisations and donors, the situation is a cruel inversion of the Chinese proverb about teaching a man to fish. 'Give a poor man a fish and you feed him for a day,' so the proverb goes. 'Teach him how to fish and you give him an occupation that will feed him for a lifetime.' 'Put that man under occupation and take away his means to fish,' we might chip in for debate, 'and for both a day and all his lifetime he will remain hungry.'

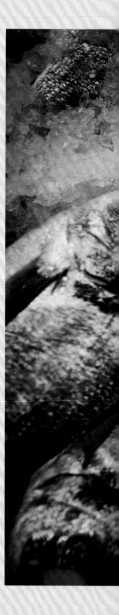

# Baked fish kubbeh
## *Kubbet samak bil siniyeh*

Kubbeh in its traditional form – shaped like little torpedos, with the bulgur casing pressed around the filling (see page 71) – is wonderful to make but does take a bit of time. Here, the same ingredients are simply baked together in a tray before being cut into individual slices. Doing this allows for the benefits of combining all the kubbeh ingredients with only a fraction of the work involved.

*Getting ahead:* This should be eaten the day it is baked, either warm or a couple of hours later at room temperature.

**Serves four generously**

190g fine bulgur
200ml boiling water
120ml olive oil, plus extra for
  greasing
2 onions, finely chopped (320g)
4 garlic cloves, crushed
450g haddock fillets (or another
  sustainably sourced firm white
  fish), skinless and boneless,
  chopped into roughly 2cm chunks
1 egg, lightly whisked
1 tsp ground cumin
½ tsp ground coriander
½ tsp ground allspice
¼ tsp ground turmeric
¾ tsp ground cinnamon
20g coriander leaves, roughly
  chopped, plus a few extra leaves
  to serve
20g parsley leaves, roughly chopped
1 green chilli, deseeded and finely
  sliced
2 lemons: finely grate the zest of
  one to get 1½ tsp, then juice to get
  1 tbsp, and cut the other one into
  wedges, to serve
2 tsp sumac
45g tahini
60g Greek-style yoghurt
Salt and black pepper

Preheat the oven to 220°C fan. Grease and line the base and sides of a 20cm square tin and brush lightly with oil.

Place the bulgur in a large bowl and pour over the boiling water. Cover the bowl with a clean tea towel or a large plate and set aside for 15 minutes. Remove the towel or plate, fluff up the bulgur with a fork and set aside to cool.

Put 2 tablespoons of oil into a large sauté pan and place on a medium-high heat. Add the onions and cook for about 10 minutes, stirring a few times, until soft and nicely browned. Add the garlic and cook for another minute. Remove from the heat and set aside to cool. Once cool, add half of the onion to a food processor along with 250g of fish, the egg, cooked bulgur, cumin, ground coriander, allspice, turmeric, ½ teaspoon of cinnamon, half of the herbs, 60ml of olive oil, 1½ teaspoon of salt and a good grind of black pepper. Blend for about a minute, until the mix comes together in a sticky ball, and then set aside.

Put the remaining onions in a bowl with the remaining fish, half of the chilli, all the lemon zest, 1 teaspoon of sumac, ¼ teaspoon of cinnamon, the remaining herbs, ⅓ teaspoon of salt, 1 tablespoon of oil and a good grind of black pepper. Mix to combine, then set aside.

Put half the bulgur-fish mixture into the base of your tin and press down firmly: it should rise about 2cm up the side of the tin. Top with the sumac-fish mixture and press down firmly. Top this with the rest of the bulgur-fish mixture, using your hands to spread it out, pressing down as you go, so that it is even and smooth. Use a small sharp knife to score the top with a cross-hatch or 'spider web' pattern, spaced about 4cm apart. Drizzle with the remaining tablespoon of oil and bake for 18 minutes, then increase the oven temperature to 250°C fan and bake for another 7 minutes, or until golden. Remove from the oven and set aside to cool for 15 minutes before gently transferring to a serving platter.

While the kubbeh is baking and cooling, put the tahini into a bowl with the yoghurt, lemon juice, 30ml of water and ⅛ teaspoon of salt. Whisk until smooth, then set aside.

Drizzle half of the tahini yoghurt over the kubbeh and sprinkle with the remaining teaspoon of sumac, the remaining chilli and the extra coriander leaves. Cut into squares and serve, with the lemon wedges and remaining tahini yoghurt in a bowl alongside for people to spoon over as they like.

# Spiced salmon skewers with parsley oil

These are quick and easy to prepare and a winner with all when served. Allow one skewer as a starter, or one or two for a main, bulked out with some rice and a green salad.

*Getting ahead:* You can get the salmon marinating a day ahead, if you like, ready to go on the skewers and be cooked. The parsley oil is also fine made a day ahead.

Put the salmon into a large bowl along with the fish spice mix, sumac, 2 tablespoons of olive oil, ¾ teaspoon of salt and a generous grind of pepper. Mix well to combine, then set aside in the fridge for at least an hour.

Put the remaining 1½ tablespoons of olive oil into a large sauté pan and place on a medium-high heat. Add the onions and cook for about 5 minutes, stirring a few times, until they are slightly softened but have not taken on any colour: don't worry if they fall apart a little bit and are no longer whole chunks. Remove from the heat and set aside.

To make the parsley oil, put the parsley, garlic, oil, ¼ teaspoon of salt and a good grind of pepper into the small bowl of a food processor. Blitz for about a minute, until smooth, then transfer to a small bowl. To prepare the lemon, use a small, sharp knife to trim off the top and tail. Cut down along its round curves, removing the skin and white pith. Release the segments from the lemon by slicing between the membranes, then roughly chop the segments. Add these to the parsley oil, stir through and set aside until needed.

Preheat the oven to 230°C fan.

To assemble the skewers, start with a tomato and then alternate the salmon chunks and onion pieces. If you have a thinner, end piece of salmon, fold it in half to form a sort of cube. Finish each skewer with a second tomato.

Place a well-greased griddle pan on a high heat.

Once the griddle pan is smoking hot, add the skewers, in two batches, and grill for 3–4 minutes, turning throughout so that all sides are charred on the outside. Transfer to a parchment-lined baking tray and continue with the remaining skewers. Transfer to the oven and bake for 6–7 minutes, or until the salmon is just cooked through.

Transfer the skewers to a large serving platter (or individual serving plates) and drizzle over the parsley oil. Serve at once, with a wedge of lemon alongside.

## Serves six as a starter or four as a main (makes 6 skewers)

800g salmon fillet, skinless and boneless, cut into roughly 4cm chunks (ideally, you want 24 pieces of salmon)
6 metal or wooden skewers (about 25cm long). If wooden, soak them in water an hour before using
1 tbsp fish spice mix (see page 190)
2 tsp sumac
3½ tbsp olive oil
2 onions, halved lengthways, peeled, then each half quartered into 4 big chunks (300g)
12 cherry tomatoes (about 150g)
Sunflower oil, for greasing the griddle pan
Salt and black pepper
1 lemon, quartered into wedges, to serve

### Parsley oil
40g parsley
1 garlic clove, finely chopped
90ml olive oil
1 lemon

# Roasted cod with a coriander crust
## *Samak mashew bil cozbara w al limon*

The combination of fish and tahini is one we find hard to resist, but this works just as well without the tahini sauce if you're looking for a shortcut or want to keep the focus on the lemon. Either way, this is as close to fast food as you can get. It's a 15-minute meal to make, beginning to end. Possibly even less time to eat.

If you are using the tahini sauce, make the whole quantity of the master recipe on page 87. It keeps in the fridge for about 4 days and is lovely to have around to drizzle over all sorts of roasted vegetables, meat, fish and salads.

*Playing around:* Any other meaty white fish works just as well here: sea bass and halibut, for example. Salmon also works well.

---

Preheat the oven to 230°C fan.

Put 2 tablespoons of oil into a small saucepan and place on a medium-low heat. Add the crushed garlic and cook for 10 seconds, then add the coriander, fish spice mix, chilli flakes, ¼ teaspoon of salt and a grind of black pepper. Cook for 4–5 minutes, stirring frequently, for the garlic to really soften, then remove from the heat.

Place the cod in a parchment-lined roasting dish, skin side down, and brush with the remaining 2 tablespoons of oil. Season lightly with salt and pepper then spoon the coriander mix on top of each fillet. Spread it out so that the whole top is covered, then top each one with a bay leaf, if using, along with 2 slices of lemon. Roast for 7–8 minutes, or until the fish is cooked through. Serve at once, with about a tablespoon of tahini sauce drizzled over, if using, and a wedge of lemon alongside.

*Pictured overleaf*

## Serves four

60ml olive oil
4 garlic cloves, crushed
50g coriander, finely chopped
2½ tsp fish spice mix (see page 190)
½ tsp chilli flakes
4 large cod loin (or another sustainably sourced white fish), skin on (about 700g)
4 large fresh bay leaves (optional)
2 lemons: cut one into 8 very thin slices, and quarter the other lengthways, into wedges, to serve
About 4 tbsp/65g tahini sauce (optional) (see page 87), to serve
Salt and black pepper

# Seared sea bass with lemon and tomato sauce

This is our favourite sort of quick fish supper, particularly if you've made the sauce in advance. Serve with some rice, crusty white bread or just a spoon, if you prefer, to scoop up all the lovely juices.

Starting with a tin of plum tomatoes and blitzing it up (rather than starting with tinned chopped tomatoes or passata in the first instance) is well worth doing: the flavour of the blitzed up plum tomatoes is wonderfully intense. With the emphasis of this dish as much on the rich sauce as it is on the fish, it's worth taking this extra step here.

*Getting ahead:* The tomato sauce keeps well in the fridge for up to 3 days or can be frozen.

**Serves four**

100ml olive oil
4 tsp fish spice mix (see page 190)
8 sea bass fillets, skin on and lightly scored, halved widthways at a slight angle (680g)
1 onion, thinly sliced (150g)
5 garlic cloves, crushed
2½cm piece of ginger, peeled and finely grated (25g)
1 green chilli, finely chopped, seeds and all (15g)
1 tbsp tomato purée
1 x 400g tin of peeled plum tomatoes, blitzed in a food processor until smooth (see headnote)
1½ tsp caster sugar
20g dill, roughly chopped
25g coriander, roughly chopped, plus extra picked leaves to garnish
400ml chicken stock
150g datterini (or cherry) tomatoes
½ a lemon, very thinly sliced into rounds, pips discarded
Salt and black pepper

Combine 2 tablespoons of oil, 2½ teaspoons of fish spice mix, 1 teaspoon of salt and a good grind of pepper together in a shallow dish. Add the scored sea bass, turning to coat, and set aside to marinate while you make the tomato sauce. You can do this up to 3 hours in advance, if you are getting ahead, but not for much longer than this, otherwise the fish will start to break down.

Put 2 tablespoons of oil into a large sauté pan and place on a medium-high heat. Once hot, add the onion and cook for about 8 minutes, stirring occasionally, until softened and browned. Add the garlic, ginger and chilli and cook for another minute or two, until fragrant. Add the remaining 1½ teaspoons of spice mix along with the tomato purée and cook for another 30 seconds. Add the tinned tomatoes, sugar, two-thirds of the dill and coriander, the stock, 1 teaspoon of salt and a good grind of pepper. Bring to the boil, then lower the heat to medium and cook for 20 minutes, stirring occasionally, or until the sauce is thick and rich. Keep warm on a low heat until needed.

In a small bowl, toss the fresh tomatoes with 2 teaspoons of oil. Place a large frying pan on a high heat and, once very hot, add the tomatoes. Cook for about 4 minutes, shaking the pan a few times, until charred all over. Add the lemon slices and cook for another 2–3 minutes, shaking the pan a few more times. Add this to the pan of tomato sauce along with the remaining herbs and keep warm until ready to serve.

Wipe clean the frying pan and place it on a medium-high heat along with 1½ teaspoons of oil. Once hot, add a quarter of the sea bass fillets, skin side down, pressing gently on the flesh so that the fish doesn't curl. Cook for 4 minutes, or until the skin is crisp and browned, then flip the fish over in the pan. Cook for another 30 seconds, then transfer to a plate. Continue with the remaining three batches, adding another 1½ teaspoons of oil to the pan before searing each batch.

Divide the sauce between four plates and top each with 4 pieces of sea bass. Sprinkle over some picked coriander leaves and serve at once.

*Pictured overleaf*

# Baked fish in tahini sauce
## *Siniyet samak bil tahineh*

Preparing fish with dairy products is not common in Arabic cuisine, as it's not considered healthy. Tahini often steps in, therefore, to fulfil the role butter or cream might otherwise have played: to enrich the fish and make the dish one to comfort. We ate far too much of this for lunch in Akka one day, minutes before Tara decided to break the 'boys only' rule when it comes to jumping off the harbour wall (see pages 186–7 for a photo of the boys). Joining the locals in a leap, Tara can confirm, is not recommended from a digestion point of view. Pair it, instead, with a crisp fresh green salad, or the spicy 'dagga' salad on page 194.

*Getting ahead:* Both the tahini sauce and the caramelised onions can be made 2–3 days in advance, if you want to get ahead. That way you're all set for a very quick-to-make supper.

---

Place all the ingredients for the tahini sauce in a medium bowl along with 60ml of water and ½ teaspoon of salt. Mix well to combine – you want the consistency to be that of thick cream – and set aside.

Put the oil for the onions into a large sauté pan and place on a medium-low heat. Add the onions and cook for about 10 minutes, stirring from time to time. Add 3 tablespoons of water and cook for another 8 minutes, until the onions have completely softened but have not taken on any colour. Remove from the heat and set aside.

Preheat the oven to 200°C fan.

Place the fish in a large shallow bowl and add the lemon zest, lemon juice, cumin, ½ teaspoon of salt and a good grind of black pepper. Mix well with your hands and set aside to marinate for 10 minutes, at room temperature. Don't leave it for much longer than this, otherwise the fish will start to break down.

Put 20ml of oil into a medium frying pan and place on a medium-high heat. Sprinkle the flour over a flat plate and, one at a time, lift the fish pieces and lightly dip them into the flour. Add half of the fish to the oil and cook for about 4 minutes, turning once halfway through so that both sides are golden. Transfer to a gratin dish, about 20 x 30cm, skin side down, and set aside. Add the remaining 20ml of oil to the pan and repeat with the remaining fish.

Stir the cooked onions into the tahini, along with the chillies, then pour the sauce evenly over the fish. Sprinkle with the pine nuts and roast for 8 minutes, or until the fish is just cooked. If you want some extra colour on top, switch the oven to a high grill setting for a further 3 minutes.

Serve warm or at room temperature, with a sprinkle of parsley and sumac and a wedge of lemon alongside.

### Serves four to six

### Tahini sauce
150g tahini
2 garlic cloves, crushed
2 tbsp lemon juice

### Caramelised onions
60ml olive oil
2 very large (or 3 large) onions,
  very thinly sliced (400g)

### Fish
6 cod loins or fillets (or any
  sustainably sourced white fish:
  hake or halibut both work well),
  skin on (900g)
2 lemons: finely grate the zest to get
  1 tbsp, then juice to get 2 tbsp
1½ tsp ground cumin
40ml olive oil
About 3 tbsp plain flour, for dusting
  the fish
2 green chillies (deseeded or not,
  depending on whether you like
  things spicy), thinly sliced
20g pine nuts
Salt and black pepper

### To serve
10g parsley leaves, roughly chopped
1 tsp sumac
1 lemon, cut into wedges

# Whole baked mackerel in vine leaves
## *Samak bil waraka*

**Serves four**

2 lemons, sliced into ½cm-thick rounds
50g coriander leaves, roughly chopped, plus about 5g extra leaves to serve
25g parsley leaves, roughly chopped
1 onion, roughly chopped (150g)
6 garlic cloves, crushed
2 red chillies, roughly chopped (20g)
1 tbsp fish spice mix (see page 190)
100ml olive oil
4 whole mackerel (about 220–230g each), cleaned and gutted, or whole seabass, trout, sea bream or snapper, as an alternative
About 36 jarred vine leaves, drained of their liquid (about 180g)
150g cherry tomatoes
Salt and black pepper

As befits all sorts of things wrapped up in a package before being presented, this is a dish for a celebration! It's impressive to make, and mackerel is always rich so sides can be kept simple: some roast potatoes and a simple green salad are all that you need.

*Getting ahead:* This is very dinner-party-friendly, as all the prep work can be done up to about 4 hours in advance. Take the fish up to the point where it's sitting on the tray ready to go into the oven and it can wait around from there.

---

Roughly chop half of the lemon slices, discarding any pips as you find them, and place in a food processor along with the coriander, parsley, onion, garlic, chillies, spice mix, 70ml of olive oil, 2 teaspoons of salt and a good grind of black pepper. Blitz for about 20 seconds, to form a coarse mix, and set aside. Set aside the remaining lemon slices: these are added to the tray when the fish is baked.

Preheat the oven to 180°C fan.

Pat the fish dry and thinly score the outside about three times on each side. Sprinkle the inside and outside of the mackerel with salt – about ¼ teaspoon per fish – then fill and cover the fish with the herb paste: about half in the cavities and half rubbed over the outside. Working on a clean work surface, lay 3 vine leaves in a horizontal line – don't worry about removing the stalks – shiny side down and one slightly overlapping the next. Repeat with another 2 rows of vine leaves, again 3 per row, to form one large rectangle of vine leaves, about 28 x 26cm, with no gaps in between.

Place one mackerel in the centre of the vine leaves, belly facing towards you and head and tail lying either side of the rectangle. Gently fold the vine leaves over the mackerel, rolling over and wrapping the body of the fish completely, with the head and tail exposed at either end. Transfer to a large parchment-lined roasting tray and repeat with the remaining vine leaves and mackerel. Once all the mackerel are in the tray, space them about 4cm apart and scatter over the tomatoes and reserved lemon slices. Drizzle with the remaining 2 tablespoons of olive oil and bake for 35 minutes, or until the fish is cooked through and the vine leaves have taken on some colour.

Transfer to a serving platter and pour over any juices. Garnish with the extra coriander leaves and serve at once. The paper-thin vine leaves will be charred and crisp, so eat this with your hands, if you are happy to be informal, sandwiching together a chunk of fish between two of the charred leaves.

# Prawn and tomato stew with coriander sauce

This is another fish dish where the holy trinity of Gazan cuisine – dill, garlic and chilli – makes it sing so boldly and loud. Big thanks to Noor Murad for this one. Serve this as it is, with some crusty white bread to mop up the juices, or dot some cubes of white feta or black olives (or both) on top. A crisp green salad with a lemony dressing on the side and you're all set.

*Getting ahead:* Batch-make the base for the stew here, if you like: this freezes well and keeps in the fridge for a good few days. That way you can just char your cherry tomatoes and pan-fry the prawns in minutes. The coriander pesto can also be made up to 3 days in advance and kept in the fridge.

---

Place a large sauté pan on a high heat. Toss the cherry tomatoes with 1 teaspoon of oil and, once the pan is very hot, add the tomatoes. Cook for about 5 minutes, shaking the pan once or twice, until blistered and heavily charred on all sides. Remove from the pan and set aside.

Wipe the pan clean, add 2 tablespoons of oil and replace it on the stove on a medium-high heat. Add the onion and cook for about 8 minutes, stirring occasionally, until softened and lightly browned. Add the garlic, ginger, chilli, spices, dill and tomato purée and cook for another 2 minutes, until fragrant. Add the plum tomatoes, 300ml of water, 1½ teaspoons of salt and a good grind of black pepper. Bring to a simmer, then lower the heat to medium and cook for about 25 minutes, or until the sauce has thickened and the tomatoes have completely broken down.

While the sauce is cooking, make the coriander pesto. Put the coriander, chilli and pine nuts into a food processor and pulse a few times until the pine nuts are roughly crumbled. Transfer to a bowl and add the lemon zest, oil, ¼ teaspoon of salt and a grind of black pepper. Mix to combine, then set aside.

Pat the prawns dry and mix them in a bowl with ¼ teaspoon of salt, 1 tablespoon of oil and a good grind of black pepper.

Put 2 teaspoons of oil into a large frying pan and place on a high heat. Once hot, add the prawns in batches and fry for a minute on each side, until cooked through and nicely browned. Set each batch aside while you continue with the remaining prawns. When the sauce is ready, stir in the prawns and charred tomatoes and cook on a medium heat for about another 3 minutes, to heat through. Serve either straight from the pan or spoon into wide shallow bowls. Scoop out the cardamom pods before serving, if you like: they are there to flavour the dish rather than to be eaten. Dot with about half of the pesto and serve at once, with the lemon and remaining pesto in a bowl alongside.

## Serves four

250g cherry tomatoes
60ml olive oil
1 large onion, finely chopped (180g)
4 garlic cloves, crushed
2cm piece of ginger, peeled and
  finely grated (15g)
1 green chilli, finely chopped
2 tsp coriander seeds, lightly
  crushed in a pestle and mortar
1½ tsp cumin seeds, lightly crushed
  in a pestle and mortar
8 cardamom pods, lightly bashed
  in a pestle and mortar
20g dill, finely chopped
2 tsp tomato purée
6 plum tomatoes, roughly
  chopped (500g)
600g peeled raw king prawns
Salt and black pepper

### Coriander pesto
30g coriander, roughly chopped
1 green chilli, finely chopped
50g pine nuts, lightly toasted (see
  page 339)
1 lemon: finely grate the zest to
  get 1½ tsp, then cut into wedges,
  to serve
80ml olive oil

# Fisherman's dish
## *Sayyadieh*

**Serves six**

40g unsalted butter, diced
30g pine nuts
30g flaked almonds
105ml olive oil
4 large onions, thinly sliced (700g)
3 cinnamon sticks
1 green chilli, finely chopped (20g)
4 garlic cloves, crushed
¾ tsp ground allspice
280g basmati rice, washed
   until the water runs clear, then
   drained well
650ml boiling water
¼ tsp saffron threads
600g grey mullet (or another
   sustainably sourced firm white
   fish such as halibut, cod or
   monkfish), skinless and boneless,
   chopped into 4cm pieces
¼ tsp ground cinnamon
¾ tsp ground cumin
12 large raw tiger prawns, head and
   tail intact but the remaining shell
   and back vein discarded (about
   500g)
2 lemons: juice one to get 1½ tbsp,
   and cut the other one into 6
   wedges, to serve
10g parsley leaves, roughly chopped
Salt and black pepper

'Sayyadieh' translates as 'fisherman's catch' or 'fisherman's dish'. The combination of spiced rice and pan-fried fish is a Palestinian favourite in the coastal towns of Jaffa, Haifa and Akka. The choice of fish depends, traditionally, on what's been caught that day. Here, we've used a combination of white fish and prawns, but other combinations – calamari and prawns or two kinds of white fish, for example – also work well.

*Getting ahead:* The nuts can be toasted and the onions can be caramelised with the cinnamon sticks a day ahead, if you like. Doing this will take 30 minutes off your prep time when it comes to making the dish.

*Playing around:* Tahini sauce (see page 87) is lovely drizzled on top before serving, for a rich addition.

Place a small frying pan on a medium heat and add 10g of butter. Once melted, add the nuts and fry for about 7 minutes, stirring almost constantly, until golden. Transfer to a plate lined with kitchen paper and set aside.

Put 3 tablespoons of oil and 20g of butter into a large, high-sided sauté pan, for which you have a lid, and place on a medium-high heat. Add the onions and cinnamon sticks and cook for about 30 minutes, stirring often, or until sweet, softened and deeply browned. Add the chilli, garlic and allspice and cook for 1 minute. Add the rice, stir through and cook for another 90 seconds, to toast. Add the water, saffron, 1½ teaspoons of salt and a good grind of black pepper. Bring to the boil, then reduce the heat to low and cook, covered, for 12 minutes.

While the rice is cooking, put 1½ teaspoons of oil into a large frying pan and place on a high heat. Put the fish into a large bowl and combine with the ground cinnamon, ¼ teaspoon of cumin, ¾ teaspoon of salt and a good grind of black pepper. Once hot, add half the fish and fry for about 2–3 minutes, turning halfway through, or until golden on both sides but not cooked through. Transfer to a plate lined with kitchen paper, then add another 1½ teaspoons of oil to the pan and continue with the remaining fish. Wipe out the pan: you'll be using this again for the prawns.

Once the rice is ready, uncover the pan and add the fish, gently pushing the rice around to tuck half the fish into the rice – the rest can sit on top. Increase the heat to medium, cover, and cook for another 5 minutes. Remove from the heat, add the remaining 10g of butter, and set aside, covered, for 10 minutes.

In a large bowl, mix the prawns with 1 tablespoon of oil, the remaining ½ teaspoon of cumin, ½ teaspoon of salt and a good grind of pepper. Place your frying pan on a high heat, add the remaining 2 tablespoons of oil and fry the prawns, in two batches, for 2–3 minutes, until golden and cooked through. Transfer to a medium bowl, mix through the lemon juice and half the parsley, and set aside.

To serve, transfer half the rice to a large serving platter along with the white fish. Top with half the nuts and half the prawns and follow this with the remaining rice, nuts and prawns. Sprinkle with the remaining parsley and serve, with the wedges of lemon alongside.

MEAT

As a kid, Sami used to be sent to the neighbourhood butcher by his mother, Na'ama, with a bag full of meat chunks, a peeled onion, a bunch of parsley and some mixed spices. Sami's job was to take the meat, all wrapped up in a paper sachet, to their butcher, who'd then mince it up in his shiny electric machine. Na'ama had her own manual meat mincer at home but it wasn't big enough to mince the amount needed to feed everyone sitting around the large family table. Such was the quality of the raw meat that Sami could never resist sneaking a few mouthfuls of the mix as he strolled back. Once it was home, the meat would be shaped into kofta or meatballs, spooned into dumplings or cored-out vegetables, piled into pitas or on to open pies, or spread out in an easy one-tray bake.

Well over half our recipes in this chapter start with minced meat. This is a tribute, in part, to the memory of Sami's strolls and the food he ate growing up. More generally, though, it's a testament to how convenient minced meat is for the home cook. It's a good way to stretch meat out, it cooks easily and quickly and lends itself to all sorts of family-friendly dishes. Pasta and other traybakes, for example (see pages 254 and 256), chicken arayes (see page 228), shush barak (see page 220), meatballs (see pages 239 and 243), kofta (see pages 230 and 234): these are just some of the dishes in *Falastin* which can be eaten with simply a fork or a spoon. And there's something about this – about the lack of need for a knife to cut with, and all the 'formal table manners' a double set of cutlery suggests – that just makes these things so inherently comforting and nurturing.

If minced meat recipes are often those to fall back on for everyday cooking, starting with a whole chicken, lamb shoulder, lamb neck or oxtail is, generally speaking, associated more with celebratory meals. These are very often the signature dishes of Palestine: the upside-down dish maqlubeh, for example (page 264) or Gaza's sumaqqiyeh (page 273). Maftoul (see page 267) is another dish whose appearance at the table so often marks a celebration, signalling to those around the table that the cook has been in the kitchen for a good while.

It doesn't all need to be too epic on the part of the cook, though. As with so much cooking, it's so often just about getting a bit organised and planning in advance. Open the freezer of all home cooks in Palestine and it will be full of sealed bags of dumplings, for example, ready to be cooked in yoghurt, or sfiha (see page 226), the open pies topped with various things, ready to go straight into the oven when needed. If not the freezer, then there are all those dishes which are happy to sit in the fridge for 2–3 days, ready to be eaten over several meals. The stews and slow-cooked chicken thighs, for example (see page 260), the meatballs and kofta: these are so often the dishes whose flavour actually improves when all the ingredients have had time to sit around together overnight.

As with all ingredients, but particularly with meat, start with the best-quality you can.

# Meat dumplings in yoghurt sauce
## *Shush barak*

These ravioli-like dumplings, cooked in a rich yoghurt sauce, go by a couple of other names: taqiyet elyahoodi, which means 'Jew's hat', or dinein qtat, which means 'cat's ears'. Whichever their shape resembles more – hats or cats – few dishes take Sami so quickly back home. They're his real madeleine moment. They're a labour of love, but, as is often the case with the food which reminds us of home, the result is pure comfort and nurture.

*Getting ahead:* You can make these in advance, as they freeze well. Put them straight into the yoghurt from frozen: they'll just need a couple more minutes in the pan.

First make the filling. Put the olive oil into a medium frying pan and place on a medium heat. Add the onion and cook for about 6 minutes, stirring a few times, until slightly golden. Add the meat, baharat, turmeric, ¼ teaspoon of salt and a grind of black pepper, and continue cooking for about 5 minutes, stirring and breaking up the meat with a wooden spoon so that it does not form into clumps, until the meat is cooked through and any liquid released has evaporated. Stir in the coriander and set aside until completely cool.

For the dough, put the flour, oil and water into a medium mixing bowl with ¼ teaspoon of salt. Using your hands, gather the dough together into a shaggy and somewhat sticky ball. Transfer to a lightly floured work surface and knead for about 4 minutes, until the dough is elastic and smooth. Shape into a ball, cover with a clean tea towel and leave to rest for about 10 minutes, at room temperature.

On a lightly floured surface, roll out the dough to form a 35 x 45cm rectangle; it should be quite thin, about 3mm. Using a 7cm cookie cutter, cut the dough into circles – re-rolling the scraps about three or four times, you should be able to make about 25. Working with one piece at a time, take a round of dough and flip it over so that the stickier underside is now facing upwards. Doing this will make it easier to seal the dumplings. Spoon about ½ teaspoon of the meat filling into the centre of each circle. Fold the dough in half and then pinch tightly around the outside to form a half-moon shape. Next, pinch together the edges so that they overlap slightly, resembling tortellini. To help you with this, either keep a bowl of water beside you, dipping your fingers once or twice as you go along, to prevent them from becoming sticky, or use a clean brush on the rim, dipped in water, to help with the seal. Arrange the dumplings on a parchment-lined tray while you continue with the remaining batch.

Preheat the oven to a 200°C grill setting.

Once all the dumplings are shaped, grill them for 8 minutes – placing them in the middle of the oven rather than directly under the grill, to prevent them burning – or until slightly golden.

## Serves four

### Filling
1 tbsp olive oil
½ an onion, finely chopped (70g)
200g beef mince (or lamb, or a combination of both)
½ tsp baharat (see page 190)
¼ tsp ground turmeric
5g coriander leaves, finely chopped
Salt and black pepper

### Dough
150g plain flour, plus extra for dusting
1 tbsp sunflower oil
About 65ml lukewarm water

### Yoghurt sauce
1kg Greek-style yoghurt
1 egg yolk
1 tbsp cornflour
300ml chicken stock

### Adha
60ml olive oil
5 garlic cloves, crushed
30g coriander leaves, roughly chopped
1 tsp Aleppo chilli flakes (or ½ tsp regular chilli flakes)

Meanwhile, put the yoghurt, egg yolk, cornflour and stock into a free-standing blender. Blend on a medium speed for about a minute, until the mixture is smooth and runny, then transfer to a large saucepan, along with 1½ teaspoons of salt, and place on a medium-low heat. Cook for about 5 minutes, stirring often, until the yoghurt comes to a gentle boil. Add the dumplings and continue cooking for about 18 minutes, stirring gently a few times and keeping an eye on the sauce to make sure it does not split, until the dumplings have cooked through and the sauce resembles a thin béchamel.

To make the adha, put the oil and garlic into a small frying pan and place on a medium-high heat. Cook for about 4 minutes, stirring often, until the garlic is lightly golden. Remove from the heat, transfer to a bowl and stir in the coriander.

To serve, divide the dumplings and sauce between four bowls and drizzle the adha on top. Sprinkle with the chilli flakes and serve at once.

# Cooking in Aida refugee camp, Bethlehem

Islam Abu Aouda lives in a refugee camp in Bethlehem and her firstborn is severely disabled. Her home is humble. The needs of her husband and six children come before her own. Frankly, it would be easy to feel sorry for Islam. Spending time with her, though, you don't feel sorry. You feel inspired, energised and happy. This is a lady with the best hug in town who sure knows how to giggle.

To make ends meet, Islam, along with five other ladies in Aida refugee camp, gives cookery lessons and hosts home-stays once or twice a month to interested visitors. Their group, formed in 2010, is called the Noor Women's Empowerment Group. The money they make from these lessons and home-stays goes towards making life better for the disabled kids in the camp. They might buy some equipment a child needs to get around or use the money to give a group of kids an experience they've never had. The visitors, in return, get a slice of Palestinian kitchen life and a good meal to boot. Women rule the roost, stockpots are enormous and, regardless of how many guests are expected, enough food is made to feed a small wedding. In time-honoured fashion, the world is put to rights over a chopping board.

Going to Aida refugee camp for the first time, a visitor can be struck by how normal it all feels. The very foundations of the camp are abnormal, clearly – refugee camps only exist for those who've been uprooted from their home – but, with everyone going about their business, it all feels strangely everyday. Socio-economic conditions are poor, population density is high, basic infrastructure is insufficient, and the smell of tear gas is familiar but, still, kids go to school, parents do what work they can, babies are born, the elderly are cared for, plays are put on, pictures are painted, meals are cooked. Just like every other teenager in the world, the older kids hang around on street corners, hankering after cool trainers and mobile phones.

It is this apparent ordinariness that results in the incredulity frequently voiced by visitors when they see a refugee doing something as 'everyday' as pulling out their mobile phone. 'Yes, I'm a refugee,' they find themselves having to explain, 'and yes, I have a mobile. Yes, I am on Instagram.' Their circumstances may be irregular and not normal but refugee camps are full of regular people doing normal things. To an outsider, it's what makes people like Islam seem so extraordinary.

When we spent the morning with Islam we prepared shush barak, little lamb-filled dumplings Sami had been craving. Dough was made, rolled, shaped, filled and then cooked in a yoghurt sauce made from kishek (see page 337), a

sharp-tasting fermented yoghurt. It's a Marmite ingredient: people either love it or hate it. For Tara, the jury is still out. For Sami, it's the Proustian 'madeleine moment' which takes him straight back home.

Islam's husband, Ahmed, was with us in the kitchen, not necessarily getting his hands covered in flour but obviously supportive of his wife. He gave Sami a semi-jovial hard time, undermining Sami's great success as a chef and traveller by saying that none of it meant anything unless a man had 'a wife and lots of kids'. As Sami and Ahmed discussed the respective paths of 'tradition' versus 'passion', Tara and Islam watched on smiling, as they rolled and shaped and filled their dumplings, entertained by two grown men having the conversation about whether one can truly 'have it all' – a conversation women are themselves so well versed in.

In terms of having it all – or just getting to dream a little – a visitor might expect Islam to voice the dream of all refugees: 'the right to return' to the place they call home. For today, though, Islam's bucket list is more the kind you take to the beach. Her dream is to make a trip to the sea, to watch the sun set over the horizon. She may live just a two- or three-hour drive from the coastal town of Haifa but, in her mid-thirties, the ocean is still something Islam has never actually seen with her own eyes. Freedom to travel from A to B (quite literally, in the case of the region's division into areas A, B and C – see the Tent of Nations profile on page 130, which goes into more detail on this) is limited for people like Islam. Getting in the way is the paperwork needed, the visa often denied, the checkpoint queues so long and humiliating, the regular and real demands of her family. For now, then, the horizons Islam is focused on are closer to home: feeding visitors to make money to provide for her extended family in the camp.

This is just a snapshot of Islam's story. Islam is just one of about 3,000 refugees living in Aida camp. Aida camp is just one of the three camps in Bethlehem. These three camps are themselves just three of the fifty-eight recognised refugee camps throughout the region of Jordan, Lebanon, the Syrian Arab Republic, the Gaza Strip and the West Bank, including East Jerusalem. These camps are home to about 5 million refugees, and 5 million different life stories.

# Open meat (or cauliflower) pies
## *Sfiha*

These easy-to-make 'open' pies are loved by kids and grown-ups alike. They are perfect party food: great to snack on and also really practical, as they can be batch-made and then baked from frozen. They're also lovely for a light meal, served with a fattoush (see page 99) (or any other) salad.

Thanks to Sami's sister, Sawsan, for creating the recipe for the dough here. It turned out so well that it's used, again, for the za'atar bread (see page 285) and sambousek (see page 294) as well.

*Getting ahead:* The dough can be made up to 2 days in advance and kept in the fridge after proving. Just bring it back to room temperature the day you are rolling it out. You can also make the pies up in full, topping and all, and freeze them before baking. They can go into the oven straight from frozen.

*Playing around:* There are two toppings to choose from here: one meat and one veggie. Make either one or the other, or a mixture of the two. If you want to serve both, you'll need to either double the quantity of dough or halve the quantities for the toppings.

---

First make the dough. Put the yeast, sugar and water into a small bowl and whisk to combine. Set aside for 5 minutes, until it starts to bubble.

Put the flour, milk powder, turmeric, if using, and ¾ teaspoon of salt into the bowl of a free-standing mixer with the dough hook in place. Mix for 1 minute, just to incorporate, then add the yeast mixture, followed by both oils. Work on a low speed for about 2 minutes, to bring everything together, then increase the speed to medium. Continue to mix for 5–6 minutes, until the dough is soft and elastic. It will feel very soft and almost sticky, but this is how it should be. Tip the dough on to a clean work surface and bring together to form a ball. Grease the mixing bowl with 1 tablespoon of oil and return the dough to the bowl. Turn it a couple of times so that it's completely coated in oil, then cover the bowl with a clean tea towel. Set aside somewhere warm for 1 hour, until it's doubled in size.

Roll the dough out into the shape of a sausage, about 30cm long, and cut into 12 even pieces, about 45g each. Roll each piece into a ball, place on a large plate, cover with a clean tea towel and set aside for 20 minutes, to rest.

If making the veggie topping, preheat the oven to 180°C fan.

If making the meat topping, put all the ingredients for the topping, apart from the pine nuts and lemon wedges, into a separate bowl. Add 1¼ teaspoons of salt and mix well to combine: doing this with your hands is the best way. Set aside.

For the veggie topping, put the cauliflower, onion, peppers, oil and spices into a large mixing bowl with ¾ teaspoon of salt. Mix well, then spread out on a parchment-lined baking tray. Bake for 25 minutes, or until the vegetables are golden brown and tender. Remove from the oven and allow to cool slightly, then chop the cauliflower into ½cm chunks. Finely chop the peppers – there is no need to peel them – and place all the vegetables in a medium mixing bowl along with the tahini, lemon juice, parsley and ¼ teaspoon of salt. Mix to combine, and set aside.

**Makes 12 pies, to serve four to six as a snack or for lunch**

**Dough**
1½ tsp fast-action dried yeast
1 tsp caster sugar
170ml lukewarm water
320g plain flour
1 tbsp milk powder (also known as dried skimmed milk)
⅛ tsp ground turmeric (optional)
3 tbsp sunflower oil
3 tbsp olive oil, plus extra for greasing
Salt

**Meat topping**
250g lamb mince
1 small onion, chopped (100g)
1 medium tomato, finely chopped (120g)
3 tbsp tahini
½ tsp ground cinnamon
¾ tsp ground allspice
¾ tsp Aleppo chilli flakes (or ½ tsp regular chilli flakes)
15g parsley, finely chopped
1 tbsp lemon juice
1 tbsp sumac
25g pine nuts

*Ingredients continued opposite*

Increase (or preheat) the oven temperature to 200°C fan.

Arrange the dough balls on two large parchment-lined baking trays, spaced well apart. Using your fingers, flatten each ball into a round disc, about 10cm wide and 2–3mm thick. Spoon 2 heaped tablespoons (about 50g) of whichever topping you are using into the centre of each disc and spread it out evenly, leaving a 1cm border clear around the edge. Sprinkle over the pine nuts, if you are doing the meat topping, and set aside for another 10 minutes. Bake for 17–18 minutes, rotating the trays around halfway through (or even switching around the position of the trays if it looks like the pies on the top tray are taking on too much colour), or until the sfiha are cooked and the edges are golden brown. Remove from the oven and serve warm or at room temperature, with a wedge of lemon alongside.

## Veggie topping

½ a cauliflower, cut into roughly 5cm florets and any stalk cut into roughly 1cm pieces (500g)
1 large onion, thinly sliced (180g)
2 red peppers, halved, core and seeds removed and then thinly sliced (200g)
60ml olive oil
¾ tsp Aleppo chilli flakes (or ⅓ tsp regular chilli flakes)
¾ tsp baharat (see page 190)
¼ tsp ground turmeric
2 tbsp tahini
2 tbsp lemon juice
5g parsley, finely chopped

## To serve

2 lemons, cut into wedges

# Spiced chicken arayes

Arayes is the plural of the word for 'bride', in Arabic, which is 'aroos'. There are various tales as to why this particular name is given to this snack: one is that the white bread represents the white dress of the bride wrapped around a dark tuxedo (typically a lamb filling) of the groom in a deep embrace (!). Thinking slightly more practically, for those with an appetite arayes are essentially pan-fried pita bread sandwiches. They're great either for snacking on before a meal or as a meal in themselves, served with a fresh chopped salad (see page 92) and some sumac yoghurt (see page 259).

*Getting ahead:* The filling can be made ahead of time – up to 3 days if you just make the tomato sauce and up to a day if you've added the chicken – ready for the arayes to be filled and fried to serve.

---

Put 2 tablespoons of oil into a large sauté pan and place on a medium-high heat. Add the onions and ½ teaspoon of salt and cook for about 8 minutes, stirring often, until soft and golden. Add the garlic, spices and tomato purée and cook for another minute, until fragrant. Stir in the tomatoes and cook for about 8 minutes, stirring often, until they have completely broken down and the mixture is quite thick. Remove from the heat and set aside to cool. Once cool, transfer the mix to a medium bowl along with the chicken, coriander, 1 teaspoon of salt and a good grind of black pepper. Mix well to combine and set aside.

Preheat the oven to 180°C fan.

Using a serrated knife, slice the pitas open to create two separate rounds. Place them on a clean work surface, cut side up. Spread one of the rounds with about 140–150g of the chicken mix – it should be about ¾cm thick – then place an unfilled pita on top, pressing down gently to make a sandwich. Continue with the remaining chicken mixture and pita slices to make 4 sandwiches in total.

Put 10g of butter and 1 tablespoon of oil into a large frying pan and place on a medium-high heat. Add 2 of the sandwiches to the pan and cook for 2–3 minutes, turning after a minute or so until both sides have taken on some colour. Transfer to a large parchment-lined baking tray and blot gently with some kitchen paper to soak up any excess oil. Continue with the remaining sandwiches, adding another 10g of butter and tablespoon of oil to the pan with each batch. Once they are all pan-fried, transfer the tray to the oven and bake for 7 minutes, or until cooked through. Remove from the oven and set aside to cool for about 5 minutes before slicing each pita into 4. Serve warm, with a wedge of lemon and some tahini sauce alongside to dip into, if using.

## Serves four as a snack

60ml olive oil
2 onions, finely chopped (300g)
6 garlic cloves, crushed
1½ tsp caraway seeds, roughly
  crushed in a pestle and mortar
1½ tsp cumin seeds, roughly
  crushed in a pestle and mortar
¾ tsp ground cinnamon
½ tsp chilli flakes
2 tsp tomato purée
2–3 plum tomatoes (250g), coarsely
  grated and skins discarded (see
  page 129 for method) (200g)
350g minced chicken thighs
  (either ask your butcher to mince
  these for you, or put skinless
  and boneless thighs in a food
  processor and blitz a few times)
25g coriander leaves, roughly
  chopped
4 pitas (about 16 x 10cm), shop-
  bought or see page 278 for
  homemade
20g unsalted butter
Salt and black pepper

## To serve
1 lemon, cut into wedges
Tahini sauce (see page 87)
  (optional)

# Baked kofta with aubergine and tomato
## *Kofta bil batinjan*

Kofta – meat patties – are something of an obsession throughout the Middle East. Baked, fried, grilled, braised; stuffed into pita and drizzled with tahini, for example, or baked in a tomato sauce and served with rice. We offer two versions: one baked with tomato and the other, a richer version, baked in a tahini sauce (see page 234). They are both simple meals to comfort – perfect for a midweek supper served with some bread or rice to mop up the juices – rather than to wow with their elegant looks.

*Getting ahead:* The tomato sauce (which can be easily doubled or tripled, if you want to freeze a batch) keeps well in the fridge for up to 4 days. The meat mix can also be made a day ahead, kept in the fridge and waiting to be cooked. Once baked, these are also lovely (or even better, as is often the case with meatballs) the next day. Either warm them through or just bring back to room temperature.

---

Preheat the oven to 220°C fan.

Place the aubergine slices in a large bowl. Sprinkle with ½ teaspoon of salt and a good grind of black pepper and pour over the oil. Mix well to combine, then spread out on a large parchment-lined baking tray. Bake for 25 minutes, or until golden brown and cooked through. Remove from the oven and set aside.

Reduce the oven temperature to 200°C fan.

While the aubergines are roasting, make the tomato sauce. Put the oil into a medium saucepan and place on a medium-high heat. Add the onions and cook for about 6 minutes, stirring occasionally, until they have softened and lightly browned. Add the garlic and tomato purée and cook for another 30 seconds. Stir in the tinned tomatoes, sugar, mint, chilli flakes, 60ml of water, ½ teaspoon of salt and a good grind of black pepper. Bring to the boil, then turn the heat to medium-low. Cook for 20 minutes, stirring occasionally, until the sauce is thick and rich. Remove from the heat and set aside until ready to use.

Put all the ingredients for the kofta into a large bowl, along with 1¾ teaspoons of salt and a good grind of black pepper. Mix well, then divide the mixture into 12 large balls. Shape into burger-shaped patties – about 7cm wide – and set aside.

## Makes 12 kofta, to serve six as a main or more as a side

2 very large (or 3 large) aubergines, as wide as possible (850g), peeled in alternate long strips (to look like a zebra), then cut widthways into 12 slices, about 2½cm thick
60ml olive oil
3 large beef tomatoes, cut widthways into 12 slices, about 1cm thick (500g)
1 large green chilli, thinly sliced (20g)
Salt and black pepper

### Tomato sauce
2 tbsp olive oil
1 onion, finely chopped (150g)
6 garlic cloves, crushed
2 tsp tomato purée
1 x 400g tin of chopped tomatoes
¼ tsp caster sugar
1 tsp dried mint
½ tsp Aleppo chilli flakes (or ¼ tsp regular chilli flakes)

### Kofta
350g beef mince (15–20% fat)
350g lamb mince (15–20% fat)
30g parsley, very finely chopped
1 onion, coarsely grated (120g)
2 garlic cloves, crushed
3–4 plum tomatoes, coarsely grated and skins discarded (200g)
1 tsp tomato purée
2 tsp ground cinnamon
1 tbsp ground allspice
¼ tsp grated nutmeg
½ tsp Aleppo chilli flakes (or ¼ tsp regular chilli flakes)
1 tbsp olive oil

*Ingredients continued opposite*

**To garnish**
5g coriander leaves, roughly
   chopped
12 small picked basil leaves,
   (or larger leaves, shredded)
25g pine nuts, toasted (see
   page 339)

Arrange the slices of aubergine in a single layer in the bottom of a large, deep baking dish, about 20 x 30cm. Place one patty on top of each slice and place a slice of tomato on top of this, to create a kind of sandwich. Spoon a generous tablespoon of the thick tomato sauce on top of each sandwich, spreading it out slightly so that it drizzles down the sides. Sprinkle over the green chilli, cover the dish tightly with foil and bake for 20 minutes. Then increase the oven temperature to 230°C fan, remove the foil and bake for a final 18 minutes.

Remove from the oven and, using a spatula, lift the kofta out of the liquid (don't discard the liquid, though), trying to keep the aubergine slices intact. Place on a large platter or individual serving plates, then pour the cooking juices from the pan into a medium sauté pan. Bring to the boil on a high heat and cook for 7 minutes, stirring frequently, until the liquid has thickened and reduced by half. Spoon the sauce over the kofta and sprinkle with the coriander, basil and pine nuts. Serve warm or at room temperature.

*Pictured overleaf*

# Kofta with tahini, potato and onion

*Playing around:* This is a rich dish, thanks to the tahini. If you want to lighten things up, the potatoes can be replaced with florets of cauliflower. Other vegetables also work: cubes of butternut squash or pumpkin, for example. If you do this, the cauliflower will need 5 minutes less in the oven than the potatoes and the squash or pumpkin will need about 5 minutes more.

Preheat the oven to 220°C fan.

In a medium bowl, toss the potatoes with 2 tablespoons of oil, ¾ teaspoon of salt and a good grind of black pepper. Transfer to a parchment-lined baking tray and bake for 25 minutes, tossing halfway through, until golden and cooked through. Remove from the oven and set aside.

Increase the oven to 230°C fan.

Meanwhile, put all the ingredients for the kofta mixture into another medium bowl with 1 teaspoon of salt and a generous grind of black pepper. Shape into 12 little torpedo-shaped pieces, each weighing about 55–60g. Set aside while you prepare the sauce.

To make the sauce, put the tahini, yoghurt, lemon juice, vinegar and garlic into a medium bowl with 125ml of water, ¾ teaspoon of salt and a good grind of black pepper. Whisk together well, until smooth and slightly runny, and set aside until needed.

Put the remaining tablespoon of oil into a large ovenproof sauté pan and place on a medium-high heat. Add the kofta and the sliced onion and cook for about 5 minutes, or until the kofta are lightly coloured and the onion has softened. Transfer the pan to the oven and bake for 4 minutes, or until the kofta are cooked through and the onions have lightly browned. Remove from the oven, stir in the potatoes and pour over the tahini sauce. Swirl the pan, so that the sauce gets distributed, and return to the oven for a final 4 minutes, or until the sauce is bubbling. Remove from the oven and leave to cool for 5 minutes before topping with the picked parsley, pine nuts and chilli. Serve directly from the pan.

## Serves four

3 baking potatoes (500g), peeled and cut into roughly 1½cm dice (470g)
3 tbsp olive oil
125g tahini
80g Greek-style yoghurt
1½ tbsp lemon juice
¾ tbsp cider vinegar
2 garlic cloves, crushed
1 onion, thinly sliced (150g)
5g picked parsley leaves
25g pine nuts, lightly toasted (see page 339)
½ tsp Aleppo chilli flakes (or ¼ tsp regular chilli flakes)
Salt and black pepper

### Kofta
250g lamb mince (at least 20% fat)
250g beef mince (at least 20% fat)
½ an onion, coarsely grated (75g)
1 large plum tomato, coarsely grated and skin discarded (90g)
1 tsp tomato purée
2 tsp olive oil
¾ tsp ground allspice
¾ tsp ground cinnamon
1 tsp Aleppo chilli flakes (or ½ tsp regular chilli flakes)
10g parsley, roughly chopped
2 garlic cloves, crushed

# Lamb bolognese with okra
## Sinniyat bamia bil lahmeh

This is essentially a lamb mince bolognese baked with okra. It's simple, comforting and completely delicious. Eat it as it is, with a salad alongside, or else with some plain rice or spaghetti.

*Getting ahead:* This is a lovely one to bake ahead and have in the fridge for the working week. It keeps well in the fridge, for 2–3 days, ready to be warmed through before serving.

*Cooking note:* As ever with okra (if you don't want a dish to become 'slimy'), don't trim the pods so much that you end up seeing the seeds. If you can see them then they'll be able to seep out. If you can't, then they won't, and anyone accusing okra of being 'gloopy' can be called out as just plain wrong.

---

Preheat the oven to 180°C fan.

Put 1 teaspoon of oil into a large frying pan and place on a high heat. Once smoking hot, add half the okra and cook for 3 minutes, shaking the pan once or twice, until nicely coloured on all sides. Transfer to a plate, then repeat with another teaspoon of oil and the remaining okra. Set aside until needed.

Put 2 tablespoons of oil into a large sauté pan and place on a medium-high heat. Add the onion and cook for 5 minutes, stirring a few times, until soft and lightly coloured. Add the crushed garlic, chilli, coriander, cumin and allspice and cook for another minute, until fragrant. Add the lamb mince and cook for 2–3 minutes, using a spoon to break up any chunks, or until no longer pink. Add the passata, chopped plum tomatoes, sugar, 150ml of water, 1¼ teaspoons of salt and a good grind of black pepper. Reduce the heat to medium and cook for 20 minutes, stirring occasionally, until the sauce is thick and rich.

Stir in 15g of the fresh coriander, half the sliced tomatoes and half the okra, then spread out in a large baking dish, about 28 x 20cm. Top with the remaining okra and tomatoes, scattered roughly over, cover with foil and bake for 30 minutes. Increase the oven temperature to 220°C fan, remove and discard the foil and continue cooking for another 20 minutes, or until the okra and tomatoes have taken on some colour and the sauce is bubbling. Remove from the oven and set aside to rest for 10 minutes.

Meanwhile, put the sliced garlic and the remaining 2 tablespoons of oil into a small frying pan. Set the heat to medium and cook for about 10 minutes, stirring from time to time, until the garlic is golden and crispy. Drain into a sieve set over a bowl and set aside: you don't need the oil for this dish, so either discard it or save it to add to your next salad dressing.

When ready to serve, sprinkle over the fried garlic, along with the remaining chopped coriander.

## Serves four to six

70ml olive oil
500g okra, lightly trimmed (see headnote)
1 onion, sliced in half, then each half cut into 4 wedges (160g)
10 garlic cloves, 5 crushed and the remaining 5 very thinly sliced
½ tsp chilli flakes
1½ tsp coriander seeds, roughly crushed in a pestle and mortar
1½ tsp cumin seeds, roughly crushed in a pestle and mortar
½ tsp ground allspice
300g lamb mince (at least 20% fat)
300g tomato passata
6 plum tomatoes (550g), 2 roughly chopped and the remaining 4 sliced into 1cm thick rounds
2 tsp caster sugar
20g coriander leaves, roughly chopped
Salt and black pepper

# Chicken meatballs with molokhieh, garlic and coriander

This is somewhere between a stew and a soup. A stoup, maybe. Comforting and hearty, certainly, served with some rice or crusty white bread. For more on molokhieh see pages 150 and page 339.

*Getting ahead:* The meatballs can be made up to a day or two in advance and kept in the fridge, ready to fry. The molokhieh can also be made a day or two in advance. You can also make up the whole thing well before serving: it keeps in the fridge for 2 days.

*Playing around:* If you want to make this dish gluten-free, replace the breadcrumbs in the meatballs with grated courgette. The resulting meatballs aren't quite as firm as those made with bread, but this, arguably, makes them even more comforting.

---

**Serves four**

**Meatballs**

50g crustless sourdough, finely blitzed into crumbs (or 1 large courgette (220g), coarsely grated (200g) – see headnote)
500g minced chicken (or turkey) thighs
2 garlic cloves, crushed
1½ tsp ground cumin
1 tsp ground cinnamon
½ tsp ground allspice
¼ tsp chilli flakes
10g coriander leaves, roughly chopped
10g parsley leaves, roughly chopped
10g mint leaves, roughly chopped
1 lemon: finely grate the zest to get 1½ tsp, then quarter, lengthways, to serve
2 tbsp olive oil, to fry, plus extra for greasing your hands
Salt and black pepper

**Molokhieh**

2 garlic cloves, crushed
1 lemon: shave the rind to get 4 strips, then juice to get 1½ tbsp
450ml chicken stock
800g frozen molokhieh (or 800g frozen chopped spinach plus 200g okra, thinly sliced – see pages 150 and 339)
½ tsp ground cinnamon
10g parsley leaves, roughly chopped
20g coriander leaves, roughly chopped

**Fried garlic**

60ml olive oil
6 garlic cloves, crushed
½ tsp chilli flakes
10g coriander leaves, roughly chopped

First make the meatballs. Place the breadcrumbs in a small bowl and cover with water. Stir, then drain through a colander, squeezing out most of the moisture from the bread (if using grated courgette, toss it with ½ teaspoon of salt and place in a sieve set over a bowl. Leave to sit for 20 minutes, then use your hands to squeeze out as much liquid as possible).

Transfer to a large bowl with the chicken, garlic, spices, herbs, lemon zest, ¾ teaspoon salt and plenty of pepper. Using well-oiled hands, shape into about 30 small balls, roughly 25g each.

Put 1 tablespoon of oil into a large non-stick sauté pan, for which you have a lid, and place on a high heat. Once hot, add half the meatballs and fry for 2–3 minutes, turning throughout until golden brown all over. Transfer the meatballs to a tray and set aside. Keep the pan on the heat and continue with one more tablespoon of oil and the remaining meatballs in the same way.

To make the molokhieh, return the same pan to a medium-high heat. Add the 2 cloves of garlic, the lemon rind and chicken stock and bring to the boil: this should take about 3 minutes. Add the molokhieh (or the spinach and okra combination), cinnamon, 2 teaspoons of salt and plenty of black pepper, then lower the heat to medium and cook, covered, for about 20 minutes, or until the molokhieh is bubbling and completely defrosted. Add the meatballs, parsley and 10g of coriander and cook, covered, for another 10 minutes, or until completely cooked through. Stir in the lemon juice.

Meanwhile, put the 60ml of olive oil into a small frying pan on a medium-high heat. Add the garlic and cook for about 3 minutes, stirring occasionally, or until golden and crispy. Add the chilli flakes, then remove from the heat and pour into a bowl. Stir in the coriander and set aside.

Divide the soup between four bowls and top with the fried garlic and herbs and the remaining coriander. Serve at once, with a wedge of lemon alongside.

# Stuffed turnips with turkey, freekeh and spicy tamarind sauce
## Mahshi lift

### Serves six

2kg turnips
90ml sunflower oil, to fry
60g pomegranate seeds
  (from ½ a pomegranate)
1½ tbsp olive oil
Salt and black pepper
150g Greek-style yoghurt,
  to serve (optional)

### Stuffing

80g cracked freekeh (also known
  as greenwheat) (see page 336),
  washed well, drained and picked
  of any stones
250g minced turkey thighs
¾ tsp baharat (see page 190)
¾ tsp ground cumin
¾ tsp ground cinnamon
10g dill leaves, roughly chopped,
  plus 1 tbsp extra to serve
10g parsley leaves, roughly
  chopped, plus 1 tbsp extra to serve
10g tarragon leaves, roughly
  chopped, plus 1 tbsp extra to serve
1½ tbsp olive oil
1 lemon: finely grate the zest to get
  1½ tsp
1½ tsp tomato purée

### Tamarind sauce

80g dried tamarind pulp (see page
  341), soaked in 250ml boiling
  water for 30 minutes
1 onion, finely diced (150g)
6 garlic cloves, crushed (25g)
1 large green chilli, deseeded and
  finely chopped (20g)
2 tbsp olive oil
½ tsp ground cumin
½ tsp ground coriander
½ tsp ground cinnamon
1 tsp baharat (see page 190)
6 plum tomatoes, coarsely
  grated (400g)
1½ tsp tomato purée
1 tbsp caster sugar

Stuffing vegetables is commonplace in Palestinian cooking. As well as being delicious, celebratory and comforting, the resulting dishes are often a practical way of making meat stretch further than it would otherwise do. Stuffing vegetables is, however, time-consuming: sauces and fillings need to be made, vegetables need to be hollowed out, the cooking time required is often relatively long. This is not to dissuade you from making a recipe like this – the results are wonderful – but to explain why there are not lots more recipes for stuffed vegetables in *Falastin*. Traditionally, coring and stuffing vegetables is done as a group activity, with the time spent divided between (equally important) coring and chatting duties.

*Getting ahead:* The turnips can be cored up to a day in advance: just keep them in plenty of cold water with some lemon juice squeezed in (to prevent discoloration). The whole dish can also be cooked a day ahead of serving, if you like, then just warmed through to serve: the flavours actually improve the next day.

---

First make the stuffing. Bring a medium pan with plenty of water to the boil. Add the freekeh and cook for about 15 minutes, or until just cooked through. Drain through a sieve, run under cold water, then set aside for about 15 minutes, to completely drain.

While the freekeh is cooking, put the remaining stuffing ingredients into a bowl along with 1 teaspoon of salt and good grind of black pepper. The freekeh can be added once it is drained and dried. Mix well to combine and set aside.

Peel the turnips, trim the top end so that it sits flat, then, using a manakra (see page 338) or a swivel peeler (as opposed to a y-shaped peeler), core them out. Pierce through one end of the turnip with your manakra or peeler, then twist to increase the cavity's circumference as you go along. Stop short before you get to the base, though: you don't want to pierce it all the way through. You should end up with a cavity which is about 3cm wide, with edges which are about ¾cm thick. Don't worry too much if you do pierce through the bottom, though; the trimmings can be used to seal the ends if needed. Any trimmings beyond this can be used to make turnip mash (see page 138).

Pour the sunflower oil into a large sauté pan. Place on a medium-high heat and, once hot, carefully add the turnips, in batches of 2 or 3, to the pan. Fry for about 8 minutes, turning occasionally to brown on all sides. Transfer to a tray lined with kitchen paper and continue with the remaining batches. Once the turnips are cool enough to handle, use your hands or a small spoon to fill the cavities with the freekeh mixture, pushing it down gently as you go.

*Continued overleaf*

To make the sauce, use your hands to break apart the tamarind pulp as much as possible. Strain the mixture through a sieve, pushing gently with a spoon, to get out as much tamarind liquid as you can: you should have about 260ml. The pulp and seeds can be discarded. Put the onion, garlic and chilli into a food processor and pulse a couple of times: you want the mixture to be finely minced but not to become a complete paste.

Put the oil into a large sauté pan, for which you have a lid, and place on a medium-high heat. Add the onion mixture and cook for about 7 minutes, stirring from time to time, until softened and lightly coloured. Stir in the spices and cook for a few seconds, then add the tomatoes, tomato purée, 2 teaspoons of salt and a good grind of black pepper. Cook for another 5 minutes, for the mixture to thicken, then add the sugar, tamarind liquid and 500ml of water. Cook for another 10 minutes, stirring occasionally.

Remove the pan from the heat and gently lower in the turnips, filling side up. Return to a medium-low heat and leave to simmer gently, covered, for about 70 minutes, or until the turnips are easily pierced with a knife. Remove from the heat and set aside, uncovered, for about 10 minutes, to slightly cool.

While the turnips are cooking, combine the pomegranate seeds, olive oil and extra herbs in a bowl. Spoon this over the turnips before serving them, straight from the pan, with a spoonful of yoghurt if desired.

# Meatballs and peas in tomato sauce

This is a dish to both comfort and surprise. Comfort in a way that only baked meatballs can, and surprise at the amount of flavour packed into both the balls and the sauce. Serve with some plain rice, mashed potato or crusty white bread, to mop up the juices, along with a crisp green salad.

*Getting ahead:* The sauce can be made in advance – it keeps well in the fridge for up to 3 days or can be frozen for longer – and the meatballs can be shaped in advance and either kept in the fridge overnight or pan-fried, ready to be warmed through. You can also just make the whole dish up to a day in advance, ready to warm through before serving.

*Playing around:* Meatballs often call for a bit of bread, to keep them spongy and light. If you want to, the bread can be replaced with an equal weight of coarsely grated courgette. Once grated, place the courgette in a sieve or colander and give it a good squeeze to extract some of the liquid. If you use the courgette, you won't need the milk.

## Serves four

50ml olive oil, plus extra for
 greasing your hands
1 onion, finely chopped (120g)
4 garlic cloves, crushed
1 tsp cumin seeds, roughly crushed
 in a pestle and mortar
6 cardamom pods, roughly bashed
 in a pestle and mortar
1 cinnamon stick
½ tsp chilli flakes
2 tsp tomato purée
8 plum tomatoes (800g), coarsely
 grated and skins discarded (600g)
250ml chicken stock
1½ tsp caster sugar
300g frozen peas, defrosted
150g feta, roughly broken into
 4–5cm chunks
Salt and black pepper
2 spring onions, thinly sliced (25g),
 to serve

## Meatballs

2 slices of white bread, crusts
 removed, torn into roughly 1cm
 chunks (60g) (or 1 small courgette,
 coarsely grated, for a gluten-free
 alternative – see headnote)
50ml whole milk (you don't need
 this if you are starting with
 courgette instead of breadcrumbs)
1 onion, roughly chopped (120g)
2 garlic cloves, crushed
500g beef mince (at least 15% fat)
2 tsp ground cinnamon
1 tsp ground allspice
15g parsley, roughly chopped, plus
 a few extra leaves to serve
10g mint leaves, roughly chopped
1 large lemon: finely grate the zest
 to get 1½ tsp
70g pitted green olives, roughly
 chopped

First make the meatballs. Put the bread and milk into a large bowl, mash together with your hands until the bread has completely disintegrated, then set aside. If starting with grated courgette, you don't need the milk and don't need to soak.

Put the onion into the bowl of a food processor and pulse a few times until very finely chopped but not liquidised. Tip the onion into the bowl of bread and add the garlic, beef, spices, herbs, zest, olives, 1¼ teaspoons of salt and a good grind of black pepper. With lightly oiled hands, shape the mixture into golfball-size balls, about 40g in weight: you should be able to make about 22.

Put 2 tablespoons of oil into a large sauté pan and place on a high heat. Add the meatballs in batches – you don't want to overcrowd the pan – and fry for about 3 minutes, turning so that all sides get nicely browned. Transfer the balls to a separate plate and set aside while you continue with the remaining batches.

Preheat the oven to 220°C fan.

To make the sauce, return the same pan to a medium-high heat and add 1 tablespoon of oil. Add the onion and cook for about 6 minutes, scraping the pan for any flavour gathered at the bottom, until softened and nicely browned. Add the garlic, cumin, cardamom, cinnamon, chilli and tomato purée and cook for another minute, or until fragrant. Add the tomatoes, stock, sugar, 1¼ teaspoons salt and a good grind of black pepper and cook for about 20 minutes, until reduced by a third. Remove from the heat, stir in the peas, then transfer the mixture to a large ovenproof dish, about 28 x 20cm. Top with the meatballs, scatter over the feta and drizzle with the remaining 1 teaspoon of oil. Bake for 20 minutes, or until the meatballs are cooked though, the sauce is bubbling and the feta has taken on some colour. Leave to sit for about 10 minutes, then sprinkle over the spring onions and picked parsley and serve.

# Stuffed aubergines and courgettes in a rich tomato sauce
## Baatingan w kusaa bil banadoura

Stuffing vegetables is such an everyday event in the Palestinian kitchen that most cooks have a special knife to help them with the task. It's called a manakra, with a thin blade curved into a semicircle and both sides serrated. You can get them online or in specialist shops but, for a good alternative, a swivel peeler (the straight ones, as opposed to the y-shaped ones) or a corer both work very well. Sami and Tara were also shown how to use a power drill, by some ladies serving lunch out of a garage in a car park in Jerusalem, to core carrots and courgettes, but such a recommendation comes with obvious health and safety warnings!

Serve these either as a side or as a main, with a salad or some other cooked vegetables alongside. Some bread is also good, to mop up the juices.

*Getting ahead:* The stuffing mixture can be made up to a day ahead. The tomato sauce keeps well in the fridge for up to 3 days, and also freezes well. Double the recipe for the sauce, if you can, so that you have a batch ready to go when you next need it.

---

First make the sauce. Put the oil into a saucepan or casserole pan for which you have a lid – about 25cm wide – and place on a medium heat. Add the onion and cook for about 10 minutes, stirring frequently, until soft and caramelised. Add the rest of the ingredients for the sauce, along with 2½ teaspoons of salt and a good grind of black pepper. Simmer on a medium heat for about 10 minutes, stirring from time to time, then remove from the heat and set aside.

While the sauce is cooking, place all the ingredients for the stuffing in a large bowl with 50ml of water, 1½ teaspoons of salt and a good grind of black pepper. Mix well, using your hands to make sure that everything is well incorporated. If making in advance, keep in the fridge until ready to use.

To hollow out the aubergines, trim off the stalks, then insert your manakra (or peeler or corer – see headnote) into the aubergine: you want it to be very close to the skin – about 2–3mm away – but not so close that it tears and won't hold its shape when it's stuffed. Scoop out the flesh to create a generous cavity. You don't need the flesh any more, but keep it for another recipe: it can be cut into cubes and steamed, for example, or added to your next omelette. If your aubergines are particularly large, slice them in half, widthways, and scoop out the flesh using a regular small serrated knife: be sure to keep one end of each half intact, so that the stuffing does not fall out!

To prepare the courgettes, do the same: use a manakra or a swivel peeler to scoop out the flesh. Keep about 2–3mm of flesh attached to the skin inside the courgettes and about 1cm from the end intact: they need to be robust enough to keep the stuffing inside. Again, keep the scooped-out flesh to use elsewhere.

**Serves six as a main or twelve as a side**

700g aubergines (between 3 and 6, depending on size)
700g courgettes (between 3 and 6, depending on size)
Salt and black pepper
250g Greek-style yoghurt, to serve

**Sauce**
2½ tbsp olive oil
2 onions, finely diced (350g)
1kg tomato passata
350g ripe tomatoes (2 large), coarsely grated
750ml chicken stock (or water)
1 tbsp caster sugar

**Stuffing**
175g Egyptian rice (see page 336), or pudding rice
250g lamb mince (or beef mince or a mixture of both)
60ml olive oil
½ tsp ground cinnamon
¾ tsp ground allspice
½ tsp ground cumin
About 3 spring onions, finely sliced (35g)
15g mint leaves, roughly chopped
15g parsley leaves, roughly chopped
20g dill, roughly chopped
1 red chilli, deseeded and finely diced (10g)
1 lemon: finely grate the zest to get 1 tsp

*Ingredients continued opposite*

Using your hands, so that you can push in a bit of stuffing at a time, fill all the aubergine and courgette cavities. Stop filling them about 1cm from the top of each vegetable: the stuffing needs some space to expand inside the vegetables when they are cooking.

Gently lower the stuffed vegetables into the sauce. They won't fit in a single layer, but try to avoid too much overlap and submerge them in the sauce as much as you can. Return the sauce to a medium heat and, once simmering, reduce the heat to low. Cover the pan and very gently simmer for 90 minutes, or until the rice is completely cooked through and soft: test it is ready by sticking a knife into the middle of one of the vegetables – it should go in very easily. Don't worry if some of the rice/stuffing tips out into the tomato sauce: this can happen and it will be fine when served.

Meanwhile, prepare the adha. Put the oil into a small frying pan and place on a medium heat. After about a minute, add the garlic and lower the heat to medium-low. Cook for about 5 minutes, stirring very often, until the garlic is golden and crispy. Keep a close eye on the pan here: you don't want the oil to get too hot and for the garlic to burn. Reserving the oil as you pour, strain the garlic through a sieve. Set the garlic aside – it will crisp up as it cools down – and return the oil to the pan. Add the coriander seeds and chilli and cook for about 1 minute, stirring a few times, until fragrant. Remove from the heat, transfer to a separate bowl and set aside until needed.

When the vegetables are cooked and the sauce is thick and rich (but still pourable), use a slotted spoon to carefully lift the vegetables out of the pan. Pour the sauce on to a large serving platter (or individual serving plates) with a rim and top with the stuffed vegetables. Spoon over the adha: the coriander and chilli oil first, followed by the fried garlic slices, fresh herbs and spring onion. Serve warm or at room temperature, with the yoghurt spooned alongside.

**Adha**

100ml olive oil
6 garlic cloves, finely chopped
1 tbsp coriander seeds, lightly
 crushed in a pestle and mortar
1 red chilli, deseeded and finely
 diced (10g)
5g parsley leaves, roughly chopped
5g mint leaves, roughly torn
5g dill, picked
1 spring onion, thinly sliced (5g)

# Chicken musakhan

Musakhan is the hugely popular national dish of Palestine: growing up, Sami ate it once a week, pulling a piece of chicken and sandwiching it between a piece of pita or flatbread. It's a dish to eat with your hands and with your friends, served from one pot or plate, for everyone to then tear at some of the bread and spoon over the chicken and topping for themselves.

Traditionally, musakhan was made around the olive oil pressing season in October or November to celebrate (and gauge the quality of) the freshly pressed oil. The taboon bread would be cooked in a hot taboon oven (see page 341) lined with smooth round stones, to create small craters in the bread in which the meat juices, onion and olive oil all happily pool. It's cooked year-round, nowadays, layered with shop-bought taboon or pita bread, and is a dish to suit all occasions: easy and comforting enough to be the perfect week-night supper as it is, but also special enough to stand alongside other dishes at a feast.

*Playing around:* The chicken can be replaced with thick slices of roasted aubergine or chunky cauliflower florets, if you like (or a mixture of both), for a vegetarian alternative. If you do this, toss the slices or florets in the oil and spices, as you do the chicken, and roast at 200°C fan for about 25 minutes for the cauliflower and about 35 minutes for the aubergine.

## Serves four

1 chicken (about 1.7kg), divided into 4 pieces (1.4kg) or 1kg chicken supremes (between 4 and 6, depending on size), skin on, if you prefer
120ml olive oil, plus 2–3 tbsp extra, to finish
1 tbsp ground cumin
3 tbsp sumac
½ tsp ground cinnamon
½ tsp ground allspice
30g pine nuts
3 large red onions, thinly sliced 2–3mm thick (500g)
4 taboon breads (see headnote), or any flatbread (such as Arabic flatbread or naan bread) (330g)
5g parsley leaves, roughly chopped
Salt and black pepper

### To serve
300g Greek-style yoghurt
1 lemon, quartered

Preheat the oven to 200°C fan.

Place the chicken in a large mixing bowl with 2 tablespoons of oil, 1 teaspoon of cumin, 1½ teaspoons of sumac, the cinnamon, allspice, 1 teaspoon of salt and a good grind of black pepper. Mix well to combine, then spread out on a parchment-lined baking tray. Roast until the chicken is cooked through. This will take about 30 minutes if starting with supremes and up to 45 minutes if starting with the whole chicken, quartered. Remove from the oven and set aside. Don't discard any juices which have collected in the tray.

Meanwhile, put 2 tablespoons of oil into a large sauté pan, about 24cm, and place on a medium heat. Add the pine nuts and cook for about 2–3 minutes, stirring constantly, until the nuts are golden brown. Transfer to a bowl lined with kitchen paper (leaving the oil behind in the pan) and set aside. Add the remaining 60ml of oil to the pan, along with the onions and ¾ teaspoon of salt. Return to a medium heat for about 15 minutes, stirring from time to time, until the onions are completely soft and pale golden but not caramelised. Add 2 tablespoons of sumac, the remaining 2 teaspoons of cumin and a grind of black pepper and mix through, until the onions are completely coated. Remove from the heat and set aside.

When ready to assemble the dish, set the oven to a grill setting and slice or tear the bread into quarters or sixths. Place them under the grill for about 2–3 minutes, to crisp up, then arrange them on a large platter. Top the bread with half the onions, followed by all the chicken and any chicken juices left in the tray. Either keep each piece of chicken as it is or else roughly shred it as you plate up, into two or three large chunks. Spoon the remaining onions over the top and sprinkle with the pine nuts, parsley, 1½ teaspoons of sumac and a final drizzle of olive oil. Serve at once, with the yoghurt and a wedge of lemon alongside.

# Olive trees and olive oil

Palestinian olive oil is delicious. It's rich, it's green, it's grassy, it's all sorts of words one normally associates with the tasting of fine wines. So why does no one, really, know about it outside Palestine? Why is the terrain of extra-virgin olive oil generally held to be Italy, or Greece, or Spain?

The answer lies in logistics – more particularly, the logistics of getting to be a well-known product in an export market. It's about marketing, selling, pricing and all sorts of other practical factors. But if out-and-out quality were the judge in a simple blind taste test of 'which olive oil really knocks your socks off', a lot more people would know a lot more about Palestinian olive oil.

It is there, though, and it is available outside Palestine, so that's the good news. The less good news is that challenges are also there: challenges to the trees themselves, to the farmers who pick the olives and to the producers who make, distribute and export the oil. As ever, there are as many stories and challenges as there are trees. Just a snapshot, then, below, telling the story from the points of view of an olive tree guardian, an olive oil producer and distributor, an olive farmer and lastly a small social enterprise company in the UK which imports and sells Palestinian olive oil.

To start with: the tree. Half of the farmed land in Palestine is planted with olive trees. Some of them are very old – around 1,000 years – so they play a huge part in the link between the people, their history and their land. With the olives generating nearly a quarter of Palestine's agricultural output, they also play a huge part in the country's productivity and economy.

The olive harvest, from mid-October to early November, is a crucial time and every year all the farmers, along with their families and visitors, head to the groves for long days of picking. Everyone gets involved, kids too, pulling at the low-hanging olives or climbing up little ladders leaning on the trees to reach for the higher branches. A big net stretches out on the ground, collecting and protecting those olives that have fallen down by themselves. It's an event which goes on for about three weeks, with everyone stopping all together for a big lunch under the shade of one of the trees.

It all sounds rather idyllic. Indeed, it *would* be idyllic were it not for the extent to which these trees (and therefore this way of life) are threatened. The main threats come in the form of bulldozers or intentional fires, both of which are employed to make way for the building of Israeli settlements or as a means to

destroy Palestinian income. Furthermore, particularly ancient trees are being dug up for sale to the highest Israeli or international bidder, who then replants them in, say, their front garden. The irony of the situation – that olive trees are being dug up from the land they've been part of and nurturing for so many years in order to showcase, precisely, an ancient connection with the land – is intense.

Another reason olive trees are being destroyed is to make way for the continued building of the separation wall. A tree said to be one of the oldest olive trees sits in the village of al-Walajeh, located near the Green Line (see page 337), south of Jerusalem. At about 12 metres high and 25 metres wide, it's ten times the size of an average olive tree. It's believed to be over 4,000 years old. Salah Abu-Ali's family has been farming the land since the 60s. Since observing the threat to the existence of the tree by the building of the wall, Salah has taken it upon himself to sit guard as the tree's protector. Now known locally as 'the guardian of the olive tree', his post under the shade of its wide branches is near permanent. It's clear, doing the maths, that Salah spends more time in the company of his tree than that of his wife. His wife's presence (and presumably, if plates of food could speak, support) makes itself known only in the form of a large tray of stuffed vine leaves, rolled long and thin, which appear to accompany our time spent with Salah in the shade of his tree. As well as protecting the tree, and making oil from the large olives he harvests in the autumn, he also hosts visitors who make a pilgrimage to his shrine, to hear his story and, in so doing, spread the word far beyond the reach of the branches. 'Post my story on Facebook,' Salah calls out, as we go on our way.

Notwithstanding these threats and challenges, the story is not all doom and gloom. As ever, the vision, commitment and enthusiasm of just one individual can be enough to transform the status quo. In the world of olives, in the world of Palestine, Nasser Abufarha – olive oil producer and distributor – is one such man (pictured opposite).

Trained as an anthropologist and working in America for many years, Nasser returned to Palestine around the beginning of the year 2000, to set up Canaan Fair Trade. Canaan is, as the name suggests, a fair trade organisation and social enterprise project which works with local farmers to produce some of the best olive oil, almonds, maftoul and freekeh the country has to offer. It started in 2004 and began exporting in 2008. Today, Canaan has a network which, collectively, works with fifty village-based co-operatives of farmers and women across Palestine.

Very much wearing two hats at once, Nasser manages to bring together the needs of the farmers to have productive conditions to work in and, at the same time, the needs of a business to make a profit in order to grow and market itself to the outside world. Walking around Canaan, there's a real buzz. The factory is there, of course, doing its work to press olives and sort almonds, but there's also an impressive shop selling olive oil, tapenade, almonds and grains to visitors. A big café space is being developed to host workshops and provide a venue for functions. Working alongside this profit-generating and thoroughly 'modern' buzz, though, sits the large and very traditional working taboon oven (see page 341), all lit up inside and on the go. Stopping by to whip up some open pies for a mid-morning snack, Nasser brings baladi ('from the land') eggs, wild asparagus, zalabeed (the tender and sweet shoots of the middle of the onion) and fresh za'atar from his bag. Munching on the pies fresh from the taboon oven, watching the building work for the new café going on, the possibility of combining the best of all worlds – the traditional and the future-looking – feels very real. It's all about olives, yes, but it's also about so much more. 'Olive oil is important for our food security and our cultural representation,' says Nasser. 'It is [also] a symbol of our identity. The trees connect us to our land, to the place, to the history, and to past generations [. . .] They represent the continuity of a nation and our rootedness in the land.'

Just one of the farmers producing olives (among other things) for Canaan is Khadir Khadir (pictured overleaf), living and working in the village of Nus Ijbail. Khadir came to farming initially as a means to get out of working in (and sleeping

on the floor of) an Israeli plastics factory. Conditions were tough and life was not good, so Khadir had to find a plan B. After an uncle asked him to help him out with the harvest, Khadir quickly got the farming bug and now has, while still being one of the youngest members of the village, something of the 'unelected mayor' feel about him. The population of the village is only about 350 and, also, is ageing, as most young people have left. Khadir sees it as his mission to stay and help, though. Making the village productive and viable is not just about keeping alive the old ways of co-operative farming. It's about keeping alive the old ways of people looking out for each other and caring and holding on to a sense of identity and pride.

The logistical challenges to productivity and morale for farmers like Khadir, working the land under the conditions of occupation, are very real. The three main challenges Khadir faces day-to-day are demolition orders, insufficient access to water and the lack of freedom of movement. He remains, though, as upbeat and resilient. 'I consider myself a very lucky man,' he says. Again, the symbolism of the olive tree – a tree so resilient and independent that it is able to both self-pollinate and live off little or no water – is hard not to note. The trees play as a big a part in the Palestinian sense of identity and spirit – which has resilience at its core – as they do in the agricultural input of the country.

After people like Khadir have picked the olives and people at Canaan have produced and packaged the oil, the challenge is then to get over and around all the logistics that get in the way of selling it to the export market. One importer of Palestinian Fair Trade products is a social enterprise company called Zaytoun (which translates from Arabic as, appropriately, 'olive').

Zaytoun was set up in 2004 by Manal White and Heather Masoud. It started off as a grass-roots volunteer initiative with a focused remit to import products such as olive oil, almonds, za'atar, freekeh and dates from Canaan and sell these to the UK market. For all the challenges of getting it to market, Manal is enthusiastic about the continued and expanding demand for Palestinian oil (among other products) in markets outside Palestine.

The market is there, then, as are the olives, the farmers, the producers, distributors and importers. The product is incredibly good and the passion is very real. With barriers to export and other logistical, political factors looking like they are not going to change any time soon, it's up to the customer to use their purchasing power to seek it out. It is there – online, in specialist stores, in well-stocked greengrocers – and, if it's not, ask for it. Create the market, which the supplier will then want and need to supply. Buy Palestinian olive oil not just because it is deliciously rich, green and grassy. Buy it because it's a way to keep oiling the logistical cogs that could be turning a lot more smoothly to get this product to market.

# Lemon chicken with za'atar

As anyone who has cooked the chicken traybakes from Sami's previous cookbooks – *Ottolenghi: The Cookbook* and *Jerusalem* – knows, the secret weapon behind so many (seemingly) effortless dinners is a make-ahead chicken dish which can just be put into the oven when needed. All the work is done in advance, which means that on the night there is little fuss, and happy feasting. It's a complete winner every time.

*Ingredients note:* We tend to start with a whole chicken (so that chicken stock can be made from the carcass), but it's absolutely fine, of course, to start with chicken supremes or legs if you prefer.

---

Slice 2 of the lemons into ½cm-thick slices and place in a large mixing bowl. Finely grate the zest of the remaining lemon (to get 1½ teaspoons of zest) and set this aside for later. Squeeze the same lemon to get about 1½ tablespoons of juice and add this to the mixing bowl along with the chicken, onions, garlic, sumac, allspice, 2 tablespoons of za'atar, 2 tablespoons of oil, the stock or water, 1½ teaspoons of salt and a good grind of black pepper. Mix well to combine, then cover with a large plate and leave to marinate in the fridge for at least 2 hours (or overnight, if you have time).

Half an hour or an hour before baking, take the chicken out of the fridge: it should be at room temperature before going into the oven.

Preheat the oven to 200°C fan.

Transfer the chicken to a large baking tray, skin side up, and pour over all the marinade and lemon slices. Drizzle the chicken with a tablespoon of oil and bake for about 45 minutes, giving everything a bit of a stir halfway through, until the chicken is golden and cooked through and the onions have taken on some colour. Transfer to a serving platter along with the lemon slices and any juices that have collected at the bottom of the tray. Some people will love to eat the lemon slices and others won't. Either way, serve them up with the chicken: they look great.

Towards the end of the cooking time for the chicken, combine the parsley, lemon zest, the remaining 2 tablespoons of za'atar and the remaining 3 tablespoons of olive oil in a bowl. Spoon this over the chicken, finish with the almonds and serve.

## Serves four

3 lemons
1 whole chicken (1.3kg), segmented into legs, thighs and breasts (or about 1kg of chicken legs or supremes, skin on, if you prefer)
2 onions, peeled, sliced in half, then each half cut into 3 wedges (260g)
2 heads of garlic, skin on, sliced in half, widthways
2 tsp sumac
¾ tsp ground allspice
4 tbsp za'atar
90ml olive oil
200ml chicken stock (or water)
5g parsley, finely chopped
30g flaked almonds, toasted (see page 339)
Salt and black pepper

# Spicy pasta bake

Sami, like so many kids – Middle Eastern or otherwise – did a lot of his growing up at home on pasta bakes. There's quite a kick in our version, but the chilli flakes can be reduced or left out if you prefer. Don't skimp on the time the bolognese sauce sits on the stove, though. It's this which gives the dish such depth and makes the house smell like home.

*Getting ahead:* The bolognese sauce can be made up to 2 days before assembling the dish, and it also freezes well. Bring it back to room temperature or gently warm through before adding the cooked macaroni and assembling the dish: it will be too firm to mix if you don't. The whole dish can be assembled a day in advance as well, ready to go into the oven and, again, also freezes well. If you are baking from frozen it will need 5 or 10 minutes longer in the oven.

---

First make the bolognese. Put the onion, celery and green peppers into a food processor and pulse a couple of times, until finely chopped. Put the butter and oil into a large cast-iron saucepan, for which you have a lid, and place on a medium-high heat. Tip in the onion mixture and cook for about 7 minutes, stirring from time to time, until softened. Add the garlic, tomato purée, oregano, spices and bay leaves and cook for another minute, until fragrant. Add the beef and cook for another 3 minutes or so, using a spoon to break the meat apart into fine crumbles, until no longer pink. Add the tinned and fresh tomatoes, red peppers, sugar, 100ml of water, 2¼ teaspoons of salt and a good grind of black pepper. Bring to a simmer, then cover the pan, reduce the heat to medium-low and leave to simmer very gently for 2½ hours, stirring every half hour or so, until the sauce is thick and rich. Lift out and discard the bay leaves, stir in the parsley and set aside until needed.

To make the béchamel, put the butter into a medium saucepan and place on a medium-high heat. Once melted, whisk in the flour and cook for a minute or so, until pale golden and beginning to smell like popcorn. Gradually pour in the milk, whisking continuously as you do so to avoid any lumps. Reduce the heat to medium, add the nutmeg and 1 teaspoon of salt, and cook for 5 minutes, whisking continuously, until the flour has cooked out and the sauce is completely smooth. Remove from the heat and set aside for about 10 minutes, then stir in the yoghurt and egg yolks until fully incorporated.

Preheat the oven to 200°C fan.

Bring a large pan of salted water to the boil and add the macaroni. Cook for about 7 minutes, or according to the packet instructions, until al dente. Reserving 60ml of the cooking water, drain the macaroni through a sieve and then add it to the bolognese sauce along with the reserved cooking water. Mix well to combine, then transfer to a baking dish, about 30 x 22cm and 8cm deep, then pour over the béchamel and spread it out evenly. Sprinkle over the feta and bake for 25 minutes, or until golden and bubbling. Leave to cool for 10–15 minutes, then serve, with a final sprinkle of parsley and chilli flakes and a drizzle of oil.

## Serves six generously

### Bolognese sauce
1 onion, roughly chopped (150g)
3 sticks of celery, roughly chopped (150g)
2 green peppers, stalk, core and seeds removed, flesh roughly chopped (150g)
25g unsalted butter
2 tbsp olive oil, plus a drizzle to serve
5 garlic cloves, crushed
1 tbsp tomato purée
2 tbsp oregano leaves, finely chopped
1 tbsp ground cumin
1 tbsp ground cinnamon
2 tsp ground allspice
1¼ tsp chilli flakes
2 bay leaves
500g beef mince (15–20% fat)
1 x 400g tin of chopped tomatoes
5–6 plum tomatoes (500g), coarsely grated and skins discarded (400g)
2 red peppers, stalk, core and seeds removed, flesh cut into roughly 3cm dice (260g)
1 tsp caster sugar
20g parsley, roughly chopped, plus extra to serve
Salt and black pepper

### Béchamel sauce
45g unsalted butter
60g plain flour
500ml whole milk
A pinch of ground nutmeg
130g Greek-style yoghurt
2 egg yolks

### Pasta and toppings
350g macaroni pasta
180g feta, roughly crumbled
¾ tsp Aleppo chilli flakes (or ⅓ tsp regular chilli flakes), to serve

# Pulled lamb shawarma sandwich

Slow-cooked lamb, piled into a warm pita with all the condiments you care for: this is the ultimate shawarma sandwich. Once cooked, the lamb keeps in the fridge so don't worry if there are fewer than eight of you for that first sandwich. The lamb is also great as a proper meal, rather than a sandwich, served as it is with a selection of sides: fattoush (see page 99), butternut squash (see page 86) and a crisp green salad makes just one great combination.

*Getting ahead:* The lamb can be cooked a day or two ahead, ready to be warmed through when serving.

---

## Serves eight

3 onions, 1 roughly chopped and
  the other 2 quartered (and peeled,
  as always) into wedges
2 heads of garlic, 1 cut in half,
  horizontally, and 8 cloves from the
  second head roughly chopped
2½cm piece of ginger, peeled and
  roughly chopped (25g)
20g parsley, roughly chopped
1½ tbsp ground cumin
1½ tbsp ground coriander
2 tsp smoked paprika
2 tsp ground turmeric
2 tsp ground cinnamon
¼ tsp ground cloves
3 tbsp cider vinegar
60ml olive oil
2–2.5kg lamb shoulder, bone in
700ml chicken stock
½ a lemon
Salt and black pepper

## Sumac yoghurt
200g Greek-style yoghurt
60g tahini
1½ tbsp lemon juice
2 tsp sumac

## To serve (any or all of the following)
2 plum tomatoes, thinly
  sliced (200g)
1 red onion, thinly sliced into
  rounds (120g)
10g picked parsley leaves
5g picked mint leaves
100g shatta (see page 73)
8 pita breads (shop-bought or see
  page 278 for homemade)

First make the spice paste. Put the chopped onion into a food processor along with the chopped garlic and ginger. Pulse until finely minced, then add the parsley and spices. Pulse for about 10 seconds, until just combined. Scrape down the sides, then add the vinegar, oil, 2¼ teaspoons of salt and a generous grind of black pepper. Pulse to form a coarse paste, then transfer to a non-metallic container large enough to hold the lamb.

Pat the lamb dry and pierce liberally all over with a small, sharp knife. Add it to the spice paste and coat generously, so that all sides are covered. Cover with foil and leave to marinate, refrigerated, overnight.

Take the lamb out of the fridge about an hour before going into the oven: you want it to be more like room temperature rather than fridge-cold.

Preheat the oven to 140°C fan.

Put the remaining onions and head of garlic into the centre of a large roasting tray and pour over the chicken stock. Sit the lamb on top of the vegetables, cover tightly with foil and bake for 4 hours. Remove from the oven, discard the foil and bake for 90 minutes more, increasing the oven temperature to 160°C fan towards the last 30 minutes of cooking time. The lamb is ready when it is fork-tender and easily pulls away from the bone. Set aside to cool slightly, about 15 minutes, before using two forks to roughly shred the lamb directly in the pan, gathering as much of its juices as possible. Transfer the shredded lamb, onions, garlic cloves and any of the pan juices to a serving bowl. Squeeze over the lemon juice and set aside.

While the lamb is in the oven, prepare the sumac yoghurt. Put the yoghurt, tahini, lemon juice, 2 tablespoons of water, the sumac and ¼ teaspoon of salt into a bowl and whisk well to combine.

When ready to serve, lay out all the various condiments, along with the pita, to let everyone make up their own shawarma sandwich.

# Chicken shawarma pie

Spiced marinated chicken thighs, slow-cooked until meltingly tender, layered with baked potato slices and rich tahini sauce, all wrapped up in thin-as-a-feather butter-brushed filo. This is a wow of a pie. Serve it either warm or at room temperature, with a crisp green salad and some pickles alongside.

*Getting ahead:* The chicken can be made a day or two ahead of assembling the pie. Keep it in the fridge and just bring it back to room temperature before putting the dish together.

*Playing around:* The layer of potatoes at the base makes this pie comforting and hearty, but, for a slightly lighter version, you can leave them out. You can also just make the chicken part of the dish. As it is, it makes a delicious stew, served with steamed rice or piled into a pita or wrap. If you do this, keep the tahini sauce: it's always a welcome addition.

---

Put the chicken into a large bowl with the garlic, ginger, ground spices, 1 tablespoon of oil, the vinegar, 1 teaspoon of salt and a generous grind of black pepper. Mix to combine, then leave to marinate for at least half an hour (or overnight in the fridge).

Preheat the oven to 180°C fan.

Mix the potatoes with 1½ tablespoons of oil, ¾ teaspoon of salt and a good grind of black pepper. Transfer to a parchment-lined baking tray and spread out so that they are not overlapping. Bake for 20 minutes, then increase the oven temperature to 220°C fan. Remove the tray from the oven, carefully flip over each potato slice, then return to the oven for another 10 minutes, or until golden. Remove from the oven and set aside until needed.

Reduce the oven temperature to 180°C fan again (or turn the oven off for now and preheat to 180°C fan before baking).

Put 15g of butter and 1½ tablespoons of oil into a large sauté pan and place on a medium-high heat. Once hot, add the onion and cook for 5 minutes, stirring occasionally, until softened. Add the chicken and cook for about 10 minutes, until lightly brown, then add the stock, ¼ teaspoon of salt and a good grind of black pepper. Bring to the boil, then lower the heat to medium. Simmer gently for 25 minutes, or until the chicken is just cooked through. Increase the heat to medium-high and continue to cook for about 8 minutes, or until the liquid has thickened and reduced to about 4 tablespoons. Remove from the heat and leave to cool for about 10 minutes, then use two forks to shred the chicken into large chunks. Stir in the herbs and set aside.

To make the tahini sauce, put the tahini, yoghurt, garlic, lemon juice, ⅛ teaspoon of salt and 2 tablespoons of water into a bowl. Whisk together until smooth, then set aside.

## Serves six

750g chicken thighs, skinless and boneless
4 garlic cloves, crushed
2cm piece of ginger, peeled and finely grated (15g)
2 tsp ground cumin
2 tsp ground coriander
¾ tsp smoked paprika
½ tsp ground turmeric
¾ tsp ground cinnamon
⅛ tsp ground cloves
90ml olive oil, plus extra for greasing
2 tbsp cider vinegar
2 baking potatoes (450g), unpeeled and cut into ½cm-thick rounds
45g unsalted butter
1 onion, thinly sliced (150g)
200ml chicken stock
5g parsley leaves, roughly chopped
5g coriander leaves, roughly chopped
8 (30 x 38cm) sheets of good-quality filo (170g)
1 tsp nigella seeds
¾ tsp Aleppo chilli flakes (or ⅓ tsp regular chilli flakes)
Salt and black pepper

## Tahini sauce
50g tahini
80g Greek-style yoghurt
2 garlic cloves, crushed
1 tbsp lemon juice

Melt the remaining 30g of butter and combine with the remaining 2 tablespoons of oil. Line the base of a 23cm springform cake tin with baking parchment and lightly grease the sides with some of the butter mixture. Lay a sheet of filo out on a clean work surface and brush with the butter. Transfer this to the tin so that the base is covered and the filo rises up and over the tin's sides. Repeat with the next sheet of filo, brushing it first with butter, then arranging it in the tin, rotating it slightly so that the excess hangs at a different angle. Continue in this fashion, brushing each piece generously as you go, until you have used up 6 pieces of filo in total and the base and sides are all covered.

Next, add the potato slices, overlapping slightly, so that the base of the pie is completely covered. Top with the chicken mixture and gently push down to even out. Lastly, spoon over the tahini sauce, spreading it gently to coat the chicken layer. Brush a piece of filo with butter and fold it in half horizontally, like a book. Place this over the tahini layer, tucking in the filo around the filling. Brush the top with the butter mixture, then repeat with the last piece of filo, angling it to cover any exposed areas. Now fold over the overhang, crinkling up the filo to create a nice 'crumpled' effect on the top. Brush the top with the remaining butter, sprinkle with the nigella seeds, place on a tray and bake at 180°C fan for 60 minutes, or until deeply golden.

Leave to cool for about 15 minutes before removing from the tin. Sprinkle with the chilli flakes and serve.

*Pictured overleaf*

# Upside-down spiced rice with lamb and broad beans
## Maqlubet el foul el akdhar

Maqlubeh is one of Palestine's key national dishes. This 'upside down' dish, made in one pot before being inverted on to a plate to serve, carries with it a real 'ta da!' thrill. However many times you've made it (or if you're making it for the first time), there's always a moment of 'eeek' before the pot gets flipped. Tap the base, count to three and be quick and confident that all will be well! Serve with a chopped salad (see page 92), some pickles, if you like, and a spoonful of thick yoghurt.

*Getting ahead:* You can make the stock and cook the lamb a day ahead. Keep it in the fridge overnight, and just warm through before proceeding.

---

Begin by washing the rice until the water runs clear, then leave it to soak in plenty of cold water with 2 teaspoons of salt for at least 2 hours (or overnight).

Put the oil for the lamb into a large saucepan, about 25cm wide and 10cm high, for which you have a lid, and place on a medium-high heat. Toss the lamb pieces with ½ teaspoon of salt and a good grind of black pepper and, once hot, add to the saucepan along with the onions, garlic, cardamom, peppercorns, bay leaves and limes, if using. Cook for about 8 minutes, stirring occasionally, or until the lamb has taken on some colour and the onions are soft and golden. Add the tomatoes, tomato purée, chillies and ground spices and cook for about 4 minutes, until slightly thickened and fragrant. Add 1.4 litres of water and 2 teaspoons of salt, bring to the boil, then cover with the lid, lower the heat to medium-low and cook for 1 hour and 40 minutes, or until the lamb is tender and practically falling off the bone. Remove from the heat and use a pair of tongs to pick out the lamb, transferring it to a bowl and leaving it to cool slightly before pulling the meat apart into large chunks, discarding the bones. There is a fair amount of fat here, but don't discard it: it can be added to the meat. Leave the stock and aromatics in the pan.

While the meat is cooking, prepare your vegetables. Put 1½ tablespoons of oil into a large sauté pan on a medium-high heat. Add the squash, ⅛ teaspoon of salt and a grind of black pepper, and cook for about 10 minutes, turning as needed, until golden and softened. Transfer to a large parchment-lined tray. Add another 1½ teaspoons of oil to the same pan, followed by the runner beans, green pepper, ¼ teaspoon of salt and a good grind of black pepper. Cook for about 8–9 minutes, stirring often, until the vegetables have charred and softened. Transfer to the same tray, keeping them separate from the squash. Add another 1½ teaspoons of oil to the pan, along with the onion. Cook for about 3 minutes in total, until browned and slightly softened, before transferring to the same tray, separate from the rest.

Drain the rice through a sieve. Return the stock and aromatics to the stove and place on a medium heat. Bring to a simmer, add the rice and cook for 6 minutes, or until al dente, draining it through a sieve set over a bowl. Measure out 150ml of stock, saving the rest for another use.

**Serves eight**

2½ tbsp olive oil
750g lamb neck (4–5 pieces), bone in
1 onion, sliced 1cm thick (150g)
8 garlic cloves, peeled
10 cardamom pods, roughly bashed in a pestle and mortar
20 black peppercorns, roughly crushed in a pestle and mortar
3 bay leaves
2 dried Iranian limes (if you can find them, or else leave them out), roughly stabbed with a small knife
5 plum tomatoes (450g), roughly chopped
2 tsp tomato purée
2 green chillies, halved lengthways
2½ tsp ground allspice
2½ tsp ground cinnamon
¾ tsp ground turmeric
Salt and black pepper

**Maqlubeh**
350g basmati rice
3½ tbsp olive oil
300g butternut squash, unpeeled and cut into 1cm-thick half-moons
400g runner beans, trimmed, then cut at an angle into 4cm pieces
1 green pepper, deseeded and cut into roughly 3cm cubes (150g)
1 large onion, cut into 1cm-thick rings (180g)
40g unsalted butter, cut into 1cm dice
1 large lemon, cut into 2mm-thick slices, pips discarded (100g)
150g green peas (fresh or frozen), defrosted
200g broad beans (podded but still in their shells), fresh or frozen and defrosted

*Ingredients continued opposite*

## To serve
1 tbsp olive oil
30g whole blanched almonds
20g pine nuts
1 red chilli, finely chopped
10g coriander, roughly chopped
300g Greek-style yoghurt

To assemble the maqlubeh, wipe out your saucepan, then coat the bottom and sides with the remaining tablespoon of oil and 15g of the butter. Spread the lemon slices out over the base of the pan, followed by the squash, onion, chunks of meat, runner beans and green pepper and, finally, the peas and broad beans. Sprinkle with ⅛ teaspoon of salt and a grind of black pepper, then give everything a good press, pushing down to compact the vegetables. Top with the rice and push down again to compress. Use the skinny handle of a wooden spoon to make 4 or 5 small holes through the rice, then pour in the 150ml of stock. Cover the pan tightly with foil, followed by the lid, and place over a medium-high heat, cooking for about 7 minutes before turning the heat to low and leaving to cook, undisturbed, for 40 minutes. Uncover, dot with the remaining 25g of butter, then replace the lid and leave to cook for 10 minutes more. Remove from the heat and let sit for about 20 minutes to cool slightly.

Meanwhile, toast the nuts. Put the olive oil into a small frying pan placed on a medium-high heat. Once hot, add the almonds and cook for 3–4 minutes, stirring continuously until golden. Add the pine nuts and cook for another 30–60 seconds. Using a slotted spoon, remove the nuts from the pan and set aside to cool. The oil can be discarded.

Once ready to serve, remove the lid and place a large flat serving dish over the open pot. Quickly invert the pot, so that the plate is now at the base. Tap the bottom of the pot (which is now at the top!) to gently help the maqlubeh slide out. Garnish with the nuts, red chilli and coriander and serve, with a spoonful of yoghurt alongside.

*Pictured on previous page*

# Fragrant Palestinian couscous
## *Maftoul*

Maftoul is one of the key players in Palestinian cuisine. It's the centrepiece of whatever table it arrives at, turning a family meal into a feast. It's big on flavour, great on looks and wonderfully satisfying to eat.

*Getting ahead:* The chicken can be marinated a day ahead (but does not need to be).

**Serves four generously**

**Chicken**
4 chicken legs (or supremes,
  if you prefer), skin on (1kg)
2 tbsp olive oil
1½ tsp ground cumin
1 tsp ground coriander
1 tsp ground cinnamon
¾ tsp ground turmeric
2 tsp fennel seeds, slightly crushed
Salt and black pepper

**Maftoul**
3 tbsp olive oil
2 medium onions, each cut
  into 8 wedges (350g)
1 tbsp tomato purée
½ tsp caster sugar
2 large carrots, peeled and cut
  into 2cm-thick slices (320g)
½ a butternut squash (400g),
  peeled, deseeded and cut into
  3cm chunks
1 x 400g tin of cooked chickpeas,
  drained and rinsed (240g)
8 large cloves of garlic, sliced in
  half lengthways (25g)
750ml chicken stock
250g maftoul (or mograbiah or
  fregola, as an alternative)
2 tbsp lemon juice
5g parsley leaves, roughly chopped

Preheat the oven to 200°C fan.

Place the chicken in a large bowl and add the olive oil, 1 teaspoon of salt and a good grind of black pepper. Toss to coat, then transfer to an oven dish or tray lined with baking parchment, skin side up. Put the cumin, coriander, cinnamon, turmeric and fennel seeds into a small bowl and mix to combine. Sprinkle just a quarter of this over all the chicken, then roast for 45 minutes, or until nicely browned and cooked through.

While the chicken is in the oven, put the oil for the maftoul into a large pot (about 25 x 12cm), for which you have a lid, and place on a medium-high heat. Add the onions and 2½ teaspoons of salt and cook for about 5 minutes, stirring from time to time. Add the tomato purée and sugar and cook for another minute. Add the carrots and squash and cook for another 3 minutes, stirring a few times, then add the chickpeas, the remaining spice mix, the garlic and stock. Bring to the boil, then reduce the heat to low and simmer for about 15 minutes, covered, or until the vegetables are just cooked. Making sure you reserve the stock, strain the vegetables and keep them somewhere warm. Return the broth to the same pot – you should have about 600ml – then add the maftoul and bring to the boil. Reduce the heat to low, then cover and cook on a low heat for 10 minutes, or until the maftoul is just cooked. Turn off the heat and set aside for 10 minutes, with the pot still covered. After 10 minutes, fluff up the maftoul with a fork and add the vegetables to the pot, along with the lemon juice and half the parsley.

To serve, spoon the maftoul into a large deep serving dish. Top with the chicken, sprinkle over the remaining parsley and serve.

## Baseema Barahmeh and the Anza co-operative

Baseema Barahmeh lives in a village called Anza, south-west of Jenin. She is a wife and a mother of four. She's also a farmer, a board member of the Palestinian Fair Trade Association (PFTA), a village council member, an expert in hand-rolled maftoul and co-ordinator of the Anza women's co-operative. Anza means 'the hard rock', a description which could as well apply to Baseema, in fact, a serene but independent force of nature who is making good things happen in her village. How on earth does she fit it all in, we wondered aloud. She starts her day at 4 a.m., we're told.

Established in 1992, the Anza co-operative rolls maftoul, sun-dries tomatoes, shells and cracks almonds, blends za'atar and supplies olive oil to Canaan Fair Trade (see page 250), who then sell it to the local and international market. More locally, they bake savoury manakeesh (page 278) and other pastries to sell to schools. It was Baseema's idea to do this, seeing it as a way to give the kids access to healthy food and, also, for the co-operative to have year-round work rather than be tied to the olive or za'atar harvesting season. She needed government funding to subsidise the plan and, after a bit of persuasion, they agreed. Other co-operatives are now taking Baseema's lead and seeking to roll out similar programmes in their own districts.

At its biggest, the co-operative had 100 members, all aged between forty and sixty. As government funding for it decreases year on year, though, so too do the numbers of women. When we met there were just twenty-five. The women of Anza village are well educated, so most of those under forty are choosing jobs in government, for example, rather than working with their hands. It's not just about the work, though, it's about the community and women coming together. 'And laughing,' says Baseema. 'We arrange ourselves into groups of four and make sure that each group has both an organised person and a funny person who tells all the stories. It's this balance that ensures productivity!'

The problem with dwindling numbers for the co-operative is not just the loss of camaraderie and productivity in the short term. It's about a loss of traditional skills in the long term. Hand-rolling maftoul is a skilled art. There's no better way to feel foolish, in fact, than trying your hand at rolling maftoul with someone who's been doing it all their life. Maftoul is made by adding flour and water to tiny balls of bulgur wheat and rolling it in the palms of your hands until it becomes slightly less tiny. It seems simple enough. Predictably, it's not. In the time that it took Tara to fail to make a tablespoon of maftoul, Baseema had pretty much made lunch for twenty. Even by Palestinian standards, though, Baseema sets the bar high. There are only twelve women in the co-operative, in fact, who are able to make maftoul properly, and even within those twelve there are some whose job it is to just steam rather than roll the grain.

The Palestinians' reputation for hospitality, and for showing this hospitality through food, is well known. The quantity of food offered by Baseema, however, along with her son and daughter-in-law, was frankly intimidating. There were just three of us at the table eating. There was enough food for twenty. Small bowls of molokhieh, large trays piled high with manakeesh, pasta, pastries, stuffed vine leaves, steamed rice, warm pita, one large bottle of Coke, another one of Fanta, and a large thermos of strong Arabic coffee squeezed in between. Hard as we tried to make a dent, our efforts literally didn't register.

We talked, among other things, about Fair Trade. Having been a member of the PFTA since 2008, Baseema is a proud advocate. The model provides financial security and sustainable work for farmers, cooks and producers like herself. Fair Trade premiums, for example, enable members to buy tools and materials for harvesting which they wouldn't otherwise be able to do. It also enables women like Baseema to become independent, to provide for their families. 'I don't have to ask my husband's permission,' she says. 'I can just go ahead and do things for myself.' It's unusual, for example, for a family to be represented on the village council by a woman, but, says Baseema, 'I wanted the independence, and to see the results of my work. I am proud of my work; I want it to be in my name.' Her son agrees, leaning back on his chair and lighting another cigarette. He is proud, clearly, but also worries that his mother takes on too much and does not look after herself. 'And she wakes up at 3 a.m.,' he says, 'not 4.'

# Meaty vine leaf pie

Rolling individual vine leaves stuffed with meat and rice is wonderful – the leaves melt in the mouth and their making often signals a celebration – but it's a time-consuming business. Here, we've taken a fair bit of the work out of the equation by making one big pie. Serve with any (or all) of the following: a spoonful of yoghurt, a squeeze of lemon or some flatbread.

*Getting ahead:* This can be served warm or at room temperature, the day it is made or for up to 2 days after.

*Cooking note:* Brining vine leaves: we don't always boil our leaves before using them, but here we do. This is because the leaves and stalks remain intact (rather than the stalks being discarded) and we want everything to be super soft and tender when eaten.

---

Preheat the oven to 180°C fan. Line the base of a high-sided 20 x 30cm baking dish (or 26cm round baking dish) with baking parchment and set aside.

Fill a medium saucepan three-quarters full of water and bring to the boil on a medium-high heat. Loosely unravel the clumps of vine leaves – it's fine that they're stuck together – and add them to the pan. Lower the heat to medium and simmer for 15 minutes. Drain them through a sieve and run under cold water for about 2 minutes, until the leaves are no longer warm to the touch. Set aside to drain completely.

Put 1 tablespoon of oil into a small frying pan and place on a medium heat. Add the almonds and cook for 2 minutes, stirring often. Add the pine nuts and cook for another 4–5 minutes, stirring frequently, until golden. Tip the nuts out on to a plate lined with kitchen paper and set aside.

Mix the tomatoes with the remaining 1½ tablespoons of olive oil and spread out on a parchment-lined baking tray. Roast for 12 minutes, until softened but still retaining their shape. Remove from the oven and set aside until needed.

To make the filling, put the oil into a large sauté pan and place on a medium-high heat. Add the onion and cook for 5 minutes, stirring from time to time, until it is golden brown. Add the garlic and cook for another 30 seconds, then add the beef and lamb. Continue to cook for another 6 minutes or so, stirring and breaking up any lumps of the meat so that it is browned all over. Add three-quarters of the nuts, the tomato purée, baharat, rice, 2 teaspoons of salt and a good grind of black pepper. Continue to cook for another 2–3 minutes, stirring frequently. Remove from the heat and set aside to cool for 10 minutes before stirring in the mint and parsley.

*Continued overleaf*

## Serves eight

450g jar of vine leaves in brine, drained (250g)
2½ tbsp olive oil
50g blanched whole almonds, roughly chopped
50g pine nuts
4 plum tomatoes, sliced into 1cm-thick rounds (400g)
Salt and black pepper
250g Greek-style yoghurt, to serve (optional)

## Filling

2 tbsp olive oil
1 onion, finely chopped (150g)
3 large garlic cloves, crushed
350g beef mince
150g lamb mince
2 tbsp tomato purée
2½ tsp baharat (see page 190)
350g Egyptian rice (or pudding or risotto rice, as an alternative)
30g mint leaves, finely shredded
50g parsley, finely chopped, plus extra picked leaves to garnish

## Sauce

900ml boiling water
80ml lemon juice (from about 2 lemons)
1 tbsp olive oil

To assemble the dish, transfer the cooked tomatoes from the baking tray to your parchment-lined dish. Place them side by side, so that the base of the dish is covered. Next, line the base and sides of the baking dish with just under half the vine leaves, shiny side down, overlapping the leaves so that there are no gaps or holes in between. Spoon over a third of the filling and spread it out in an even layer. Add another layer of leaves, overlapping them slightly to just cover the filling, then repeat the process so that you have three layers of filling in total. Finish with the vine leaves, this time letting them drape over the sides of the dish. Tuck them into the dish, like you're wrapping them around the pie, so that the filling is totally sealed.

Whisk together all the ingredients for the sauce with 1 teaspoon of salt and a good grind of black pepper. Pour this very gently over the bake – it will almost cover the top – and seal the dish tightly with aluminium foil. Put the dish on a tray (in case there is any leakage) and bake for 80 minutes, until the liquid is mostly absorbed and the rice is completely cooked through. Remove from the oven – don't remove the foil yet – and set aside for 20 minutes. Remove and discard the foil, then invert the dish on to a large platter or board. The best way to do this is to place a chopping board or large platter on top of the pie, then boldly flip it over so that the board or platter is at the bottom. The pie should detach itself easily from the baking parchment: don't worry if any tomatoes have stuck to the parchment, just remove these by hand and place on top of the pie. Sprinkle with the remaining nuts and a handful of parsley and set aside for 15 minutes. Serve warm or at room temperature, with a spoonful of yoghurt, if desired.

# Oxtail stew with chard, sumac and tahini
## *Sumaqqiyeh*

**Serves four generously**

2 onions, roughly chopped (300g)
6 garlic cloves, roughly chopped
2 green chillies, deseeded and thinly
    sliced (40g)
1 tbsp sunflower oil
1.5kg oxtail
2 tbsp olive oil
2–3 plum tomatoes, finely
    chopped (300g)
1 tbsp tomato purée
1 tbsp ground cumin
1 tbsp ground cinnamon
1 tbsp baharat (see page 190)
1½ tsp caster sugar
1 x 400g tin of chickpeas, drained
    and rinsed (240g)
500g Swiss chard, stalks removed
    and roughly chopped into 2½cm
    pieces, leaves roughly shredded
1 tbsp dill seeds (or celery seeds, as
    an alternative)
15g parsley, roughly chopped
2 tbsp sumac
20g dill, roughly chopped
Salt and black pepper

**Tahini sauce**
75g tahini
1½ tbsp lemon juice

The green chilli, the dill seeds, the tahini sauce: the roll-call of typical Gazan ingredients makes this a classic Gazan dish. In Gaza, the tahini would be red tahini, which is nuttier and richer than regular tahini. The difference between the two is the sort of heat the sesame seeds are roasted with: steam heating in the case of regular tahini, and roasting with direct heat in the case of the red tahini. As long as you are starting with what we call 'proper tahini', though (see page 288 for the sermon), any regular creamy Arabic tahini is just fine.

*Getting ahead:* The oxtail needs a long time cooking – 4 hours – in order to ensure that it falls off the bone as much as you want it to. You can make it a day or two in advance, though, taking it up to the point before the chard leaves and fresh dill get added. These should always go in at the last stage, so that they retain their colour and freshness.

---

Put the onions, garlic and two-thirds of the green chillies together into a food processor. Pulse a few times, until finely minced but not so much that it turns to a purée. Set aside until ready to use.

Put the sunflower oil into a large heavy-based saucepan, for which you have a lid, and place on a medium-high heat. Pat the oxtail dry and sprinkle with ½ teaspoon of salt and a good grind of black pepper. In two batches, sear the oxtail for 5–6 minutes, turning so that all sides get nicely browned. Once all the meat is browned, transfer it to a separate plate, pour off the excess oil, wipe the pan clean, and add the olive oil. Add the onion, garlic and chilli mix and cook for about 4 minutes, stirring often, or until softened. Add the tomatoes and tomato purée and cook for another 4 minutes, or until the tomatoes have broken down. Stir in the spices, then add the oxtail, sugar, 1½ litres of water, 2¼ teaspoons of salt and a generous grind of black pepper. Bring to the boil, then lower the heat to medium-low, cover the pan and leave to simmer gently for 4 hours, stirring every so often, or until the meat is tender and almost falling off the bone.

Put the ingredients for the tahini sauce into a bowl with 75ml of water and ⅛ teaspoon of salt. Whisk until smooth and set aside.

After about 4 hours, use a pair of tongs to remove the oxtail from the pan. Set it aside to cool slightly, and add the chickpeas and chard stalks to the pan. Increase the heat to medium-high and cook for 20–25 minutes, stirring often, until the sauce has thickened and reduced by half.

Meanwhile, once the oxtail is cool enough to handle, tear off the meat and fat in large chunks, discarding the bones: you should be left with about 650g. Return this to the pan, along with the chard leaves, dill seeds, parsley, 1½ tablespoons of sumac and all but a handful of dill. Cook for about 5 minutes, or until the leaves have wilted and the meat has heated through.

Transfer the stew to a large serving platter and drizzle with a third of the tahini sauce. The remaining sauce can be served in a bowl alongside. Top with the remaining dill, chillies and the last 1½ teaspoons of sumac, and serve at once.

# BREADS AND PASTRIES

The idea of bread piled high doesn't really mean anything until you spend time in Palestine. Not a meal goes by without platters of flatbread in attendance, ready to be pulled apart and handed around to signal the start of a meal. There's often no need for cutlery once a piece of flatbread has been shaped into a scoop in one hand, ready for the other hand to pile food directly on to it. For those who like eating with their hands, it's a legitimised form of hands-on heaven. If the bread is not being used as a scoop then it's turned into a mini shovel ploughed into bowls of warm, creamy hummus.

Just as bread is there on every table – ice breaker, utensil, scoop and shovel – it's also there on every street corner. The sounds of ka'ak carts on the cobbled streets of East Jerusalem are near-permanent, accompanied by the cries of vendors selling their freshly baked goods from sunrise to sunset. Jerusalem sesame bread in the morning, pita bread and manakeesh as the day goes on. For Palestinians everywhere, bread is the sight, sound, smell and taste of home. The Arabic word for this is 'taghmees'. Bread is not just something to eat or something to help scoop up other food to eat. For Palestinians, it's a way of life.

Traditionally, flatbread is cooked in an outdoor oven called a taboon oven (see page 341). Lining the base of the conical or dome-shaped taboon oven are lots of little stones or pebbles which get very, very hot. Once the flatbread is placed on top of the stones, the dough bakes very quickly and, also, takes on the shape made by the stones. It looks almost moon-like when it's pulled out from the oven with a long-handled paddle, indentations like mini craters all over. These then become little pools for olive oil or tahini to drizzle into and wallow in. Taboon bread is divine in a dish like chicken musakhan, for example (see page 247). Try as we might, though, taboon is not something we found easy to create without said outdoor oven and a sack full of stones. We tried the stones in a regular oven – Sami was a sight walking back from the garden centre with his shopping bag spilling over with little rocks! – and also using our fingers to make indentations in the dough, but the results weren't good enough to showcase the bread. You'll just have to go to Palestine to try proper taboon bread for yourself! The dough is the same dough used to make pita, though (which in turn can lead you on to the manakeesh – see page 278), so there's more than enough to get going with and share around in the meantime. Rolls filled with tahini and cinnamon (see page 287), Jerusalem sesame bread (see page 282), pies to snack on or take on a picnic (see page 296), little buns filled with fresh oregano and za'atar (see page 285), big rolls filled with sumac onions (see page 292). For everyone, everywhere: the smell of fresh bread baking is what makes a house a home.

# Pita bread
## *Khubez*

*Who put the pocket in the pita?*

Pita is the Arab bread khubez adi ('ordinary bread') or khubez kimaaj (taken from the Turkish and translating as 'bread cooked in the ashes'). Before indoor ovens became the norm, this 'ordinary' dough would be quickly rolled into an oval shape and then either thrown against the very hot inside walls of the outdoor oven or into the ashes of the direct flame itself. The intense heat of the flame, and its rapidly vaporising steam, then does the job that a leavener would otherwise do, creating lots of little air bubbles which cause the dough to quickly rise. It rises quickly and it also cooks really quickly, but, once out of the oven, deflates just as quickly! The speed with which all this rising and deflating happens is what causes the split between the two layers of dough and the empty 'pocket' to remain. It's this pocket which distinguishes pita from other flatbread and which, happily, makes it such a welcome home to all sorts of fillings: falafel (see page 62), shawarma (see page 259), ijeh (see page 24) and so on.

*Getting ahead:* Fresh pita is pillowy and soft and likes to be eaten the day it is baked. Anything older than a day, though, can be pulled apart to use in fattoush, for example (see page 99), or pan-fried in a mix of olive oil and butter to add to any soup or leafy salad as you would a crouton. Make the full quantity here even if you are not going to eat all twelve at once. Pitas can be frozen once baked, then warmed through in the oven or toasted to serve.

*Playing around:* Pita dough is the same dough used to make manakeesh, when the dough is rolled out as if making pita but is then brushed or topped with various things before being baked, as if making a pizza. For manakeesh za'atar, mix 120ml of olive oil with 100g of za'atar and brush about 1½ tablespoons of this on top of each pita. Sprinkle some finely chopped tomato on top of this, if you like, then carefully transfer to two or three preheated baking trays. Bake at 250°C fan for 8–10 minutes, rotating the trays halfway through, until slightly golden, and serve at once.

*Ingredients note:* We've used 100 per cent plain flour, but you can use a mix of plain and wholemeal, if you prefer. The result won't be as pillowy and soft but has a toothsome, wholesome bite that can appeal.

**Makes 12 pitas**

2 tsp fast-action dried yeast
1 tbsp caster sugar
About 420ml lukewarm water
750g plain flour (or a mix of 600g plain flour and 150g wholemeal flour), plus extra for dusting
35g milk powder (also known as dried skimmed milk)
2 tsp salt
2 tbsp olive oil, plus extra for greasing

---

Put the yeast, sugar and 200ml of lukewarm water into a separate small bowl or cup. Set aside for about 4 minutes, or until the mixture starts to bubble up.

Place the flour, milk powder and salt in the bowl of a free-standing mixer with the dough hook attachment in place. Mix on a low speed for just a minute, for the ingredients to combine. Increase the speed to medium, then, slowly, pour in the warm yeast mixture, followed by the oil: it will start to form a shaggy mess at first, but keep the machine running for about 7 minutes, slowly adding the remaining water, for the dough to come together as a ball. You want it to be smooth and elastic and for the dough not to stick to your fingers when pinched.

Transfer the dough to a lightly oiled bowl, cover with a clean tea towel, and place somewhere warm (close to a stove which is on, for example) for about 1 hour, until the dough has risen by a third.

Transfer the dough to a lightly floured work surface, cut into 12 pieces, and shape into round balls, each weighing about 100g. Cover with a clean, slightly damp tea towel and leave to rest for 10 minutes: you won't see any change in size or shape after 10 minutes but it's still important for the dough to have this 'rest'.

After 10 minutes, flatten the balls of dough one at a time, first with your fingers and then using a rolling pin to shape them into 15–18cm-wide circles: use more flour to dust the work surface, if you need to, to prevent them sticking as you roll. Take care not to have any tears in the dough, as this will allow steam to escape in the oven and prevent the pitas puffing up. Continue until all the balls of dough are rolled out, covering them with a damp tea towel once rolled, to prevent them from drying out. Set aside to prove for a final 20 minutes.

While the dough is proving, preheat the oven to 250°C fan. Place the trays you are going to bake the bread on in the oven at this stage to heat up. Fit as many trays as you can into your oven: you will only be able to fit 2 or 3 pitas on to each tray, so you will need to do them in batches.

When ready to bake, remove the hot trays from the oven and place 2 or 3 pita rounds on each (depending on how many you can fit without any dough overlapping), top side down: flipping them over at this stage allows for the baked pitas to be equally 'pillowy' on both sides. Bake for 4–5 minutes, or until they puff up and their tops are slightly golden. You don't want them to take on too much colour, as this will lead to the bread being hard.

Arrange the pitas in a large tray or shallow bowl and cover them with a clean tea towel while you continue baking the remaining batches of dough. Covering them with the towel is important for keeping the bread moist and pillowy while you continue with the remaining batch of dough. Serve warm.

*Pictured overleaf*

# Jerusalem sesame bread
## Ka'ak Al Quds

Ka'ak Al Quds are stacked high on street corners all over Jerusalem, sold by men young and old, from sunrise to sunset. Pomegranates or oranges often sit on a table alongside, ready to be freshly squeezed. This is breakfast on the go, Jerusalem-style. They are great for breakfast, eaten as they are, but just as good made into a sandwich for lunch or, as Sami used to, to snack on walking home from school.

These are long and thin (rather than round and thick) so, when shaping the dough, you'll need to pull a bit more than feels natural. It might want to spring back into a round shape, but be assertive and the dough will do what you want. Don't skip out on any of the resting stages, either: there are quite a few, so these are a good thing to make when you have something else to do at home or in the kitchen.

*Getting ahead / keeping notes:* In an ideal world these are eaten freshly made and warm from the oven. It doesn't always work like that, though, with all the proving and resting and so forth. Warmed through in the oven or lightly toasted the next day they are also delicious. These are very happy to be frozen, once shaped into their oval rings. Baked straight from frozen, they'll just need a minute or two extra in the oven.

---

Put the yeast, sugar and 120ml of the lukewarm water into a small bowl. Mix to combine, then set aside for 5 minutes, until the mixture has frothed.

Place both flours, the milk powder, baking powder and 2½ teaspoons of salt in the bowl of a free-standing mixer with the dough hook in place. (If you don't have one you can knead by hand: it will just take a bit longer to work the dough.) Mix on a medium-low speed for 1 minute, to incorporate, then add the oil, the yeast mixture and the remaining 150ml of lukewarm water. Mix on a medium speed for 3 minutes, until the dough has come together and formed a smooth ball. Remove the dough from the bowl, gently form into a ball and rub all over lightly with oil. Return it to the mixing bowl, cover with a tea towel, and set aside in a warm place for an hour or so, or until doubled in size.

When the dough has risen, punch it back down and turn it out on to a lightly floured work surface. Divide the dough into 6 pieces: each one should weigh just under 150g. Shape one piece of dough at a time gently into a ball, tucking the dough under at the base to form the ball rather than rolling it between your palms, trying not to overwork it. Repeat with the remaining pieces of dough, then cover with a clean tea towel. Set aside for 10 minutes, to rest.

Dig your finger into the centre of one of the balls, to create a hole, then stretch the dough outwards to create an oval ring. Use your fingers to pull and shape the dough into a large ring: it should be about 18cm long on the outside (12cm on the inside) and 9cm wide. The dough will want to spring back into a smaller shape, but be assertive here: you want it to be nice and long.

*Continued overleaf*

## Makes 6

1 tbsp fast-action dried yeast (10g)
2½ tbsp caster sugar
270ml lukewarm water
250g plain flour, plus extra
   for dusting
250g strong bread flour
2 tbsp milk powder (also known
   as dried skimmed milk)
1 tsp baking powder
3 tbsp sunflower oil, plus extra
   for greasing
Salt

## Topping
60g white sesame seeds (untoasted)
1 egg
2 tbsp whole milk (or water)

Transfer to a piece of baking parchment as large as your tray and continue forming the rest of the dough in the same way: you should be able to get 2 rings on each sheet of paper, spaced 4–5cm apart. Cover and set aside to rest for a further 15 minutes.

Preheat the oven to 220°C fan.

Spread the sesame seeds out in a large shallow dish, about 30 x 22cm, and set aside. In a small bowl, whisk together the egg and milk (or water) and set aside.

Place three large baking trays in the oven to warm up (or just two, if that's what you have, and you can then bake in batches).

Brush the tops of each ring with the egg mixture, then dip them into the sesame seeds, egg-wash side down, so that the top is well coated. Return to the baking parchment, cover and set aside to rest for another 10 minutes.

Remove the hot trays from the oven, then drag the baking parchment, with the rings on top, carefully on to the trays. Bake for about 15 minutes, rotating the trays once during baking to ensure an even cook, until the rings are a deep golden brown.

Remove from the oven and set aside for 10 minutes to serve warm, or longer, if serving at room temperature.

# Za'atar bread
## *Aqras za'atar*

Za'atar bread is also known as 'fatayer fallahi', which means 'villagers' pie'. Traditionally, it's made in spring, when the season for collecting fresh wild za'atar begins. We've used fresh oregano and dried za'atar, though, freeing up the option to make this year round. The bread can be shaped all sorts of ways: into a flatbread, a loaf or individual buns, as here. Either way, it should always be super soft – almost moist – in the middle, with a really crunchy crust.

Serve this either warm, fresh from the oven, or at room temperature the same day, with some labneh (or feta), fresh chopped salad (see page 92), olives, or Hassan's easy eggs (see page 22).

*Getting ahead:* The dough can be made up to 2 days ahead and kept in the fridge, ready to be rolled and baked. Once baked the buns also freeze well, ready to be toasted or warmed through in the oven straight from frozen.

**Makes 12 rolls**

### Dough
1½ tsp fast-action dried yeast
1 tsp caster sugar
170ml lukewarm water
320g plain flour, plus extra
   for dusting
1 tbsp milk powder (also known
   as dried skimmed milk)
1⅛ tsp ground turmeric
1¼ tsp salt
3 tbsp sunflower oil
3 tbsp olive oil, plus 1 tbsp extra
   for greasing
2 tbsp white sesame seeds, plus
   1½ tsp for sprinkling
1 tbsp nigella seeds, plus ½ tsp for
   sprinkling
15g picked oregano leaves
120g feta, crumbled
2 tbsp Greek-style yoghurt
1 tbsp za'atar

First make the dough. Put the yeast, sugar and water into a small bowl and whisk to combine. Set aside for 5 minutes, until it starts to bubble.

Put the flour, milk powder, turmeric and salt into the bowl of a free-standing mixer with the dough hook in place. Mix for one minute, just to incorporate, then add the yeast mixture, followed by both oils. Work on a low speed for about 2 minutes, to bring everything together, then increase the speed to medium. Continue to mix for 3 minutes. Add the sesame seeds, nigella seeds and oregano leaves and mix for another 4 minutes, until the dough is soft and elastic and the oregano leaves have been incorporated in the dough. It will feel very soft and almost sticky, but this is how it should be. Tip the dough on to a clean work surface and bring together to form a ball. Grease the mixing bowl with 1 tablespoon of oil, then return the dough to the bowl. Turn it a couple of times so that it's completely coated in oil, then cover the bowl with a clean tea towel. Set aside somewhere warm for 1 hour, until it's doubled in size.

Roll the dough out into the shape of a sausage, about 30cm long, and cut into 12 even pieces, about 50g each. Roll each piece into a ball, place on a large plate, cover with a clean tea towel and set aside for 20 minutes, to rest.

Preheat the oven to 200°C fan.

On a clean, lightly floured work surface, use your fingers to flatten each ball into a round disc, about 10cm wide and 2–3mm thick. Spoon 2 heaped teaspoons (about 10g) of the crumbled feta cheese into the centre of each disc. Draw all the sides upwards and press together to form a ball. Arrange the buns on a parchment-lined oven tray, pinched side down and spaced well apart. Brush the balls all over with yoghurt, as you would egg-wash, and sprinkle with the extra sesame seeds, nigella seeds and the za'atar. Set aside to rest for 5 minutes, then bake for about 20 minutes, or until the buns are cooked and the bottoms are golden brown. Remove from the oven and serve either warm, at once, or at room temperature.

# Sweet tahini rolls
## *Kubez el tahineh*

The journey of these rolls can be traced through Lebanon to Armenia, where these kubez el tahineh come from. They are simple to make, impressive to look at and loved by all. They're a particular favourite with kids. Eat them as they are, or sliced and spread with dibs w tahini, the Palestinian equivalent of peanut butter and jam, where creamy tahini is mixed through with a little bit of grape or date molasses (see page 336).

*Keeping notes:* These are best eaten fresh on the day of baking but are also fine for 2–3 days once baked, warmed through in the oven. They also freeze well, after they've been baked and left to cool: you can pop them into the oven straight from the freezer until warmed through.

---

**Makes 10 rolls**

### Dough
1½ tsp fast-action dried yeast
1 tsp caster sugar
110ml whole milk, lukewarm
300g plain flour, plus extra
  for dusting
75g unsalted butter, melted
1 egg, lightly beaten
Olive oil, for greasing
Salt

### Filling
100g caster sugar
1 tsp ground cinnamon
120g tahini

### Topping
1 egg yolk, beaten
1 tbsp white sesame seeds

First make the dough. Put the yeast, sugar and milk into a small bowl and mix to combine. Set aside for 5 minutes, until it starts to get frothy.

Meanwhile, put the flour and ½ teaspoon of salt into the bowl of a free-standing mixer, with the dough hook in place. Mix on a low speed, then slowly pour in the yeast mixture. Add the melted butter and continue to mix for about a minute.

Add the egg, then increase the speed to medium and leave for 5 minutes, for the dough to get well kneaded. Using your hands, scrape the dough into a ball: it will be slightly sticky and elastic. Place it in a lightly oiled bowl, turning it a couple of times so that the dough gets well greased. Cover the bowl with a clean tea towel and leave to rest in a warm place for about 1 hour, or until almost doubled in size.

Put the sugar and cinnamon for the filling into a small bowl. Mix well to combine, then set aside.

On a lightly floured surface, roll out the dough into a large rectangle, about 35 x 50cm. Drizzle the tahini over the dough, then, using the back of a spoon or a spatula, spread it out evenly, leaving 1cm clear of tahini at both the shorter ends. Sprinkle the sugar mixture evenly over the tahini and leave for 10 minutes, until the sugar looks all wet.

Starting from one of the long sides, roll the dough inwards to form a long, thin sausage. Trim away about 2cm from each end, then slice the dough into 10 equal pieces: they should each be just over 4½cm long. Sit each piece upright, so that its cut side is facing upwards, then, using your hands, gently flatten out to form an 8cm-wide circle. Cover with a damp tea towel and leave to rest for 15 minutes.

Preheat the oven to 160°C fan.

Transfer each roll of dough to a large parchment-lined baking tray, spaced 2–3cm apart. Brush all over – just the top and sides, not the base – with the egg yolk, sprinkle with sesame seeds, and bake on the middle shelf of the oven for 18 minutes, or until cooked through and golden. Remove from the oven and set aside for about 20 minutes – you don't want them to be piping hot – then serve.

# The art of tahini: one man's quest to get it just right

Behind every great Palestinian dish lies a swirl of tahini. Maybe not every *single* dish and maybe more or less than a swirl, but, still, it's the absolute golden stuff, very often there in the foreground, background or alongside a dish.

In the foreground you'll see it drizzled over anything to come near it without an umbrella: baked kofta, grilled meat or fish, roasted vegetables, shakshuka. In the background, meanwhile, you won't see it but you'll be wondering how it is that a chilled cucumber soup, for example, can be so rich and nutty until you have that 'ta-da! ta-ha-ini!' moment. All manner of dressings and sauces or spreads and stews will have a tablespoon or two of tahini in them, there to make the dish rich and creamy and utterly moreish. Sometimes it can just be sitting there alongside a dish, providing the silky and luxurious element to a freshly fried fritter or falafel. It doesn't look like much, certainly, but – once loosened up with a bit of lemon juice and water, crushed garlic and salt – it becomes the thoroughly addictive secret behind so much of the country's cooking.

The challenge, with all this evangelical talk, is to make those who've never started with 'proper' Middle Eastern tahini understand what on earth is being talked about. 'Tahini: isn't that just what you add to chickpeas to make hummus?' Yes! And also to have around to drizzle on your toast and on your yoghurt and ice cream and salad and salmon and lentils and, and, and...

For us, the difference between the tahini made inside the Middle East and the tahini made outside the Middle East is enormous. Much of the tahini made outside the Middle East has, for us, both a 'claggy' texture and a bitter taste which don't encourage very wide use in the kitchen. Even though the ingredients are the same – sesame seeds ground down to form a thick paste – there are so many factors which lead one version of the product to be smooth, creamy and rich and the other product to be, well, not.

Someone who knows the difference between one tahini and the next is Kamel Hashlamon. Kamel is a man on a mission. After a decade or so making his name and reputation in various hotel and restaurant kitchens in Jerusalem and Tel Aviv, he decided to step back, hone his craft and become very, very good at one thing. Luckily, for those who love tahini, that one thing was the grinding of sesame seeds.

Becoming very good at grinding sesames requires several things. Using the best sesame seeds, for starters, commissioning the making of the best millstone

which can then grind them and, of course, providing the perfect conditions for the seeds to be ground as finely, smoothly and gently as possible. The seeds are the Humera variety, from Ethiopia. The millstone would come from Syria, via Turkey, and the perfect conditions would include a temperature of 60°C, cold-pressing techniques and a rate of production not much faster than a trickle. These are the steps that Kamel would perfect in pursuit of his mission – to make the best tahini around.

Kamel's first stop was Nablus, in the north, where he spent nine months learning the trade from one of the several old families in the city making tahini. Second stop was Turkey, to meet Mohammed Halabi, the Syrian stonemason Kamel had heard about who could make him the exact bespoke traditional millstone he was after: it had to be wider than the stonemason had ever made before and, using black granite, smoother than any baby's bum. Third stop: West Jerusalem, to find the right site. Not the obvious location for a Palestinian who grew up in Shuafat in East Jerusalem, of course. A very canny choice, however, for someone who wants to make the best possible tahini and wants to make enough of a buck to stay in business and be able to build on his dreams to grow. And in 2017, Kamel realised his dream and set up shop in Abu Ghosh, West Jerusalem.

The excellent tahini that he produces on site and sells in his shop is somewhere between a paste and a liquid and truly good enough to drink. He makes only 30–40 litres a day (as opposed to the 2 tonnes a large factory would produce), and it is made so slowly and with such care that the tahini does not 'split' in the jar like most mass-produced tahini, where the oil separates and sits on top of the thick sesame paste below. 'Tahini splits when it's nervous,' Kamel says gently. Alongside the tahini he makes on site, Kamel also sells an intoxicating range of halva, made off-site but using his tahini. It's beautifully displayed inside a glass counter, luring customers in off the street to try and buy.

Appealing to a primarily Israeli (but also Palestinian) market is enough to make some think he has 'sold out', but Kamel is happy to take the observation on the chin and bat it right away: 'We are all living in *the result* of the game,' he says, 'we are not in the game.' It's a point of view many who still see their day-to-day as a struggle or even a battle would take issue with, certainly. Talking about the situation for Palestinians as a 'game' is not an expression you often hear. For a chef who has had a lot of challenges and barriers to the growth of his career, though, as a result of the politics of being Palestinian, Kamel's response to the situation is the equivalent of a massive cheffy charm offensive. Rather than bemoaning his lot or wringing his hands, Kamel has chosen to make the most irresistible product, package it beautifully, display it in a small, stunning shop, and now be the artisanal producer selling it with a smile.

Israelis and Palestinians stand side by side at the counter, looking through the glass, debating little more than which halva to buy.

# Sumac onion and herb oil buns

The inspiration for this recipe is less tradition itself than sumac onions: one of the sweet, sharp and heavenly flavours of the very traditional chicken musakhan (see page 247).

*Getting ahead:* Get going the day before you want to eat these, so that the dough can rest in the fridge overnight. Once baked, they can be eaten warm or at room temperature for up to 2 days.

Put the flour, sugar and yeast into the bowl of a free-standing mixer, with the dough hook in place. Mix on a low speed for a minute. Whisk together the eggs and 120ml of water and add these to the mixer. Work on a low speed for just a few seconds, then increase the speed to medium. Continue to work for 2 minutes, until the dough comes together. Next, add ½ teaspoon of salt and start adding the butter, a few cubes at a time, until it all melts together into the dough. Continue kneading for about 10 minutes, on a medium speed, until the dough is completely smooth, elastic and shiny. Place the dough in a large bowl brushed with sunflower oil, cover with a clean tea towel and leave in the fridge for at least half a day or, preferably, overnight. It will increase in volume by just under 50 per cent.

To make the filling, put 3 tablespoons of oil into a medium sauté pan and place on a medium-low heat. Add the onions and cook for 15 minutes, stirring frequently, until the onions are completely soft and golden brown. Add the cinnamon and cook for another minute. Remove from the heat and set aside to cool before adding the remaining 55ml of olive oil, the sumac, oregano, thyme, sugar and 1 teaspoon of salt.

Grease and line a 20 x 30cm baking tray. On a lightly floured surface, roll the dough out into a rectangle, about 55 x 35cm. Spread the sumac onion mixture all over the dough, taking it right up to the edges.

With the long end facing towards you, gently roll up the dough as you would a Swiss roll, using both hands to gently press the roll as you go along. Trim about 2cm off both ends so that it becomes a perfect sausage. Then cut the sausage widthways into 12 even slices, each about 4cm wide. Carefully arrange the slices on the baking tray, evenly spaced apart and cut side facing up so that the filling is showing. Cover the tin with a slightly damp tea towel and leave to rise in a warm place (near a stove, for example) for 1½ hours. The rolls will rise by 20–30 per cent.

About 30 minutes before the buns have finished rising, preheat the oven to 180°C fan.

Remove the tea towel and place the tray of buns on the middle shelf of the oven. Cook for 30 minutes, until the buns are golden brown. Remove from the oven, cover loosely with foil and return the buns to the oven for about another 20 minutes, or until the dough is cooked through.

Remove the buns from the oven and set aside to cool for half an hour while you combine all the ingredients for the herb oil in a bowl with a small pinch of salt. Once the buns have cooled, pour this evenly over the top of them. Sprinkle lightly with sumac and serve.

## Makes 12 buns

### Dough
530g plain flour, plus extra
   for dusting
35g caster sugar
2 tsp fast-action dried yeast (6g)
3 large eggs
150g unsalted butter, at room
   temperature, cut into 2cm dice
Sunflower oil, for greasing
Salt

### Sumac onion filling
100ml olive oil
3 onions, finely chopped (600g)
2 tsp ground cinnamon
½ tbsp sumac, plus 1 tsp extra
   for dusting
30g oregano leaves, roughly
   chopped
15g thyme leaves, roughly
   chopped
1 tsp caster sugar

### Herb oil
15g parsley leaves, finely chopped
1 red chilli, deseeded and
   finely chopped (15g)
1 tsp finely grated lemon zest
120ml olive oil

# Arabic samosas
## *Sambousek*

Indian samosas, Hispanic empanadas, Cornish pasties, Bosnian burek: there are so many ways to encase various fillings with pastry before the whole thing gets baked or fried. Sambousek is the Palestinian way. Traditionally they're fried but we've baked ours here.

*Getting ahead:* These can be made in full in advance and kept in the freezer. You'll need to defrost them overnight (just transfer them to the fridge the night before baking) and bake them as normal.

---

First make the dough. Put the yeast, sugar and water into a small bowl and whisk to combine. Set aside for 5–10 minutes, until it starts to bubble.

Put the flour, milk powder, turmeric and ¾ teaspoon of salt into the bowl of a free-standing mixer with the dough hook in place. Mix for 1 minute, just to incorporate, then add the yeast mixture, followed by both oils. Increase the speed to medium and mix for 6 minutes, until the dough is soft, sticky and elastic. Tip the dough on to a clean work surface and bring together to form a ball. Grease the mixing bowl with 1 tablespoon of olive oil and return the dough to the bowl. Turn it a couple of times so that it's completely coated in oil, then cover the bowl with a clean tea towel. Set aside somewhere warm for 1 hour, until doubled in size.

Meanwhile, make the filling. Roughly crush the chickpeas with the back of a fork, leaving about half of them whole. Put the oil into a medium saucepan and place on a medium-high heat. Add the onion and garlic and cook for 8 minutes, stirring a few times, or until softened and browned. Add the meat, spices and ¾ teaspoon of salt and cook for 90 seconds, stirring constantly. Add the chickpeas and cook for another 2 minutes. Remove the pan from the heat, stir in the parsley and set aside to cool.

Place all the ingredients for the mint yoghurt in a bowl with ¼ teaspoon of salt. Mix to combine, and keep in the fridge until ready to serve.

Cut the dough into 12 even pieces, about 45g each. Roll each piece into a ball, cover with a clean tea towel and set aside for 20 minutes, to rest. Preheat the oven to 180°C fan.

Taking one ball at a time, roll it into a circle, about 12cm wide. Spoon 2 tablespoons of the cooled chickpea mixture – about 35–40g – into the middle of the dough and fold the dough over itself to form a half-moon shape. Press down the edges with your fingers and seal with a fork. Continue with the remaining batch and arrange on 2 large parchment-lined trays, spaced well apart.

Brush the top of the sambousek with the egg wash and sprinkle evenly with the nigella and sesame seeds. Bake for about 20 minutes, until they are cooked through and golden brown. Leave to cool for about 10 minutes and then serve warm or at room temperature with the yoghurt alongside.

## Makes 12 samosas

### Dough
1½ tsp fast-action dried yeast
1 tsp caster sugar
170ml lukewarm water
320g plain flour, plus extra
    for dusting
1 tbsp milk powder (also known
    as dried skimmed milk)
⅛ tsp ground turmeric
3 tbsp sunflower oil
3 tbsp olive oil, plus extra for
    greasing
Salt

### Filling
1 x 400g tin of chickpeas,
    drained and rinsed (240g)
3 tbsp olive oil
1 onion, finely chopped (150g)
4 garlic cloves, crushed
1 sirloin steak (250g), trimmed
    of most of the fat and finely
    chopped (180g)
1 tsp ground cumin
½ tsp ground ginger
¾ tsp baharat (see page 190)
½ tsp ground cinnamon
¼ tsp Aleppo chilli flakes
    (or regular chilli flakes)
¼ tsp ground turmeric
10g parsley, finely chopped
1 egg, whisked together with
    1 tbsp water
2 tsp nigella seeds
1 tsp white sesame seeds

### Mint yoghurt (optional)
180g Greek-style yoghurt
1 tsp dried mint
1 tbsp olive oil
1 tbsp lemon juice
5g mint leaves, roughly chopped

# Spinach pies
## *Fatayer sabanekh*

These take Sami straight back home. He used to have them, once or twice a week, eaten fresh from the oven when he got home from school. The filling would vary – cheese, minced meat, mashed root vegetables – but spinach was always the firm favourite. If you want to make a meal of them, serve them with a simple chopped salad (see page 92) and a spoonful of plain yoghurt.

*Getting ahead:* Both the dough and the filling can be made up to 3 days ahead and kept, separately, in the fridge. Once assembled, the pies freeze well and can be cooked from frozen: you'll just need to add an extra minute or more to the cooking time.

*Batch cooking:* The dough here is the same dough used to make the sfiha pies (see page 226) and also the za'atar bread (see page 285), so make more than you need for this recipe and freeze what you don't use to have at the ready.

Whisk together the yeast, sugar and water in a bowl and set aside for 5–10 minutes, until it starts to bubble. Put the flour, 1 egg, the oil, the yeast mixture and ¾ teaspoon of salt into the bowl of a free-standing mixer with the dough hook in place. Work on a low speed for about 2 minutes, to bring everything together, then increase the speed to medium-high. Continue to mix for 5–6 minutes, until the dough is soft and elastic. (If you are freezing the dough, now is the time to do it.) Cover the bowl with a clean tea towel and set aside somewhere warm for half an hour, until slightly risen. Roll the dough out into the shape of a sausage, about 30cm long, and cut into 12 even pieces. Roll each piece into a ball and place on a large plate. Cover with a clean tea towel and set aside for 1 hour, to rest.

Meanwhile, put the oil into a medium sauté pan and place on a medium-high heat. Once hot, add the onions and cook for 4–5 minutes, stirring frequently until the onions are soft but have not taken on any colour. Remove from the heat and set aside for 10 minutes, then mix in the spinach, sumac, lemon juice, chilli, pomegranate molasses (if using) and 1 teaspoon of salt.

Preheat the oven to 200°C fan and brush two large baking trays (30 x 40cm) lightly with oil.

Taking one ball of dough at a time, flatten and then roll into a disc which is about 14cm wide and about 2–3mm thick. Dust with a little flour if you need to, to prevent the dough sticking to your work surface.

Spoon 3 tablespoons of the spinach mixture – about 45g – into the centre of the disc and spread it into an 11cm wide triangle. Draw the pastry in over the filling to form a triangle, press the middle to seal, then pinch the three points together firmly to form a triangle. Place on the baking tray and repeat with the remaining dough and filling, spacing the pies well apart on the trays. Brush them with the remaining whisked egg and bake for 12 minutes, until golden brown. Don't worry if a few of the pies split open while cooking – rustic is a good look here!

Remove from the oven and set aside for about 15 minutes – you want to eat them warm rather than piping hot.

**Makes 12 pies, to serve four to six as a light lunch or snack**

1½ tsp fast-action dried yeast
1½ tsp caster sugar
100ml lukewarm water
375g self-raising flour, plus extra for dusting
2 large eggs, each lightly whisked, one kept for the dough and the other for glazing the pies
75ml olive oil, plus extra for greasing
Salt

**Filling**
3 tbsp olive oil
2 onions, finely chopped (350g)
500g frozen spinach, defrosted and squeezed well to get rid of any water (about 300g)
2½ tbsp sumac
2 tbsp lemon juice
⅓ tsp chilli flakes
4 tsp pomegranate molasses (optional)

# SWEETS

Palestinians, by and large, have a very sweet tooth. No get-together is complete without the offer of something sweet. A plate of fine-crumb cookies, for example, or squares of flaky filo, or slices of sugar-syrup-drenched semolina cake, all served with a short black coffee. It's a chicken-and-egg question of which came first: the ubiquity of the sweet treat or the near-permanence of Arabic coffee on tap. Either way, the combination is heady and heavenly.

As always, our offering is a mix of traditional recipes and those which we shine a new light on. Leading the way on the traditional is knafeh (see page 302), popular throughout Palestine but a positive rock star in the city of Nablus, where its eat-me-now fragrance wafts around every street corner and down every alley (see page 78 for more on this). Ma'amoul (see page 310) and ghraybeh (see page 325) are also quintessential, there for both mid-morning coffee and, also, at every family gathering or big get-together, romanticised with tales of why they're served at one particular religious or celebratory occasion or another. The joy of the simplicity of making these cookies is that, on one hand, they can be quickly made to have around whenever needed, and on the other, they can also be scaled up in number for big occasions, so that batch after batch can be made and often frozen in advance of eating. Let it never be said that there will be a shortage of biscuits whose name translates as 'swoon' (see page 325) at a family wedding! Our no-churn strawberry ice cream (see page 312) is also very typical, with its distinctly Arabic – almost chewy! – texture, thanks to the addition of mastic to the mix.

Other recipes we have shone new light or changed the angle on, to make them more accessible to a non-Arabic audience. This can be to do with specific ingredients, such as using a hibiscus tea bag to make a hibiscus syrup (see page 327), rather than the dried hibiscus flowers many Palestinians would take for granted as an ingredient. Or the creamy, silky ishta, so common in Palestinian puddings, is replaced by a cream cheese alternative in our flaky warbat (see page 306).

Fun and rewarding though making sweet treats is, there's a real culture of guests arriving at a house with boxes full of shop-bought sweets as well. During Ramadan, for example, lots of shops close and are replaced by pop-up bakeries for the month, producing everything everyone wants to serve after the iftar, the 'breaking of the fast' meal. So much so that it's actually more usual, for many, to buy rather than make certain things. As we discovered with atayef, for example, the lace-like delicate pancakes rolled up and stuffed with ricotta. After our fourth or fifth attempt to get these perfect for *Falastin*, Sami put out an SOS phone call to his sister Sawsan in East Jerusalem. 'Oh, no one makes these any more!' she breezily assured her brother. 'Everyone just buys them ready-made from the shops and then fills them up with whatever they want at home.' Job done, then: available at all good Middle Eastern shops near you! Ditto mutabbaq khalili, the sugar and nut or grated cheese and spice-filled pastries particularly popular in Hebron and the southern West Bank.

Then there are the recipes where we've taken ingredients from the Palestinian pantry and created new dishes from them. These are the recipes with the distinct paw-prints of Noor Murad all over them. Noor has been with us every

step and every stir of the way on the recipe development for *Falastin*. Bahrain-made, New York-trained and now London-based, Noor has brought her endlessly inspired twists and turns to so many of the recipes in this book. In just this chapter alone, for example, the labneh cheesecake (see page 322), chocolate and qahwa torte (see page 317), baklava semi-freddo (see page 314) and sticky date and halva puddings with tahini caramel (see page 320) are Noor through and through: sweet of course, but at the same time punchy and totally distinct.

# Knafeh Nabulseyeh

Knafeh is a national institution, made and served all over the Middle East, and no celebration is complete without it. It's particularly associated with Nablus, where the shredded filo pastry is filled with the city's trademark firm, white, salty Nabulsi cheese. A filling of just nuts and cinnamon is called knafeh Arabiyeh – Arabic knafeh. Nabulsi cheese is not widely available, though, so we've used a combination of firm mozzarella and ricotta.

*Getting ahead:* These are best eaten the day they are drizzled with sugar syrup. They can be made up to 2 days in advance, though, if you want to get ahead. If you do this, just skip the step where the syrup is poured over and then, when ready to serve, reheat the knafeh in the oven at 180°C fan. Once they are warmed through, pour over the syrup and serve while still warm. The sugar syrup can be made well ahead of using: it keeps in the fridge for weeks. You'll have a bit more syrup than you need here (you'll make 400ml and use 250ml), but it's always good to have around, for when a touch of sweetness is needed.

---

First make the syrup. Put 245ml of water and the sugar into a medium saucepan and place on a medium-high heat. Bring to the boil and add the lemon juice, swirling the pan frequently until the sugar dissolves. Remove from the heat, stir in the orange blossom water and set aside until completely cool.

Preheat the oven to 175°C fan. Liberally grease the base and sides of a baking tray, about 30 x 20cm and 4cm high.

Place the pastry in a food processor, in three or four batches, and blitz a few times until the strands are about 2cm long. Transfer to a bowl, pour over the butter and toss evenly so that all the kataifi is coated.

Put the mozzarella, ricotta, feta, sugar, lemon zest, salt and orange blossom water into a separate bowl. Mix to combine and set aside.

Press about two-thirds of the kataifi mixture into the base of the baking tray. Press down quite firmly: you want it to be as compact as possible. It should rise about 2cm up the sides of the tray. Evenly top with the cheese mixture, spreading very gently so that the kataifi layer is covered but doesn't get moved about. Finally, top with the remaining kataifi, pressing down firmly to cover any exposed cheese. Even out the top, then cover with a piece of baking parchment about the size of the tray. Top with a separate baking dish, about the same size, so that it is compressed down. Bake for 30 minutes, then remove the dish and baking parchment and bake for another 25 minutes, or until deeply golden around the edges and browned on top.

Slide a knife around the edges of the tray and leave to cool for about 5 minutes before flipping over on to a platter or cutting board. Slowly drizzle with 250ml of the syrup (the remainder can be kept in the fridge for future use), then leave aside for 5 minutes, for the syrup to be absorbed. Sprinkle with the pistachios and serve warm, preferably, or at room temperature later on.

## Makes 15 pieces, serving six to eight

375g kataifi pastry (see page 337), defrosted and roughly pulled apart
200g unsalted butter, melted, plus extra for greasing
1 x 200g block of mozzarella (the firm kind), coarsely grated
100g ricotta
150g feta, finely crumbled
25g caster sugar
1 lemon: finely grate the zest to get 1 tsp
⅓ tsp flaked sea salt
1 tsp orange blossom water
35g pistachio kernels, roughly blitzed in the small bowl of a food processor (or finely chopped)

### Sugar syrup
400g caster sugar
2 tbsp lemon juice
1½ tbsp orange blossom water

# Filo triangles with cream cheese, pistachio and rose
## *Warbat*

Warbat is a popular snack during the month of Ramadan. Sami's childhood was spent crowding around the street vendor selling these at the corner of their street. He'd barely make it home before the flaky pastry – dripping with thick and sticky syrup and always sprinkled with vivid green crushed pistachios – was finished. The filling is traditionally made with ishta – a kind of thick, milky, silky cream – which is then drizzled with rose water or rose water syrup. Ishta is not always easy to find, though, so we've created a cream cheese filling instead.

*Keeping notes:* Once assembled, these should be served on the same day – as close to the syrup being drizzled over them as possible, ideally.

First make the syrup. Put 55ml of water and the sugar into a small saucepan and place on a medium-high heat. Mix well, using a wooden spoon, and then, once it starts boiling, add the lemon juice. Simmer gently for 2 minutes, then stir in the rose water and remove straight away from the heat. Set aside.

Preheat the oven to 180°C fan.

To make the filling, put the cream cheese, cornflour, sugar, salt and mastic (or vanilla bean paste) into a medium bowl and whisk well to combine.

To assemble, spread one filo sheet out on a work surface and brush evenly with some of the melted butter. Top with another sheet and brush with butter again. Repeat the process until you have 5 layers evenly brushed with butter. As is always the case when working with filo, you'll need to work fast when you start brushing and folding: the pastry will dry out if you don't. You should have used about a quarter of the melted butter at this stage.

Now, using sharp scissors, cut the large layered sheet of pastry into 6 even squares, all 12 x 12cm – you'll need to trim the sheets to get even squares. Taking one of these smaller squares at a time, spoon about 35g (or 2 tablespoons) of the thick filling into the centre of each square, leaving a 2–3cm border clear around the edge. Fold the pastry diagonally in half to form a triangle, press on the edges without reaching the filling (so that it stays well sealed within the pastry), then brush all over with more butter. Once all 6 triangle pastries are on a parchment-lined baking tray, repeat the whole process (brushing one large filo sheet with butter, layering it five times, cutting it into 6 squares, filling and folding and sealing each square) with the remaining pastry, butter and filling.

Once all 12 pastries are made up and spread on two parchment-lined baking trays, bake for 22 minutes or until golden and crisp: some of them will pop open, but that's okay. Remove from the oven and set aside to cool for 10 minutes. Drizzle over the syrup, sprinkle over the crushed pistachios and rose petals, if using, and serve.

### Makes 12 pastries

10 sheets of good-quality filo pastry (we use feuilles de filo), each sheet 31 x 38cm (240g)
120g unsalted butter, melted

**Syrup**
100g caster sugar
1½ tsp lemon juice
¾ tsp rose water

**Filling**
450g full-fat cream cheese
2 tsp cornflour
55g caster sugar
½ tsp flaked sea salt
¼ tsp powdered Arabic mastic gum (see page 338) or ½ tsp vanilla bean paste, as an alternative

**Garnish**
20g pistachio kernels, finely crushed in a food processor or by hand as finely as possible
About 1½ tbsp dried rose petals (optional)

# Pistachio harisa

Harisa (not to be confused with harissa, the spicy North African chilli paste!) also goes by the name basbousa or namoura, depending on where in the Levant it is being made. Either way, it's a sugar-syrup-soaked semolina cake, popular all over the Middle East. Traditionally, the dominant flavours are rose or orange blossom water, but we've replaced these flavourings with the less traditional combination of coconut and lemon zest. Our harisa is super sticky and sweet so you'll only need a small piece, as you would baklava, with a strong black coffee.

*Keeping notes:* This keeps well for up to 3 days, stored in an airtight container. It also freezes well.

Preheat the oven to 180°C fan. Grease and line a 20 x 30cm baking tray and set aside. Put 100g of pistachios into the bowl of a food processor and blitz for 1 minute, until very fine. Transfer to a separate bowl and set aside.

Place the remaining 50g of pistachios in the same food processor (there's no need to clean it) and pulse-blitz just a few times: you just want these pistachios to be coarsely chopped. Transfer to a separate bowl and set aside.

To make the sugar syrup, put 180ml of water and the sugar into a small saucepan and place on a medium-high heat. Bring to the boil, then reduce the heat to medium and simmer for 10 minutes. Stir in the lemon juice and rose water and remove from the heat. Set aside to cool.

Put the sugar, butter, oil and yoghurt into the bowl of a free-standing mixer and whisk on a high speed for about 3 minutes, until well combined and smooth. Reduce the speed to medium and add the eggs, one at a time. Whisk for another minute, then add the finely ground pistachios, semolina, coconut, baking powder, flaked sea salt and lemon zest. Continue to whisk until just combined – you don't want to overwork it – then tip the batter into the prepared baking dish. Even out with a spatula and sprinkle the coarsely chopped pistachios on top. Using your fingers, gently press the pistachios into the batter, without completely submerging them. It will feel like a lot of sugar syrup but hold your nerve! It ill seep into the cake as it cools and it's this which makes it so sticky and sweet. Set aside for 10 minutes, to rest, then bake in the middle of the oven for 15 minutes, until the cake is almost set and the sides have taken on some colour.

Remove from the oven and, using a small sharp knife, make a diagonal crosshatch pattern across the top of the batter. Space the lines about 5cm apart, doing five lines one way and five lines the other. Return to the oven for a final 10 minutes, until the surface is golden brown and a knife inserted into the centre comes out clean. Remove from the oven and set aside to cool for 10 minutes, then evenly pour the cooled sugar syrup over the cake. It will feel like a lot of sugar syrup but hold your nerve! It will seep into the cake as it cools and it's this which makes it so sticky and sweet. Set aside for an hour – swirling the tray around a few times if the sugar syrup is pooling at the edges – until completely cool. When serving, follow the indentations to cut out individual pieces.

## Serves eight to ten

75g unsalted butter, at room temperature, plus extra for greasing
150g pistachio kernels
100g caster sugar
100ml sunflower oil
160g Greek-style yoghurt
2 medium eggs
350g fine semolina
50g desiccated coconut
¾ tsp baking powder
¾ tsp flaked sea salt
2 large lemons: finely grate the zest to get 1 tbsp

### Sugar syrup
300g caster sugar
2 tbsp lemon juice
1½ tbsp rose water

# Ma'amoul bars
## Ma'amoul maad

In the days leading up to Eid, to mark the end of Ramadan, Sami's aunties, mother, grandmother and cousins would come together to make the very popular ma'amoul. Sitting on the floor in a circle, everyone would have their designated job: kneading or rolling the dough, stuffing or moulding, baking and packing. It seemed to go on for days, in Sami's imaginings, and led him to think that the process must be a long and complicated one. It was with some surprise then, when he made the cookies for himself years later, that he saw that the recipe couldn't be easier. Time set aside for festive catch-ups, Sami now sees, should be factored into the write-up of the recipe. These are traditionally cookies to mark Easter or Eid, but make them year round. They have a wonderfully crumbly shortbread-like texture: crunchy, rich and melt-in-the-mouth. Crumbs are part of the equation here, but that's how some things should be.

*Getting ahead / keeping notes:* The dough needs to rest for at least 4 hours, so it's a good idea to make this the day before you want to bake. Once made, the dough keeps well in the fridge for up to 2 days: you'll need to bring it back to room temperature before using, though, so that it is malleable. If you are using the dough the day you make it then it does not need to go into the fridge. You can also make the fillings a day ahead. Once made, the bars keep in a sealed container, at room temperature, for up to a week.

*Fillings:* We've given a choice of two fillings – one with dates and one with pistachios. If you want to make both versions, just double the quantity of the dough.

First make the dough. Put the butter into a small saucepan and place on a very low heat, for about 2 minutes, just to melt.

Put the semolina, flour, icing sugar, yeast, mahleb, ground aniseed and ½ teaspoon of salt into a free-standing mixer bowl with the paddle attachment in place. Mix on a low speed for a minute, to combine. With the mixer still on a low speed, pour in the melted butter, continuing to mix until well combined and the texture is that of sticky, wet sand. Cover the bowl with a plate and leave for about 4 hours, at room temperature, for the semolina to really absorb the fat. Letting it rest for this long makes it much easier to work with.

Preheat the oven to 180°C fan. Grease well and line the base and sides of a 30 x 20cm baking tray and set aside.

*If making the date filling:* put all the ingredients for the filling into a medium saucepan and place on a low heat. Heat for 8 minutes, stirring a few times, to form a mushy, sticky paste. Remove from the heat and set aside. If you make this in advance you'll want to warm it through a little when filling the pastry: it's much easier to spread when warm.

*If making the pistachio filling:* spread the pistachios out on a parchment-lined tray and toast for about 8 minutes. Remove from the oven and set aside until completely cool. Put the honey, orange blossom water and 3 tablespoons of water into a small bowl. Mix well to combine and set aside. Once the

**Makes about 24 cookies**

**Dough**
250g unsalted butter, plus extra for greasing
250g semolina
250g self-raising flour
60g icing sugar, plus extra for dusting
¼ tsp fast-action dried yeast
¾ tsp mahleb (see page 338) (or a tiny drop of almond extract, as an alternative)
2 tsp ground aniseed
2 tbsp rose water
2 tbsp orange blossom water
60g ghee, melted
Salt

**Date filling**
500g Medjool dates, pitted and finely chopped
¼ tsp mahleb (see page 338) (or a tiny drop of almond extract, as an alternative)
½ tsp ground cinnamon
½ tsp ground cardamom
2 tbsp sunflower oil

**Pistachio filling**
300g pistachio kernels
60g honey
1 tbsp orange blossom water
200g natural marzipan, cut into 2cm chunks
1 tsp ground cardamom
¾ tsp ground cinnamon

pistachios are cool, transfer them to a food processor, along with the marzipan, and blitz for 2 minutes. You want them to turn into fine crumbs but still have a little bit of texture. Add the honey mixture, spices and ½ teaspoon of salt, and pulse a couple of times to combine, to form a sticky paste.

To complete the dough, put the rose water and orange blossom water into a small bowl, along with 2 tablespoons of water and the melted ghee. Mix to combine, then, while kneading with one hand, gradually pour the mixture over the dough. Continue to knead for about 5 minutes (either by hand or in a food mixer with the paddle attachment in place), until the dough is soft and comes together well and is pale in colour. Add a few more drops of water, if you need to, if the dough is too dry.

When ready to assemble, divide the dough into 2 equal pieces and, working with wet fingers, press half the dough gently into the base and sides of the baking tray.

Place the date paste (or pistachio filling) in between two sheets of baking parchment (about 30 x 40cm), and gently roll with a rolling pin to form a rectangle, about 20 x 30cm: don't worry about getting the dimensions exact here, they can be adjusted in the baking tray.

Remove and discard the top layer of parchment from one of the paste sheets and then, sliding your hand under the paste to help you, flip it upside down into the baking tray. With the paper still attached (and now facing upwards), start pressing it gently on to and up the sides of the tray. Carefully pull away the paper and then flatten the paste to fill any gaps.

Repeat the process with the second half of the dough, spreading the remaining dough evenly over the filling, taking it right up to the edges. Pinch some of the excess pastry to fill any gaps and, using your fingers, seal the edges very well. Using a small, sharp knife, cut the dough (keeping it in its tray) into 4 rows and 6 columns, to make 24 squares. Take the knife right down to the bottom of the tray. The lines will close up as the dough bakes, but will help when it comes to finally cutting them. Next, use the back of a fork to press down gently into the middle of each square, to make line patterns with the tines of the fork.

Bake for 30–35 minutes, rotating the tray halfway through cooking, until the dough is golden brown, and the edges are looking crispy. Remove from the oven and allow to cool completely before cutting.

Arrange the ma'amoul squares on a serving platter, dust generously with icing sugar and serve.

*Pictured on page 318, middle right*

# No-churn strawberry ice cream
## *Bouza*

After supper in Haifa one night on our travels, Sami stopped by an ice cream shop for something sweet. Opting for what Tara thought the least delicious option – the hallucinogenic-pink bubblegum-flavoured ice cream – Sami proceeded to skip happily down memory lane, remembering the holiday treats of his childhood. Palestinian ice cream has a distinct texture, thanks to the mastic (see page 338) in the mix. It's unusual to those who haven't had it before, but the taste – that of liquorice or anise – is soon acquired. Mastic is available in Middle Eastern shops or online.

*Keeping notes:* Once made, this keeps in the freezer for a good 2 weeks.

---

Place half the strawberries in a food processor, along with the lemon juice and 1 tablespoon of sugar. Blitz for a minute, until very smooth, then set aside.

Cut the rest of the strawberries into 1cm cubes and place in a medium bowl. Add 4 tablespoons of the strawberry sauce to the bowl, mix to combine, and keep in the fridge until ready to serve.

Put the mastic and the remaining 1½ teaspoons of sugar into a spice grinder (or pestle and mortar, as an alternative). Grind for a few seconds, to form a fine powder, then transfer to the bowl of a free-standing mixer with the whisk attachment in place. Add the cream, condensed milk and orange blossom water, then whisk on a high speed for 2–3 minutes, until the mixture is airy and creamy and soft peaks form. Pour the rest of the strawberry sauce into the whipped cream and then, by hand, gently swirl it through, taking care not to overmix. Spoon the mixture into a roughly 1 litre airtight container and freeze for at least 6 hours, or overnight.

Serve straight from the freezer. Scoop the ice cream into individual glasses or bowls. Spoon over the chopped strawberries and sprinkle with the sumac, if using.

### Serves eight

400g strawberries, hulled
1 tbsp lemon juice
1½ tbsp caster sugar
1 tsp Arabic mastic gum
  (see page 338)
300ml double cream
120g condensed milk
1½ tsp orange blossom water
2 tsp sumac (optional)

# Orange blossom, honey and baklava semi-freddo

This is a real show-stopper of a dessert. There are a few elements to it but none of them are complicated. The only thing to keep an eye on is timing, as the bubbling syrup needs to be added to the eggs halfway through their being whisked. Just follow the instructions and you'll be in for a treat which sees the best part of baklava – the sticky, nutty filling – layered through a simple semi-freddo.

*Getting ahead:* This keeps well for up to 2 weeks in the freezer so you can make the whole thing well in advance.

---

Lightly grease and line the base and sides of a 20 x 10cm loaf tin. Set aside until ready to use.

First make the semi-freddo. Put the cream into the bowl of a free-standing mixer with the whisk attachment in place. Beat on a medium-high speed for about 3 minutes, or until medium peaks form. Transfer to a separate bowl and keep in the fridge until needed. Wash the bowl and whisk and return them to the mixer: they need to be clean and ready to whisk the eggs halfway through the next stage.

Put the sugar, honey and 2 tablespoons of water into a small saucepan and place on a medium-high heat. Bring to the boil, then leave to simmer for 5–6 minutes, stirring often, until bubbles form and the mixture becomes foamy and glossy. After 3 minutes, add the egg and egg yolks to the bowl of the free-standing mixer. Beat on a medium-high speed for about 3 minutes, until pale and creamy. Reduce the speed to medium-low and slowly pour in the bubbling hot syrup, which will have been cooking for 5–6 minutes by now. Once the syrup is completely incorporated, increase the speed to medium-high and continue to beat for about 6 minutes, until the mixture is pale and glossy and the bowl is cool to touch. Using a spatula, fold in the orange blossom water and whipped cream until just combined. Put half the mixture into the prepared tin – about 200g – and smooth out the top. Wrap with baking parchment and freeze for at least 2 hours. Refrigerate the other half of the mixture in a separate bowl until needed.

To make the baklava filling, put the pistachios and walnuts into the bowl of a food processor and blitz roughly until crumbled. Transfer to a small bowl and stir in the spices, flaked salt, honey and orange blossom water. Once the semi-freddo has been in the freezer for 2 hours, gently top it with the baklava filling. Spread it out so that the top is covered, without pushing it in. Remove the reserved semi-freddo from the fridge, give it a good whisk by hand, then pour it over the baklava filling. Spread it out until smooth, then wrap the pan with baking parchment and freeze overnight.

To make the salsa, if using, use a small, sharp knife to trim the tops and tails off the oranges. Cut down along their round curves, removing the skin and white pith. Release the segments by slicing between the membranes and transfer them to a bowl, discarding any pips and squeezing what's left of the membranes to release any liquid into the bowl. Just before serving, add the pomegranate seeds and mint leaves to the salsa and then either spoon it in a line along the top of the semi-freddo or serve alongside.

## Serves six to eight

### Semi-freddo
250ml double cream
70g caster sugar
40g mild runny honey
3 eggs (crack one open, then separate the yolk and white of the other two: you only need the yolks of these)
1½ tbsp orange blossom water

### Baklava filling
90g pistachio kernels, toasted (see page 339)
60g walnut kernels, toasted (see page 339)
1 tsp ground cinnamon
10 cardamom pods, shells crushed and then discarded, seeds finely ground in a pestle and mortar (or ¾ tsp ground cardamom)
¼ tsp flaked sea salt
2½ tbsp mild runny honey
1 tbsp orange blossom water

### Orange salsa (optional)
2 oranges
80g pomegranate seeds, from about 1 pomegranate
5g mint leaves, roughly torn

# Chocolate and qahwa flour-free torte

Qahwa means 'coffee' in Arabic. Arabic coffee tends to be very strong and intense, drunk in small quantities and usually paired with something sweet like a date or two. The Arabic coffee theme plays a strong note here, making this torte incredibly rich and intense. You only need a thin slice, served with some crème fraîche, vanilla ice cream or plain yoghurt alongside. No need for an extra caffeine shot.

*Keeping notes:* Once baked, this keeps for up to 3 days in the fridge.

*Ingredients note:* We've used two types of dark cooking chocolate: one with 70 per cent cocoa solids and the other (which can be called semi-sweet chocolate) with roughly 50 per cent cocoa solids. You can use all 70 per cent if you need to, but this will make it even more intense.

*Playing around:* The saffron can be dropped, if this is not to your liking, and replaced with a pinch of cinnamon. Again with the rose water, reduce or remove it (or replace it with orange blossom water, for example, or a teaspoon of vanilla extract) if you prefer.

## Serves ten to twelve

220g unsalted butter, at room temperature, cut into 1cm dice, plus extra for greasing
200g dark cooking chocolate (50% cocoa solids), broken into roughly 1cm pieces
50g dark cooking chocolate (70% cocoa solids), broken into roughly 1cm pieces
2 tbsp instant espresso powder (also known as espresso instant coffee), plus ½ tsp to garnish
⅛ tsp saffron threads, roughly crushed in a pestle and mortar (optional)
10 cardamom pods, shells discarded and seeds finely crushed in a pestle and mortar (or ¾ tsp ground cardamom)
270g caster sugar
1 tbsp rose water
5 eggs
¼ tsp flaked sea salt
2 tsp cocoa powder, to garnish
Vanilla ice cream, crème fraîche or plain yoghurt, to serve

Preheat the oven to 170°C fan. Grease and line the base and sides of a 23cm springform cake tin and set aside.

Place the butter and both types of chocolate in a large heatproof bowl. Put the espresso powder, saffron (if using), cardamom, sugar, rose water and 2 tablespoons of water into a small saucepan and place on a medium-high heat. Bring to the boil, stirring continuously – this should take about 5 minutes – then pour this over the chocolate and butter. Stir everything together until the chocolate has melted and you are left with a thick but pourable sauce.

Separate 3 of the eggs, setting the whites to one side. One at a time, add the yolks and the remaining 2 whole eggs to the chocolate sauce, stirring to incorporate.

Put the reserved 3 egg whites and the flaked salt into a free-standing mixer with the whisk attachment in place. Beat on a medium speed for about 2 minutes, until medium-firm peaks form. In two batches, gently fold the egg whites into the chocolate until just incorporated, taking care not to overmix.

Pour the mixture into the prepared tin and bake for about 50 minutes, or until a skewer inserted in the centre comes out clean. Leave to cool for about an hour, then refrigerate for at least 2 hours, or preferably overnight. Remove the torte from the fridge at least half an hour before serving: you want it to be room temperature. Transfer the torte out of the tin on to a serving platter.

Mix together the cocoa and ½ a teaspoon of espresso powder in a small bowl. Using a fine-mesh sieve, sprinkle liberally and evenly over the torte, to coat. Serve with a spoonful of ice cream, crème fraîche or plain yoghurt alongside.

# Palestinian Bakewell tart
## *Al mabroushy*

This is our take on the Bakewell tart. Kids love these, adults love these, Mr Kipling himself would have loved these, we're sure! You'll make more jam than you need here but it's lovely to have around to spread on toast. Drizzled with tahini it's the Palestinian equivalent of peanut butter and jam.

*Getting ahead:* The jam can be made up to a month ahead.

*Keeping notes:* Once baked, these keep well in a sealed container for up to 3 days.

*Shortcut:* Start with shop-bought strawberry jam, if you like: just stir in the rose water and take it from there. You'll need 250 grams.

**Makes 12 bars**

**Rose jam**
600g strawberries, hulled and
  quartered
250g preserving sugar (also known
  as jam sugar)
¼ tsp flaked sea salt
3 tbsp lemon juice
1½ tbsp rose water

**Shortbread base**
165g plain flour
75g icing sugar, plus 15g extra
  for sprinkling (optional)
¼ tsp flaked sea salt
1 lemon: finely grate the zest to
  get 2 tsp
150g unsalted butter, fridge-cold,
  cut into 1cm dice, plus extra
  for greasing

**Halva spread**
60g halva
1 tbsp tahini

**Shortbread topping**
25g flaked almonds
20g halva
1 tbsp sesame seeds
1½ tsp plain flour
½ tsp flaked sea salt

If making the jam, put the strawberries, sugar, salt and 1½ tablespoons of lemon juice into a medium saucepan and place on a medium-high heat. Cook for about 10 minutes, stirring often and skimming away the foam a few times, or until the sugar has completely dissolved and the strawberries are beginning to break down. Reduce the heat to medium and cook for another 25–30 minutes, or until the jam begins to thicken and become glossy. Remove from the heat, then stir in the rose water and the remaining 1½ tablespoons of lemon juice. Transfer the jam to a shallow baking dish – this allows it to cool and set more quickly – and set aside, at room temperature, for about 45 minutes, to set. Transfer to the fridge for at least an hour, to completely cool.

Preheat the oven to 175°C fan. Grease and line the base and sides of a 20cm square baking tin (which has a removable base) and set aside.

Put all the ingredients for the base into a food processor and pulse for about 15 seconds, until the mixture has the consistency of coarse breadcrumbs. Remove 60g of this – about an eighth – and keep in the fridge until needed. Press the remaining mixture into the lined baking tin, so that it evenly covers the base, and bake for about 25 minutes, or until cooked through and lightly golden. Remove from the oven and set aside to cool for about 15 minutes.

To make the halva spread, put the halva and tahini into a bowl along with 1½ tablespoons of water. Beat with a fork until smooth, then spread this evenly over the cooled shortbread base. Top this with 250g of jam – just under half – and set aside.

To make the topping, combine the 60g of set-aside shortbread mix in a bowl with the almonds, halva, sesame seeds, flour and salt. Using your hands, rub together until the consistency is that of crumble, and sprinkle this unevenly over the jam. Bake for a final 25 minutes, or until golden, then set aside for at least 1 hour, to cool. Remove from the tray and slice into 12 pieces, each about 6½ x 4½cm. Dust with icing sugar, if desired, and serve either warm or at room temperature.

*Pictured opposite, middle left*

# Sticky date and halva puddings with tahini caramel

These little puddings – our take on sticky toffee pudding – are a knockout, best eaten warm with a spoon of crème fraîche, yoghurt or soured cream alongside.

*Getting ahead:* The puddings can be made ahead and stored in a sealed container for up to 2 days. Reheat in a microwave as they are or in a hot oven, wrapped in foil. They can also be frozen, for up to 2 months.

*Shortcuts / playing around:* We love the tahini-rose caramel drizzled on top, but the puddings work well alone if you want to serve them with just the crème fraîche or yoghurt. The rose water can also be replaced by water, if you don't like the flavour or don't have a bottle open.

*Kit note:* Pudding moulds are widely available and useful to have, but, if you don't have them, a deep muffin tray with 8 moulds also works, as does a regular 12 hole muffin tray.

## Makes 8 or 12 puddings, depending on size of tin

### Date pudding
180g Medjool (or other good-quality) dates, pitted and roughly chopped (160g)
140ml boiling water
2 tbsp strong brewed coffee
½ tsp vanilla extract
¾ tsp bicarbonate of soda
75g unsalted butter, at room temperature, plus extra for greasing
150g caster sugar
2 eggs
175g self-raising flour, sifted
2½ tbsp white sesame seeds
85g halva, roughly crumbled

### Tahini caramel
2½ tbsp tahini
2 tbsp rose water (or 2 tbsp water, as an alternative)
150g caster sugar
125ml double cream, at room temperature
45g unsalted butter, at room temperature
1 tsp flaked sea salt

### To serve
About 120g crème fraîche (or yoghurt or soured cream)

Preheat the oven to 165°C fan. Liberally grease and line the base of eight 7½–8cm-wide pudding moulds with baking parchment and set aside. If using a regular muffin tin, line each mould with a paper liner.

First make the caramel. Put the tahini and rose water into a small bowl along with 2 tablespoons of water. Whisk until smooth and set aside.

Place a medium saucepan on a medium-high heat and, once hot, add 50g of the sugar: it will begin to melt as it hits the pan. Give it a stir once or twice and, once the sugar has completely melted, add another 50g of sugar. Continue in this way for 3–4 minutes, until all the sugar has been incorporated and has turned into an amber-coloured caramel. Remove from the heat, add the cream and butter and slowly whisk in: the sauce will splutter but this is normal. Return the pan to a medium-low heat, whisking to smooth out any lumps, then add the tahini-rose mixture, along with the flaked salt. Whisk until smooth and set aside.

To make the puddings, place the dates in a bowl along with the boiling water, coffee, vanilla extract and bicarbonate of soda. Mix to combine and set aside.

Put the butter and sugar into the bowl of a free-standing mixer with the paddle attachment in place (or alternatively use a hand mixer) and beat on medium speed for about 3 minutes, until pale and fluffy. Add the eggs, one at a time, beating to incorporate. Using a spatula, fold in the flour and 2 tablespoons of sesame seeds. Lastly, stir in the date mixture, along with all its liquid, as well as the halva. The mixture will be quite wet.

Spoon the mixture into the pudding moulds, filling them about two-thirds full. Bake for about 22–25 minutes – depending on what size mould or muffin tin you are using – or until a skewer inserted into the centre comes out clean. Leave to cool for 5 minutes, then, using a cloth to hold the moulds so that you don't burn your hand, slide a small knife around the outsides to loosen them. Transfer them on to a tray, then loosely cover the tray with foil to keep warm.

Just before serving, return the tahini caramel to a medium-high heat and bring to a simmer, stirring often. Place one pudding on each plate and pour over the caramel. Sprinkle over the remaining 1½ teaspoons of sesame seeds and serve, with a spoonful of crème fraîche alongside.

# Labneh cheesecake with roasted apricots, honey and cardamom

Cheesecake is not, traditionally, a dessert eaten in Palestine, but all the ingredients are: the labneh and filo, for example, the nuts and floral orange blossom. The base was Noor's idea: blitzing up the sheets of filo to make crumbs. Mixing this with the nuts calls baklava to mind. The result, we think, is distinct and special.

*Getting ahead:* If you are making your own labneh (which couldn't be easier: it just requires getting organised a day ahead), then it needs to be made 1–5 days before using. To get the 500g of labneh required, you'll need to start with 850g of Greek-style yoghurt, mixed with ⅔ teaspoon of salt (see page 48 for the recipe). The base and cheesecake are best baked the day before serving, so that it can chill in the fridge overnight. The apricots are best roasted and put on top of the cake on the day of serving. Once assembled, the cake is best eaten the same day.

*Playing around:* Rose water or vanilla extract can be used instead of the orange blossom water, if you like. If using vanilla in the filling, use 1½ teaspoons of vanilla paste or the scraped seeds of ½ a vanilla pod, in addition to the vanilla extract already there. Lots of other fruits – stone fruits or otherwise – work as well as the apricots here. Peaches, plums and cherries are also good, as are strawberries. As ever, with nuts, other nuts can be used apart from those we suggest: Brazil nuts, for example, or macadamia nuts. They both work well in any combination in the base: just keep the net weight the same.

---

Preheat the oven to 160°C fan. Grease and line the base and sides of a 23cm springform baking tin and set aside.

To make the base, lay out one sheet of filo on a clean work surface. Measure out a third of the butter – this will be used for brushing the sheets – and set the remaining 60g aside for later. Brush the sheet until well coated, then top with the second filo sheet. Continue in this fashion until all the filo and butter has been used up, finishing the last layer with a coating of butter. Transfer the filo stack to a parchment-lined baking tray and bake for about 20 minutes, or until golden and crispy. Remove from the oven and set aside to cool for 15 minutes (or longer) before breaking apart into large shards. In two batches, place the shards in a food processor and blitz for about 10 seconds, to form fine crumbs. Place in a medium bowl, then add the nuts to the processor. Blitz for about 20 seconds, until fine but not powdery. Add the nuts to the filo along with the flour, sugar, spices, flaked salt and remaining two-thirds of butter and mix to combine. Tip the mixture into the base of the lined tin and press it down firmly and evenly so that the whole base is covered. Bake for 12 minutes, or until lightly golden. Remove from the oven and set aside to cool.

*Continued overleaf*

## Serves ten to twelve

### Base
5 sheets of good-quality filo pastry (about 110g)
90g unsalted butter, melted, plus extra for greasing
40g walnut halves
60g pistachio kernels
1½ tbsp plain flour
50g caster sugar
10 cardamom pods, shells discarded and seeds finely crushed in a pestle and mortar (or ¾ tsp ground cardamom)
1 tsp ground cinnamon
¼ tsp flaked sea salt

### Filling
500g labneh (either shop-bought or 850g of Greek-style yoghurt, see headnote and page 48, if making your own)
500g ricotta
210g caster sugar
⅔ tsp flaked sea salt
5 eggs (2 whole, and 3 with yolks and whites separated: you will only be using the yolks of these)
2 tsp finely grated orange zest
1 tbsp orange blossom water
1¼ tsp vanilla extract
1½ tbsp cornflour

### Topping
75g runny honey
2 tsp orange blossom water
40ml orange juice
6 cardamom pods, shells on, seeds roughly bashed together in a pestle and mortar
350g ripe apricots, stones removed, cut into 6 wedges
A small handful of picked mint leaves, to garnish (optional)

To make the filling, clean out the food processor and add the labneh, ricotta, sugar and salt. Pulse for just a few seconds, to combine. Scrape down the sides of the bowl, then add the eggs, egg yolks (the spare whites can be saved for something else), orange zest, orange blossom water, vanilla extract and cornflour. Pulse for about 15 seconds, to combine, then pour the mixture into the cake tin. Bake for 60–70 minutes, or until the cake is beginning to take on some colour around the edges but still has a slight wobble in the middle. Remove from the oven and leave to cool at room temperature for an hour before refrigerating for at least 4 hours or (preferably) overnight.

On the day of serving, preheat the oven to 200°C fan and prepare the topping.

Put the honey, orange blossom water, orange juice and bashed cardamom pods into a small saucepan and place on a medium-high heat. Cook for 4–6 minutes, stirring often, until the mixture has reduced by half and is beginning to form a thin syrup. Spread the apricots out on a parchment-lined baking tray, on their side, and drizzle over half the syrup. Bake for about 8 minutes, turning the apricots over halfway through baking, until completely softened but still retaining their shape. Remove from the oven and set aside for about 30 minutes, until completely cool.

Just before serving (or up to 1 hour, if you want to prepare ahead), release the cake from its tin and transfer to a round serving platter. Top with the apricots – there should not be any overlap – and drizzle with the remaining syrup. The bashed cardamom pods can be used for garnish as well – they look nice – but these are not to be eaten. Scatter over the mint leaves, if using, and serve.

# Shortbread cookies
## *Ghraybeh*

**Makes about 35 cookies**

200g ghee or clarified butter (see
    page 336), at room temperature
80g icing sugar, sifted
370g plain white flour, sifted
¾ tsp salt
1½ tsp orange blossom water
1 tsp rose water
12g unsalted pistachio kernels
    (enough for one to go on each
    cookie)

Ghraybeh means 'swoon' in Arabic. Aptly, these little sugar cookies are often served at celebrations such as baptisms or weddings, when the air is thick with 'swooning'. They're a popular choice for large events for practical reasons also: the recipe scales up well, if there are many mouths to feed, and they are quick and easy to prepare. Use them for everyday baking as well: they're lovely to have around to snack on.

*Getting ahead / keeping notes:* The dough can be made up to 3 days in advance and kept in the fridge (or longer in the freezer). The cookies can also be shaped and frozen, then baked straight from frozen: they'll just need an extra minute in the oven. Once baked, the cookies keep well in an airtight container for up to 5 days.

*Playing around:* Play around with the shape and flavourings, if you like. We've gone for a thin bracelet with the ends 'cemented' together with a nut but a little round cake or a diamond also looks good. You can also stick two cookies together with any sort of jam – to create a sort of Palestinian jammy dodger. Flavour-wise, the orange blossom and rose water can be replaced with vanilla essence and lemon zest.

---

Put the ghee and icing sugar into the bowl of a free-standing mixer with the whisk attachment in place. Mix on a medium-high speed for about 4 minutes, until pale and fluffy. Replace the whisk with the paddle attachment. Add the flour, salt, orange blossom water and rose water and mix for another 3 minutes, until the dough is uniform and smooth. Using your hands, bring the dough together and shape into a ball. Place the dough in an airtight container and leave in the fridge for about an hour, to rest. You'll need to remove it from the fridge 10 minutes before you want to roll it out so that it has some malleability.

Preheat the oven to 160°C fan.

Pinch off a bit of the dough, about 20g, and roll it into a sausage: it should be about 10cm long and ½cm thick. Bring both ends together, slightly overlapping them and pressing down where the two ends meet. Press a single pistachio into the dough where the ends join and place on a tray lined with baking parchment. Repeat with the remaining dough, spacing the rings 1cm apart on the tray. You'll need two trays to fit them all. Bake for 15 minutes, until the cookies are cooked through but have not taken on too much colour. Remove from the oven and set aside until completely cool before serving.

*Pictured on page 318, top left*

# Muhallabieh with cherries and hibiscus syrup

This is basically Palestinian panna cotta – a simple set pudding – but even lighter and easier to make. Milky set puddings are traditionally served on New Year's Day as a symbol of prosperity and happiness. We can't vouch for the prosperity but they do make us happy. This takes minutes to prepare and is the perfect way to round off a meal.

*Getting ahead:* Both the puddings and the cherries can be made a day or two ahead of serving. Just keep them separately, in the fridge, and assemble when ready to serve.

*Ingredients note:* Traditionally, dried hibiscus flowers are used to make the syrup. We've played around with hibiscus tea bags, instead, as an easier-to-find alternative.

*Playing around:* Figs can be used instead of the cherries, if you like, and all sorts of nuts work as well as (or instead of) the pistachios: walnuts are particularly good. A sprinkle of desiccated coconut, flaked almonds or pomegranate seeds is also lovely.

## Serves four

50g cornflour
500ml whole milk
60g caster sugar
25g pistachio kernels, roughly chopped, to serve

### Cherries and hibiscus syrup
1 pure hibiscus tea bag
60ml boiling water
60g caster sugar
½ tsp picked thyme leaves
½ vanilla pod, seeds scraped (¼ tsp)
1 tsp lemon juice
100g cherries, cut in half and pitted

Put the cornflour into a small bowl along with 100ml of milk. Whisk to make a smooth paste and set aside.

Pour the remaining 400ml of milk into a medium saucepan along with 200ml of water and the sugar. Place on a medium heat for about 2–3 minutes, stirring a few times, until the sugar dissolves. When it starts to release steam, whisk in the cornflour paste and keep whisking for another 3 minutes, until the mixture boils and thickens and has the consistency of thick custard. Remove from the heat and set aside for 5 minutes, then pour into individual glass bowls, wine glasses or little tumblers. Cover with cling film (see page 342) and keep in the fridge for at least 3 hours, or overnight, to set.

To make the syrup, place the tea bag in a small saucepan and pour over the boiling water. Set aside for 5 minutes, to brew, then lift out the tea bag. Add the sugar, thyme, vanilla seeds and lemon juice to the pan and place on a low heat for 3 minutes, stirring a few times, to help the sugar dissolve. Add the cherries, then remove from the heat and set aside to cool.

To serve, top each milk pudding with a few pieces of cherry and about a tablespoon (or more, if you have a sweet tooth) of the syrup. Garnish with the pistachios and serve.

# The Walled Off Hotel, the separation wall, and the Balfour balls-up

The Walled Off Hotel, in Bethlehem, is a work of Banksy genius. That's what we think, anyway. Other opinions are available. We'll get to those in a bit. For now, here's the pitch.

The Walled Off is a nine-room hotel that sits in the shadow of the eight-metre-high wall that separates Israel from the Palestinian Territories. From the name of the hotel – a play on the 'Waldorf' – onwards, everything inside slightly skews reality and plays with the expectations of a typical hotel guest. Walking through the heavy red velvet curtains which hang at the entrance door, visitors feel as though they've entered some sort of colonial dystopian nightmare. Welcome to the hotel, the Walled Off boasts, with 'the worst view in the world'.

First impressions are of a space that feels incongruously old-school, embarrassingly English, unironically Empire-ish. Tea is drunk from little china cups, teapots are silver, pictures sit in large, gilded frames. The waiting staff wear waistcoats. A piano tinkles away, providing soothing background music.

Blink and look again, though, and the cracks soon appear. The cherubs floating over the piano are wearing oxygen masks. The kids on swings in the picture are flying around an Israeli military watchtower. The piano is eerily self-playing. The stuffed stag heads on the walls are not stag heads at all, but surveillance cameras.

The experience continues in the bedrooms, accessed via a secret door that looks, at first glance, like book-stacked shelves in a slightly dusty library. Frames hang on walls, empty of anything apart from a written description of the picture you'd *expect* to see in a days-of-Empire drawing room. 'Rural Landscape', says one, 'Dog', says another. A montage of pictures hangs together around a velvet sofa and chair, showing a 'Dog', a 'Naval Battle', 'Dog', 'Dog', 'Fruit', 'Amateur Watercolour Done by Friend of the Owner', 'Portrait of Race Horse', 'Two Dogs'.

The hotel's nine rooms are all very different from each other. One, the 'budget room', feels prison-like, filled with three sets of metal bunk beds, each separated by a thin mosquito curtain. Others are plusher. In the 'Banksy room', a mural shows an Israeli soldier and a Palestinian protester having a great big fluffy pillow fight. The Presidential Suite is the most lavish and provocative of all. A mural of four leopards reclining is positioned above a zebra-print sofa where padded entrails snake out of the cushions. Next to the sofa is a large Jacuzzi set in the floor of the room. A pineapple-shaped ice container sits, in attendance, ready to chill the requisite sun-downers. It's disconcertingly bling, completely incongruous and hugely thought-provoking. We think it is a little bit genius, a big bit stir-mongering, and all the more important and useful for that.

For anyone not quite getting the irony of it all, a visit to the small museum on the ground floor soon clarifies the hotel's genuine and serious perspective. The museum is small but massively hard-hitting in terms of the information packed in. The impact felt by visitors as they walk, read, listen and watch their way around the range of pictures, video footage and text is big. A three- or four-minute video at the outset, spoken in a plummy, military-style English-speaking voice, brilliantly summarises the British balls-up which kick-started this great big political, geographical conflict in the first place.

To summarise the summary (with an acknowledgement that doing so will only ever provide a reductive sweep over big events), there were two major things going on here – the Balfour Declaration of 1917 and the Second World War – and they came together eventually in the formation of the State of Israel in 1948, when Jewish survivors of Nazi persecution in Europe, desperate for a safe place to live, were granted a new homeland by the United Nations. Starting a national state for a population who had been persecuted, killed and tortured over centuries was not just an understandable necessity; it was a global imperative. The big mistake, of course, was ignoring the rights of the Palestinians who were already living there.

From the late nineteenth century and the birth of the Zionist movement, there had been calls for a Jewish homeland from Jews facing anti-Semitism in Europe. This movement was given legitimacy with the Balfour Declaration, when Arthur Balfour, the British foreign secretary at the time, stepped in with his magic wand and said, 'Look here, chaps, I know what, we can create a state for you here, the State of Israel, and you can all set up shop and be safe and well. Job done!' Or words to that effect.

The problem with this 'magic solution', of course, was that this piece of land was already home to about 700,000 Palestinians. The words issued by Balfour at the time have to be read to be believed – suggesting, as they did, that it was somehow possible to *view with favour the establishment in Palestine of a national home for the Jewish people'* at the same time as ensuring that *'nothing shall be done which may prejudice the civil and religious rights of existing non-Jewish communities in Palestine'*. The two halves of the sentence just don't fit, Arthur! A new carving appeared on the separation wall outside the hotel in 2017 to coincide with 100 years since Balfour's declaration. 'ER', it says (to be read either as a hesitant 'er' or as a more regal and reverent 'Elizabeth Regina') on one line, with a one-word 'SORRY' on the second. The great British Balfour balls-up indeed.

The hotel has its critics. Banksy – the anonymous graffiti artist – will always generate a degree of controversy but this is part of the point: to get people talking, discussing, disagreeing. The specific problem some locals have is the idea that the hotel, and the graffiti on the wall around and beyond the hotel, make art of (and therefore benefit from) the occupation. The view of some is that by making the occupation the subject of art, it somehow normalises or trivialises it, rendering it acceptable to the tourists who just come to Bethlehem to 'see the Banksy', 'see the Church of the Nativity', and then scoot back in their coach or taxi to Jerusalem, where they are staying.

The question of Banksy benefiting from the hotel is one refuted by the facts. The hotel is locally run, with forty-five staff on the payroll, and all profits from the hotel and gift shop next door are ploughed back into local community projects. The question of making Bethlehem a 'two-stop shop' has a point, but it's a reality faced by lots of places people tend to visit for, frankly, one of two reasons. Pisa, for example, has more to offer than just its Leaning Tower. Is it not incumbent upon enterprising locals in Bethlehem to give tourists reason to venture on beyond the hotel and the church: to see the refugee camps, to have somewhere to go for a drink and some food afterwards to take it all in? Getting a good meal in Bethlehem is, surprisingly, quite hard. Falafel and hummus – great, fine – but, at the time of writing, all the really tasty, interesting and fresh cooking is being done inside people's homes rather than being available to visitors through a restaurant.

The 'making art of the occupation' question is complex but our take is that, surely, when there are so many issues in the world – where to start? – it's better to be one being talked about than one getting no air time at all. If art helps get people to look at (and therefore think about, talk about and tell people about) the separation wall, for example, is this really such a bad thing?

Next door to the hotel, for example, sits the 'Wall Mart' shop. In it, Tara buys three T-shirts for her kids to wear back home in London. Each has an image of Banksy's Bethlehem-based art: a young girl floating upwards, holding on to a bunch of balloons; a donkey having its papers checked by an armed soldier; a masked rioter throwing, not a Molotov cocktail, but a bunch of flowers. Does this make Tara an 'occupation tourist', making light of what she has seen by a 'been there, done that, got the T-shirt' attitude? Or does it mean that her six- and ten-year-old kids are now wearing them in south London and, as an absolutely direct result, knowing about Banksy and the wall, talking to their little friends about the situation and occupation? On one hand these souvenirs are all too easy, too neat: the fridge magnet, the tote bag. But the questions and chats really do follow. 'Do donkeys need passports in Palestine?' Tara hears her daughter's friend ask. 'Why can't the girl just walk around the wall?' asks another. Getting people talking, getting kids asking questions: it's a really important part of the process of making change happen.

# Glossary: the pantry and politics of Palestine

Two notes. First, on content. The words in our glossary cover a lot of ground, all the way from the pantry to the politics of Palestine. When it comes to the politics, any attempt to compress very involved subjects down to just a line or two is, clearly, only ever going to be partial. The aim of this glossary, then, is to quickly and briefly inform: it does not do justice to the amount that can be said, from all perspectives, on all the various matters.

Second: on spelling. When Arabic words are transcribed into English, they are written out phonetically. This can lead to a lot of different ways to spell the same thing: pitta or pita, for example; hummous or humous or hummus or hommos! We have chosen the spelling which makes most sense to us and then stuck to it throughout.

**ADHA** Adha means 'pouring' or 'spilling' in Arabic. A bit like tarka in Indian cuisine or the Turkish kızgın tereyağı, it's poured over a dish just before serving, to bring a final layer of flavour, aroma and texture. Adha is made from a combination of garlic, spices and fresh herbs which are brought to the point of sizzle in a little bit of butter, oil or ghee. It can be drizzled over all sorts of dishes – stews, soups or dips, for example – so make more of it than you need. It keeps well in a sealed container at room temperature for up to a week.

**AKKAWI CHEESE** Originating from the port city of Akka, Akkawi is a slightly salty semi-hard cheese. It can be eaten either as it is – for breakfast or added to salads, as you would feta – or used in the making of sweet knafeh (see page 302), where the salty cheese contrasts so well with the sugar-syrup-drenched pastry. Before being used in a sweet dish like this, the cheese needs to be soaked in several changes of cold water. It's widely available in Middle Eastern shops, but, if you can't get hold of any, a mixture of firm mozzarella, grated, and ricotta makes a good alternative. The ratio, if you are doing this, should be two-thirds mozzarella to one-third ricotta. In a savoury context, substituting feta also works. See also **jibneh baida** and **Nabulsi cheese**.

**AKKOUB** Akkoub is the Arabic name for the *Gundelia* plant, from the daisy family, which is native to the wild hills and mountains of the eastern Mediterranean and the Middle East. The vegetable (also known as tumbleweed), with its spiny leaves and prickly thistles, is hard to get outside the area, so it's not an ingredient used in *Falastin*. Still, it's an important part of Palestinian village cuisine, added to stews or salads or pickled, once its spiny leaves and thistles have been removed.

**ALEPPO CHILLI FLAKES** Named after the Syrian city of Aleppo, these dried chilli flakes have a medium heat and sweet aroma, similar to the Turkish chilli flakes, pul biber. Aleppo flakes can be sprinkled fairly liberally over all sorts of dishes. They work particularly well with eggs and are great, also, added to a bit of melted butter or heated oil which is then drizzled over a stew or soup. If you can't get hold of any, just substitute regular chilli flakes: the hotter they are, the less you'll need.

**ALLSPICE** Allspice is an essential spice in the Palestinian pantry (as well as throughout the Levant), used in both a savoury and a sweet context. It's made from the dried, unripe berries of the *Pimenta dioica* tree. Despite its Latin name, it's not related to either black pepper or capsicums. It's called 'allspice' because of its ability to conjure up the flavours of many other popular spices: cinnamon and cloves, bay and black pepper, mace and hints of nutmeg. The berries are brown-green when picked and turn to a reddish-brown when dried.

**ANISEED** Aniseed is a versatile spice which can be used in a sweet or savoury context. The small, pale brown seeds, which smell and taste sweet, are used either whole or ground in a range of cakes, custards and cookies (see the ma'amoul recipe, page 310) – as well as, for a savoury example, fish stew. The flavour has warming notes of liquorice, star anise and fennel. Anethole is the principal essential oil and it's this which gives aniseed its distinct taste. It greets you head-on every time you have a sip of drinks such as the Greek ouzo, French pastis, Lebanese raki and Turkish arak.

**AREAS A, B AND C** These are the three areas that the West Bank is divided into. Each area has a different set-up in terms of who leads on the governance, administration and civil and security control in the area. Area A (18 per cent of the West Bank) is under Palestinian Authority (PA) control. Area B (about 22 per cent) is shared-responsibility: the PA is responsible for civil administration and Israeli jurisdiction covers security control. Area C (at about 60 per cent, the largest chunk of land) is under full Israeli civil and security control. When the plan was written up in 1993 as part of the Oslo Accords, the measure was meant to be an interim one, with full Palestinian governance achieved by 1999. Twenty years on, the division of land into areas A, B and C is still in place.

**AUBERGINES: how to char** The more you char your aubergines, the smokier the flesh, and the better your m'tabbal (see page 82), grilled aubergine and lemon soup (see page 152) and burnt aubergine and tomato salsa (see page 110) will taste. Unless you don't mind your whole house smelling of burnt aubergines, ventilation is key. Open the windows, open the door, put on the ventilator! We char our aubergines in one of two ways. The first, if you have a gas flame on an open stove top (as opposed to an induction hob) is to put one aubergine over each gas ring, switch the flame on high and leave it there for 15–20 minutes, turning halfway through with long tongs so that all sides get charred. The advantage of doing this is that it is a really quick and very effective way of getting the flesh smoky. The disadvantage is that it can cause a bit of a mess on your stove top if the aubergines leak once they've been turned and their skin gets pierced. This mess can either be cleaned up with a bit of elbow grease or minimised in the first place if you cover your stove top with aluminium foil. Make holes in the foil for the gas rings to pop through and then proceed. If you have an induction hob you'll need to heat up a chargrill pan until it is very hot – sit it on a high heat for at least 5 minutes, until smoking – then add the aubergines directly to the pan. Pierce them a few times with a sharp knife before doing so. This method takes longer than the open-flame option – around 35 or 40 minutes, again turning throughout with long tongs so that all sides get charred – but you will get the same result. At the end of the 40 minutes, transfer the aubergines to a foil-lined tray and place in a hot oven (220°C) for a final 10 minutes. Once charred (whether on a gas ring or hob), place the aubergines in a colander. Once cool enough to handle, slit them open to scoop out the flesh and place in a clean colander. Don't worry if some of the charred skin sticks to the flesh: this all adds to the smoky flavour. Set aside for an hour or so (or overnight), over a bowl, to drain. You're then all set for the smokiest of all smoky spreads, soups and salsas.

**AUBERGINES: to salt or not to salt** Opinion divides on whether or not aubergines should be salted (to release their bitterness) before cooking. For us it's more about whether we want moisture in the aubergines before cooking (rather than it being about bitterness, which we rarely find to be an issue these days). Our policy is to salt and drain when we are frying aubergine – getting rid of the moisture in the aubergine makes sense before it goes into hot oil – but not when we are roasting cubes or wedges of aubergine. In an oven, the steam generated by a bit of moisture trapped in the aubergine helps it cook for a long time without drying out.

**BAHARAT** Baharat translates literally from the Arabic as 'spices'. The combination of spices in a particular blend depends on what is championed by each region (and within each household in each region!), so no single flavour tends to dominate. Generally, though, it's an aromatic, warm spice made up of a combination of black peppercorns, coriander seeds, cinnamon, cloves, **allspice**, cumin, **cardamom** and nutmeg. It brings a sweet depth and flavour to all sorts of savoury and sweet dishes. It's widely available to buy, but if you want to make your own, place the following spices in a spice grinder or a pestle and mortar and grind until a fine powder is formed: 1 tsp black peppercorns, 1 tsp coriander seeds, 1 small cinnamon stick, ½ tsp whole cloves, ½ tsp ground allspice, 2 tsp cumin seeds, 1 tsp cardamom pods, ¼ tsp ground nutmeg. Store in an airtight container, where it will keep for 2 months.

**BALADI** Translated literally, 'balad' means 'village', 'country' or 'land'. The word conjures up more than that, though: it encapsulates the deep roots Palestinians have in their land and their feelings towards what grows out of it. The 'i' in 'baladi' makes it 'my': '*my* village', '*my* country', '*my* land'.

**BDS** This stands for 'Boycott, Divestment and Sanctions'. The movement began in 2005, when a coalition of 170 Palestinian civil society groups issued a call for 'people of conscience' to boycott (Israeli goods, universities and cultural institutions), divest (from companies which provide goods and equipment to Israel) and support the application of sanctions by other countries on Israel. The movement elicits strongly opposing opinions – those who think it does as much harm as it does good – from both Palestinian and Israeli individuals and groups.

**BESARA** Besara is somewhere between a soup and a thick, warm dip. The main ingredient is broad beans, pointing to its origins in Egypt before it spread to other Levantine countries. In Palestine, the herbs in the Egyptian version – coriander and parsley – are matched by Palestine's flavour-packed dried leaf, **molokhieh**.

Wherever it's made, a mixture of fried onion, chilli, lemon and olive oil is always spooned on top.

**CARDAMOM** Cardamom brings its distinctive flavour and aromatic sweetness to all sorts of cakes, desserts and sweets. It works as well in a savoury context and we've also added some to our breakfast granola (see page 25). Throughout the Levant, cardamom pods are also often placed in the spouts of coffee pots to flavour the hot liquid as it is poured. The aroma is intense (a result of no less than twenty-five essential oils being present in the seeds), so a little bit goes a long way. If a recipe calls for ground cardamom you can either source this ready-ground or make your own. To make your own, bash open the pods in a pestle and mortar and discard the dry outer husks. Transfer the inner small black seeds to a spice or coffee grinder (or return them to the pestle and mortar) and grind until smooth. It might seem like a lot of work but the result is a real flavour bomb – pungent, smoky, lemony and floral – so it's well worth doing.

**CHICKPEAS** See **pulses**.

**CLARIFIED BUTTER** Also known as ghee or samneh (or samna) in Arabic, clarified butter is the pure fat left over from when butter has been separated from its milk solids. It has a long shelf life so was traditionally a key part of the Palestinian pantry (see **mooneh**). Nowadays, cooks are more likely to reach for regular butter, olive oil or other vegetable oils as a healthier cooking fat.

**DATE SYRUP** Date syrup (also known as date molasses) is the dark, sticky sweet syrup made from cooking down dates. A little bit goes a long way in both sweet and savoury cooking. A teaspoon added to a meatball mixture or in a stew, for example, brings a real depth of sweet flavour. It's wonderful, also, paired with **tahini**, to be either spread on toast or spooned over yoghurt (see page 25) in the morning. On toast, it's the equivalent of the classic peanut butter and jam combination.

**DILL SEEDS** Dill seeds smell like caraway, taste like **aniseed** and bring a spicy warmth to dishes. They pair naturally with acidity – lemon juice, for example – and are ideal for pickling vegetables. Dill seeds (and dill weed) are widely used in Gazan cuisine, playing a leading role in Gaza's signature spicy tomato salad dagga, for example (see page 194). You can buy dill seeds online if you can't find them in a shop, but, otherwise, celery seeds or caraway seeds can be used as an alternative.

The seeds should be crushed in a pestle and mortar before being used in order to release their fragrance.

**DRIED IRANIAN LIMES** Small and rock-hard, these are lovely added to all sorts of soups and stews or a rice dish like maqlubeh (see page 264), infusing them with their distinct and pungent sweet-sharp aroma. Puncture them here and there with the tip of a knife before adding them to a dish, and remove them before serving: their job is to infuse rather than to be eaten.

**EGYPTIAN RICE** This looks like short-grain rice but is creamier and holds its shape more. Because of this, it works particularly well in long and slow-cooked dishes and in dishes where vegetables or vine leaves are stuffed. It's fairly easy to source, in well-stocked supermarkets or specialist stores, but can be replaced by pudding or risotto rice, if need be.

**FALAFEL SCOOP** Invest in one of these if you are planning to make a lot of falafel – they're not expensive – but, otherwise, a small ice cream scoop or just your hands can be used as an alternative to shape the falafel mix. See page 62 for the recipe.

**FATTEH** Fatteh or fatta means 'crushed' or 'crumbled' or 'broken into pieces' in Arabic. It describes a type of food preparation practised throughout the Levant and North Africa, where a piece of flatbread is torn into chunks and then layered into a dish. If the bread is fresh or untoasted, it will soak up the juices or sauce in a dish and collapse happily in with the other ingredients. If the pieces of bread are toasted they will retain their shape and crunch and can be used instead of a fork to scoop things up with and eat.

**FAVA BEANS** See **pulses**.

**FREEKEH** Freekeh is a Middle Eastern wholegrain or cracked wheat. The wholegrain wheat is just called freekeh. The cracked version sometimes goes by the name 'greenwheat'. Either way, the wheat is harvested before it is fully ripe and then roasted over an open fire so as to burn off the husks. This gives the wheat a wonderfully smoky and nutty flavour. It's widely available in well-stocked supermarkets, in specialist stores, health-food shops and online.

**GLUTEN-FREE** The 'bulgur vs. quinoa' debate is one that Sami and Tara had many times during the making of *Falastin*. 'Please! Quinoa is just *not* an ingredient used in Palestine,' Sami would point out, entirely reasonably, when discussing a dish such as the baked fish kubbeh (page 201). 'But I don't eat bulgur wheat,' Tara would respond, entirely selfishly, 'and it does work here!' For all the tussles over traditional vs. non-traditional ingredients and twists, the line was very firmly drawn, by Sami, at quinoa! While noting, therefore, that quinoa is absolutely not used in traditional Palestinian kitchens, Tara would like to whisper that the bulgur is often very happy to be replaced with the gluten-free alternative, if you are looking for one. Use the same amount of white quinoa as bulgur, throw it into boiling water for 9 minutes, then refresh under cold running water. In the case of that kubbeh on page 201, when mixing the cooked quinoa with the fish, add a couple of tablespoons of gram flour to the mix, to help everything bind together.

**GREEN LINE** The Green Line is the generally recognised boundary or dividing line between Israel and the West Bank. It is properly referred to as the 1949 Armistice line: the ceasefire line of 1949. The exact borders of Israel and a future Palestinian state are subject to negotiation between the two parties. The Palestinians want a complete end to the Israeli occupation of the West Bank, Gaza Strip and East Jerusalem, and use the phrase to mean a return to the pre-4th June 1967 borders.

**HARISSA** (Not to be confused with harisa – see page 309 – the sugar-syrup-soaked semolina cake popular all over the Middle East!) We use this spicy North African chilli paste as an alternative to shatta if we don't have a batch ready-made. Rose harissa (we like the one produced by Belazu) is what we tend to use: the addition of the rose petals softens and sweetens the kick from the chilli.

**HAWADER** Roughly translated as 'ready to eat', this is the practice of batch cooking or preparing food in advance that can then sit in the freezer or in jars on the shelf, ready to be served after heating through if needed. Hawader plays a big role in the seemingly effortless hospitality of Palestinian home cooks. If the freezer is full of ready-made kubbeh or fatayer, for example, food can always appear – as if by magic! – whenever someone turns up unexpectedly.

**JAMEED** Jameed, like **kishek**, is a dried and fermented yoghurt. There are various ways to preserve and ferment yoghurt: in the case of jameed, the yoghurt is shaped into balls and dried in the sun. This method of preservation made its way into Palestine via the Bedouins of Jordan.

**JIBNEH BAIDA** This is an umbrella term for the semi-hard, rindless, white, salt-brined Arabic cheeses which appear throughout the Middle East. They appear under various different names, depending on where they come from: jibneh Nabulsi from the city of Nablus, for example, or jibneh Akkawi from the port city of Akka. Their flavour is always pronounced, but varies according to the milk they are made from (goat's, ewe's, sheep's, cow's) and the length and strength of the salt brine. These cheeses need to be soaked in water before using, to pull back on some of their saltiness.

**JUTE MALLOW** See **molokhieh**.

**KATAIFI PASTRY** Popular across the Levant (as well as Turkey and Greece), kataifi consists of long, thin strands of shredded filo pastry. It's what is used to make our Knafeh Nabulseyeh on page 302. Being in strands makes it easy for the pastry to get wrapped around or layered with various sweet or savoury fillings before being baked or fried. This vermicelli-like pastry loves being drenched in melted butter, oil or sugar syrup and develops a wonderfully light crunch when cooked. It's the not the easiest of ingredients to find but it should be stocked in the frozen section of a good Greek, Arab or Turkish grocer.

**KISHEK** Kishek (also known as **jameed**) are preserved discs of fermented yoghurt and (though not always) wheat. The discs are made at the end of summer in Palestine (and throughout the Levant), just after the wheat harvest. First, bulgur is made by boiling, drying and crushing the wheat grain. This is then mixed with yoghurt, spread out on a tray and set aside until all the liquid has been absorbed into the grain. The kishek grains are then spread out on cloths and left to dry in the sun. Finally, these are rubbed together to produce a powder. This can then be added to soups and stews to both thicken them and bring a deep flavour. There are also wheat-free versions of kishek. These are just blocks of dried, fermented yoghurt which are crushed and then reconstituted. With or without the wheat, kishek has a deep umami flavour similar to what you'd find in a mature cheese such as tart feta or Parmesan. The taste is totally distinctive, so it's worth hunting down in Middle Eastern grocers, specialist stores or online. If you can't get it you can make a (very!) vague approximation by mixing together some sour cream or crème fraîche along with some grated Parmesan and a few very finely chopped tinned anchovies.

**LABNEH** This is an Arabic cheese made by hanging yoghurt (with salt, to draw out the liquid) until it's drained of all its liquid: the longer it is left to drain, the drier and firmer it becomes. If you are rushed you can bring it about in 6 hours: you'll just need to squeeze the ball of yoghurt a few times during that time to help the process along. Ideally, it will hang for a couple of days. Once made, it can either be spread as it is on toast, sprinkled with **za'atar** or **sumac** and drizzled with olive oil, or rolled into balls which are then preserved in oil. It keeps in the fridge for up to 2 weeks (if not preserved in oil) or, as balls covered in oil, for about 2 months. Labneh can be made with either a combination of goat's (or sheep's or ewe's yoghurt) and Greek-style yoghurt or, for a less 'tangy' version, just Greek-style yoghurt. For the recipe, to get the ratio of yoghurt to salt, see page 48.

**MAFTOUL** Also known as Palestinian couscous or giant couscous, maftoul is made from sun-dried and cracked bulgur wheat which is then hand-rolled in flour. The little balls of pasta – like couscous, but larger – are then steamed and sun-dried. Maftoul is added to soups or stews, to bulk them out, or served as it is, itself bulked out with chickpeas, alongside a piece of meat or fish. It's fairly easy to get hold of in well-stocked supermarkets but, as an alternative, fregola can be used instead.

**MAHASHI** The word mahashi or mahsi refers to stuffed food. The stuffing being the 'hashwa' (derived from the same word). This can be anything from carrots, cucumbers, courgettes and potatoes (which need to be cored), to cabbage and vine leaves (which will be rolled). Mahashi also refers to stuffed meat, from a whole lamb (or any part of the animal) to a whole chicken, which will be stuffed as it is. The stuffing can vary – a mixture of rice and meat is common, as is a mix of spiced ground meat, onion and pine nuts, or a vegetarian stuffing of bulgur, tomatoes and herbs – as can the cooking methods and sauces. Other mahashi include fish, seafood, eggs and various parts of lamb, sheep or cow.

**MAHLEB** This spice, which has a nutty, slightly bitter-almond flavour, is made from grinding the kernel of the black St Lucia cherry. The kernels are sold whole or ground to use in bread and sweet baking. It's in our ma'amoul bars, but is lovely to have around for general use. Try adding a tiny bit to any shortbread biscuits you are making, or adding it to sugar syrups for a fruit salad, or use it to flavour whipped cream. A tiny drop of almond essence can be used as an alternative, if you are looking for one.

**MANAKRA** Also known as miqwarah or miqwar, these are used to core out vegetables. They are small, long thin knives which have a thin, semi-circular serrated blade. This blade makes easy work of removing the flesh from inside a vegetable. A swivel peeler (or a power drill, as we discovered over lunch one day when cooking and eating in a garage in a car park in Jerusalem!) works well as an (non-health-and-safety-compliant) alternative.

**MANSAF** This is a stew of lamb braised in **kishek**, the fermented goat's yoghurt. It hails from the Levant: it originated from Hebron, is the national dish of Jordan and is a typical Bedouin dish. It's traditionally served at celebratory meals in Palestine: weddings and major feasts. The lamb and its tangy sauce tend to be assembled on a large serving platter, with buttery rice and paper-thin flatbread called shhrak layered in with the lamb, and a garnish of toasted nuts, such as pine nuts and almonds. Guests either pull at the bread, using this in lieu of crockery to scoop up and eat the lamb and rice, or else spoon some on to their own plate to eat with a fork.

**MASHWI** or mashawi means 'grilled', referring to grilled food which uses skewered meats (such as shuqaf, hunks of lamb), kofta (ground lamb) or shish taouk (marinated chicken). These (along with **mezzeh** dishes) are the types of food more often served in restaurants in Palestine (as opposed to the more labour-intensive 'tabeekh' cooking, usually confined to the home.

**MASTIC GUM** Mastic is a resin obtained from the mastic tree, found on the island of Chios in Greece. It is often called Arabic gum or Yemen gum (but not gum Arabic, which does not have the same taste). Mastic starts life as a sap which is then sun-dried into pieces of brittle and translucent resin. When chewed, this becomes a bright white and opaque gum. The taste is initially bitter, then transforms into something pine or cedar-like. Added to things like ice cream, jams, custards or other set puddings, mastic brings its distinct, rich flavour – a combination of fennel, **aniseed** and mint – and almost rubbery texture. In Gaza, it is also added to soups. It is available in health-food shops and online. There is no alternative!

**MAZA / MEZZEH** This refers to the large number of small plates of salads, pickles, cured meats and other appetisers that everyone can help themselves to at an informal meal or gathering. They are often served at room temperature, meaning that making them ahead works well.

**MOLOKHIEH** Also known as jute leaves or jute mallow, molokhieh is a dark green leaf, a bit like spinach. The leaves are used widely throughout the Levantine region, added to soups and stews or cooked along with meat. It tastes rather bitter before it gets cooked. A bit like okra, it has a slightly gelatinous consistency which, when blitzed, thickens things up. The molokhieh plant is available fresh in the summer, and dried or frozen for the rest of the year. Outside Palestine, bags of frozen molokhieh are available in Middle Eastern supermarkets. If you can't get hold of any, an approximation can be made by cooking together spinach and thinly sliced okra. The result, when blitzed together, is not the exact flavour of molokhieh but will get you somewhere close in terms of texture.

**MOONEH** Mooneh translates literally as 'pantry essential items': things like rice, flour, grains and sugar that always need to be well stocked, as they are used so much in the kitchen. It means more than this, though, referring to the whole process of preparing food well in advance of when it is going to be used: pickling, preserving, jamming, fermenting and so forth. This is done as a way to make certain seasonal foods available all year round, and also allows the cook to make the most of a particular ingredient when it is abundant at a certain time of the year. This sort of mooneh, where the focus is on preserving food, is often prepared in groups – mooneh gatherings – when circles of women come together to sterilise glasses, make brines, roll **labneh**, pickle vegetables, stack vine leaves, make jams and so on. This sort of sociable batch cooking allows for many a short cut to be taken in the making of everyday food.

**MUSAKHAN** This is one of Palestine's national dishes, where chicken is cooked and served with layers of olive-oil-drenched flatbread. It's traditionally made during the olive oil season, to test the quality of that year's crop. **Sumac** is also a key player, both in the marinade for the chicken and in the onions which are such a star of the dish. See page 247 for the recipe.

**NABULSI CHEESE** Like **Akkawi cheese**, this is a slightly salty semi-hard cheese. It's made with a mix of milks (traditionally ewe's and goat's milk, in equal proportions). Authentic Nabulsi is perfumed with **mastic** and **mahleb**. In a savoury context, it can be added to salads (grated or in cubes or slices) or eaten for breakfast with bread, as you would feta. In a sweet context, it comes

into its own in knafeh (see page 302), where its tangy flavour offsets the syrup-doused pastry. See also **jibneh baida**.

**NAFAS** Nafas means 'soul' in Arabic. In the context of the kitchen, the term translates loosely as 'soul cooking': cooking according to intuition, taste and senses. Recipes are often passed on through talking and sharing and eating together, rather than being written down, so this element plays a key role in the beauty of homemade food.

**NAKBA** This is the term used by Palestinians to refer to the displacement of more than 700,000 Palestinians and the establishment of Israel. It commemorates the end of the 1948 Arab–Israeli War, which Israelis refer to as the War of Independence. It is the name for the most traumatic collective memory for Palestinians, and literally means 'a catastrophe' or 'disaster'. In the Palestinian consciousness, this date represents the displacement of Palestinians, their separation from their land, and the subsequent ban on their return to what they see as their homes and properties.

**NUTS: how to toast** The best way to toast nuts is spread out on a baking tray in the oven, preheated to 160°C fan. Timings vary depending on the nut. Flaked almonds get 6–7 minutes, for example, pine nuts, walnuts and pistachios about 8 minutes and whole almonds 8–10. Always give them a stir halfway through cooking, or give the tray a shake. Toasting them in the oven is better than in a pan on the hob, which can result in one side of the nut taking on a lot more colour than the other. If you do need to toast in a pan, though, that's fine – just keep the heat low, stir often and remove the pan from the heat a minute or so before the nuts are ready: the residual heat in the pan means they'll continue to cook.

**OPT** This stands for 'Occupied Palestinian Territories'. The general phrase 'occupied territories' refers to East Jerusalem, the West Bank and, strictly speaking, the Golan Heights. Under international law, Israel is still the occupying power in Gaza, although it no longer has a permanent military presence there. The occupied territories are sometimes referred to as 'Palestinian land' to explain why the construction of settlements is considered illegal by the UN. Critics of the phrase, though, say that it is not accurate because, for example, the West Bank was captured from Jordan in the 1967 war. The phrase 'Palestinian Territories' refers, strictly speaking, to the areas that fall under the administration of the Palestinian Authority. They are difficult to work out, though, because of the way the West Bank was divided into complex security zones under the Oslo Accords and because of on-the-ground changes since the outbreak of violence in September 2000.

**ORANGE BLOSSOM WATER** This is a key ingredient in various Arab and Mediterranean cuisines. It is distilled water made from the macerated blossom of Seville oranges. It can be used in savoury cooking, a teaspoon or less added to a green leaf and herb filled soup, for example, but is most commonly used to flavour syrups which are then used in the making and soaking of cakes, baklava, or to fold into creams for desserts. There are plenty of good brands around: we use the Cortas brand. See also **rose water**.

**POMEGRANATE MOLASSES** This is made by cooking and reducing the juice of sour pomegranates down to form a thick, dark syrup. It has a sweet-sour flavour which pairs brilliantly with all sorts of marinades, meatballs, sauces, salads, stews, stuffed vegetables and salsas. There are lots of good brands available: we use either the Arabic brand Al-Rabih or the (more expensive and wonderfully astringent) Mymouné brand, which is made from 100% pomegranate molasses (with no added sugar).

**PRESERVED LEMONS** Finely chopping the skin of preserved lemons (and the flesh, if you like, making sure to discard the pips) is a wonderful way to add a pop of flavour to all sorts of savoury dishes. Preserving your own lemons is a lovely and easy thing to do – see Sami's book *Jerusalem*, if you have it (or you can look online), for the recipe – but here we use the thin-skinned Beldi preserved lemons produced by Belazu. They are widely available.

**PULSES: dried vs. tinned** You can use either dried or tinned pulses: the recipe will still work but the result will be different. Starting with dried pulses and soaking them overnight will bring about the 'best' results (the creamier hummus, for example, as you can use the cooking water when blitzing together the chickpeas), but starting with ready-cooked chickpeas will always, of course, have the advantage of almost-instant readiness. When it comes to fava beans, though, we often prefer using already cooked tinned beans rather than dried ones. For one thing they are easier to get hold of, but the dried ones can also cook unevenly and require peeling.

**QAHWA (or A'AHWAH)** This means 'coffee' in Arabic. It's strong and intense, often with a hint of cardamom, and is served at every gathering and social event in Palestine, before and after meals. It's usually served with something sweet – a date or a slice of baklava, for example – an idea we've run with in our chocolate and qahwa torte (see page 317).

**QIDREH** This literally means 'pot' in Arabic. Originally from Hebron, it refers to the richly spiced festive rice and meat dish (traditionally lamb, but beef or chicken can also be used) cooked in an unglazed copper pot. The pot sits over slow-burning coals either in the ground or in a stone oven. Home cooks don't cook this dish at home themselves: they fill their pot or urn and take it to a community qidreh oven where the owner of the oven takes care of the cooking. The pots are tightly sealed, so, in order not to get all mixed up, they are individually named with chalk. Before serving, the urn is dramatically cracked open and the fragrant, buttery rice pours out. Qidreh cooking can be replaced with a cast-iron Dutch oven (casserole dish) on a regular stove or oven.

**ROSE WATER** This is the distilled water from the Damascus rose, or ward jouri in Arabic. As with **orange blossom water**, it can be used to flavour milk puddings, ice creams, cakes and other sweets. A little bit goes a long way with these floral-flavoured waters. Always start with less than you need, with the knowledge that you can add more but can't take it away. There are various brands around. We use either the Cortas or the Mymouné brand, both of which we recommend.

**SAHLAB** Sahlab is a powder made from the tubers of wild orchids which grow in the mountains. It's used as a thickener in the making of many Arabic desserts – particularly set puddings – bringing about an almost elastic texture. It can also be dissolved in hot milk, along with some ground cinnamon, to make a thick, velvety, creamy drink. It can be found in most spice shops and Middle Eastern supermarkets. A (rough) approximation can be made by using 4–5 tablespoons of cornflour for each tablespoon of sahlab a recipe calls for (for every litre of milk).

**SAHTEIN!** The Arabic equivalent of 'bon appétit!', this translates as 'two healths' or 'may your health be redoubled'. The response is often 'al-albak': 'on your heart' or 'same to you'. At the end of a meal, guests might also say 'sufra daymeh': 'may your dining room be eternally blessed'. 'Ahlan wa sahlan,' the cook will often reply: 'welcome'.

**SAWANI** These are the equivalent of traybakes and roasts in Palestinian cooking: dishes baked, roasted or braised in large round baking tins where everything is tossed and cooked together.

**SEPARATION WALL** This is the physical barrier which Israel started to build during the second intifada, between Israel and the West Bank. Some parts of the barrier consist of a fence and surrounding exclusion zone; others of an 8-metre-high concrete fence. What the wall is called and how it is perceived depends very much on which side someone is standing. From the Israeli side, the wall was built as a response to suicide bombings. The number of violent attacks has reduced since the 'security wall' has gone up, confirming the legitimacy of the security concerns that gave rise to it. From the Palestinian side, the term 'security wall' is offensive, though, as it implies that all Palestinians in the West Bank are a potential source of suicide or other violent attacks. The barrier both prevents freedom of movement and, because it diverges from the **Green Line** to encompass a number of settlements, effectively annexes Palestinian areas into Israel proper. There are a number of Palestinians, therefore, who refer to the wall as an 'annexation wall', 'segregation wall' or even 'apartheid wall'.

**SHATTA** Made from either fresh or semi-dried green or red chillies, shatta is the must-have spicy condiment for all meals. Chillies are finely chopped, seasoned heavily with salt, then left to sit in the fridge for at least 3 or 4 days before being blitzed up with some cider (or white wine) vinegar and lemon juice. See page 73 for the recipe.

**STERILISING JARS** Glass jars or pots need to be sterilised before things which are going to be preserved are put into them: makdous, for example (see page 56) or **shatta**. This ensures that all bacteria and yeasts are removed from the jar so that the food remains fresh. There are various ways to do this. A water bath, for example (where the jars go into water, with their lids added separately, the water is brought to the boil and then the jars are 'cooked' for 10 minutes), or filling them with just-boiled water and then rinsing and drying with a clean tea towel. We tend to just put them into the dishwasher, though, and run it as a normal wash: it's a simple solution which works very well.

**SUMAC** Made from grinding down the dried sumac berry, this astringent, tangy spice is heavily used in Palestinian cooking. It can either be used as a seasoning – sprinkled over all sorts of egg dishes, for example, or roasted vegetables, meat or fish – or added to a batch of onions, cooked slowly for a long time before starring in a traditional dish like **musakhan**.

**TABOON OVEN** Taboon ovens are large outdoor (often communal) ovens made of stone. The heat is not sealed in with a door: instead it is the conical or domed shape of the oven which keeps the heat in. Little stones or pebbles line the base of the oven and, once these are incredibly hot, flatbread and other things are taken into the heart of the oven using a long flat paddle. Taboon bread takes on the shape of these pebbles, emerging looking like the surface of the moon with all its pockmarked indentations. We tried to re-create this in our regular kitchen in London (lining a baking tray with lots of stones from the local garden centre) and can confirm that this alternative does not work.

**TAGHMEES** Roughly translating as 'dipping', taghmees refers to one of the most common methods of eating in the Arabic world. It's not just about dipping a piece of flatbread in hummus, though – it's much more about a way of life: it's about making bread into a scoop-shape and using it like a utensil to pick up food. It's bread as an accompaniment, bread as a utensil, bread as an extension of the hands.

**TAHINI** This is the paste made from grinding sesame seeds. There are no other ingredients, so you'd be surprised how different one brand is from the next. We have a huge bias towards the creamy Lebanese, Israeli and Palestinian brands (rather than the Greek and Cypriot ones, which we find to be a bit claggy). The Arabic brands we love – Al Arz, Al Taj, as just two examples – are creamy, nutty and pourable, easily drizzled over a multitude of things. Roasted vegetables, fish and meat all love tahini sauce (see page 87), and tahini as it is can just be spread on your toast or spooned over vanilla or chocolate ice cream.

**TAMARIND** Tamarind brings its sharp, acidic, fruity, sweet-sour flavour to all sorts of soups, sauces and salsas. It first comes to a lot of Palestinians in the form of tamarind juice, sold ice-cold when the sun is out and hot. Ready-made tamarind paste is available in supermarkets, but these tend, on the whole, to be too acidic. For the best tamarind paste or water, start with a whole block of tamarind pulp and then soak and strain what you need from there.

**ZA'ATAR** This is the name for both the wild herb (a variety of oregano) that grows throughout the region and the iconic Palestinian spice mix (which is a blend of dried za'atar, whole toasted sesame seeds, **sumac** and salt). The leaves have a distinctive, savoury aroma and their flavour is complex. There's a connection to oregano and marjoram but also to cumin, lemon, sage and mint. It's lovely sprinkled over all sorts of things – eggs, leafy salads, grilled meat and fish – or else served as it is with a little bowl of olive oil alongside, for bread to be dipped into.

**ZAYTOUN** Zaytoun (which means 'olive' in Arabic) is a UK-based social enterprise which imports Palestinian olive oil, dates, almonds, **freekeh**, **za'atar** and **maftoul**. The company began in 2004, when volunteers brought back products from their travels and started selling them through their local churches, Oxfam shops, village fairs and so on. Although many of their sales are still made at a grass-roots level, you'll also see them in well-stocked greengrocers and high street shops. For more info see www.zaytoun.org.

**ZIBDIYEH** A zibdiyeh is a heavy, unglazed clay bowl. It's a basic but often precious item in a lot of kitchens throughout Palestine, particularly Gaza. It's often accompanied by a lemonwood pestle and, like a pestle and mortar, is used for crushing garlic to a creamy pulp or for grinding dill (or other) seeds. The insides of the bowl are always rough, rather than smooth, to facilitate this grinding. As well as being used to mash and mix ingredients, it's also used for cooking some dishes, either on the stove-top or in the oven, or for serving spicy dagga in (see page 194).

### A note on ingredients and cooking

Vegetable weights in brackets are net: that is, after peeling, chopping, etc. Our measurements are calculated on the basis that one tablespoon is equal to 15ml and there are three 5ml teaspoons in a tablespoon. Unless otherwise specified, olive oil is extra-virgin. Onions, garlic and shallots are peeled and garlic cloves are regular-size (rather than large). Chillies are used whole, or chopped, with their seeds left in. Salt is table salt, black pepper is freshly cracked and parsley is flat-leaf. Eggs are large, yoghurt is plain and full-fat, and tahini is from the Middle East. We use the Al Arz brand but Al Taj and Al Nakhil are also good. All recipes have been tested in a fan-assisted oven so, if cooking in a conventional oven, temperatures should be increased by 20°C. Start with the best-quality produce you can, taste your food as you go and, if ever in doubt, add a squeeze of lemon.

### A note on cling film

All efforts have been made to remove use of single-use plastic (i.e. cling film) in our recipes. Instead of using cling film, baking parchment (which can be wiped clean and used again) has been used. In a couple of instances, cling film is the only option we found to be properly effective. Biodegradable cling film is available.

# Index

## A

# Acknowledgements

Our biggest acknowledgement and thanks goes to Noor Murad. Noor was 'loaned' to us by the Ottolenghi test kitchen for *Falastin* and is the secret behind so many of the kitchen's successes. Noor: thank you! For everything you created, tweaked and fixed. 'Team Falasteeeeen' could not have been, were it not for you.

Big thanks also to everyone else in the test kitchen, who tried, tasted and tweaked our recipes: Yotam Ottolenghi, Gitai Fisher, Ixta Belfrage and Verena Lochmuller. Claudine Boulstridge, as well – thank you for testing and tasting all our recipes: your feedback, as ever, is a crucial part of the process. Huge thank yous also to Cornelia Staeubli and Noam Bar, for all your championing, support, help and advice.

Thank you to Felicity Rubinstein: you were the first person to make us feel so excited about *Falastin* and all the possibilities it contained. Thank you for your unstinting support. Thank you, also, to Mark Hutchinson.

Huge thanks to team Ebury. Thank you to Louise McKeever, for setting us safely on our way, and then so many thank yous to Lizzy Gray and Celia Palazzo, for taking over the reins and keeping us on such good track. You guys are a great team! Sarah Bennie, Di Riley and team: you are everything two nervous authors could dream of. Thank you also to Joel Rickett for supporting us and for cooking Ottolenghi recipes at home on a seemingly nightly basis. Thank you also to Alice Latham and Rae Shirvington, for championing *Falastin* to overseas publishers, and to Annie Lee and Kate Parker, for their clever eyes. Thanks also to Aaron Wehner, Lorena Jones, Emma Rudolph, Windy Dorresteyn and everyone at Ten Speed Press, as well as Kimberley Witherspoon, for support from across the seas. David Bond: thank you also for reminding us to enjoy the process.

For the design, photography and look of the book: thanks to Harry Bingham, Caz Hildebrand and Alex Merrett at Here Design. Jenny Zarins: we were so lucky to have you as our location and food photographer and travel companion: what a talented and totally gorgeous bean you are. And thank you for giving Tara a run for her money, appetite-wise. It was a dead heat, in the end! And Thomas Gonsard, thank you for the good vibes and two-week-long playlist. Wei Tang, thank you for working miracles on all the prop finding. For a remit to find props for a book we didn't want to 'prop', you really pulled it out of the bag.

Thank you also to Manal Ramadan White, Heather Masoud and everyone at Zaytoun, for being so interested and supportive at every stage. You guys bring the best olive oil to the party. High-fives and full respect also to Gemma Bell, Chris Rose, Nick Welsh, Katie Hagley, Jenny Baker, Veronica Pasteur and everyone waving the Amos flag.

During our travels in Palestine, thanks to Vivien Sansour – team Zaki Zaki! – and Leila Sansour: your continued interest and support in what we are cooking up has been a joy. To Raya Manaa (and to Yasmin Khan for the introduction) for showing and driving us around. The way you take those speed bumps is inspiring. To Wisam, Esme, Holly and all at the Walled Off Hotel in Bethlehem: thank you for generously putting us up. Thank you to everyone who shared their time, stories and food with us on our travels: in particular to Islam Abu Aouda, Baseema Barahmeh, Alla Musa, Daher Zeidani, Mirna Bamieh, Suzanne Matar, Kamel Hashlamon, Fadi Kattan, Amal and Daoud Nassar, Nasser Abufarha, Salah Abu-Ali, Heba Al-Lahham Nisrin Abuorf and Ronit Vered. Your hospitality floored us, your steadfastness inspired us, your food delighted us.

---

In addition, Sami would like to say: 'Thank you to my parents, Hassan and Na'ama. To Jeremy for always being there for me and for eating all of my cooking. Gianluca Piermaria and his family for adopting us and for feeding us all the delicious Italian food. A big thank you to Yotam, Noam and Cornelia for letting us do this book. For Ramzi Khamis: I'm forever grateful and humble. I don't even know where to start or how to thank you for saving my life, for your love, care and friendship, and of course Manal Khamis. Thanks to my *Falastin* journey partner Tara, for the olives, preserved lemons, tinned tuna, gallons of coffee and all things Zaki. Thanks to my brothers and sisters and their families, Sawsan, Kawthar, Olla, Adel, Adnan, Azam, Manal, Badria, Magdi, Amgad, Azza. Thanks to Alejandra Chavero: you are more than family to me. Big thank you to the lovely Basia, for caring and all things spiritual. Special thank you to Helen Goh, Maria Mok, Carmel Noy, Tali Levin, Dana Elemara, Danielle Postma, Dorit Mainzer, Eric Rodari. To the Kelly and Penny family, George, Maureen, Georgina and Louis, Bethany and Darren. Thanks so much to Karen Handler-Kermmerman, Adrien Von Ferscht, Lindy and all the lovely ladies at Ceramica Blue, Eric Treuille from Books for Cooks. Naser Tawil, Israel Vatkin. Big thank you also to my second family, all the amazing people working at Ottolenghi.'

Tara would also like to thank the following: Suzanna and Richard Roxburgh, Alison and Alec Chrystal, and Sophie O'Leary: thank you for stepping in and scooping up the kids so often and keeping the show on the road. Justin and Lex, my big brothers: thank you for being such happy Tupperware takers and, Lex, for eating so many more lemons than you might have liked to. An enormous thank you to Vicki Howard, for reading all my words (and honing a fair few of them). Sarit Packer, thank you! – for calling me in for NOPI chats when I was clearly so ill-suited for the job and for making me realise that working in a professional kitchen was *not* my hottest idea. Yotam, thank you so much: for taking a chance on me back in the day and for always believing in me (even when I didn't). I have so much to thank you for. Sami, thank you for taking me on your journey with you back home: it's been a huge privilege. We got there! Thank you for eating my share of all the bread, and I promise never, ever to mention quinoa again. Thank you to my crew: Winnie, Ellie, Jessie (who first introduced me to Bethlehem, over 20 years ago), Nicky, Katherine, Neache, Sala, Carenza, Annie and Ella: old friends, like bookends – extraordinary, bold, brilliant, women who I'd be lost without. Biggest hugs and high fives to Scarlett, Theo and Casper – I'm sorry the house smells so often of burnt aubergines! – and to Chris, as ever: sorry for springing the Palestine marathon on you when you thought you were just going for the culinary tour. Less running and more tequila shots from here on in ...

# FALASTIN

## THE PERFECT INTERACTIVE COMPANION TO THE BOOK

A gift from Sami and Tara
All of the recipes at your fingertips, wherever you are

**BROWSE**

Access all the recipes online from anywhere.

**SEARCH**

Find your perfect recipe by ingredient or browse through the chapters.

**FAVOURITES**

Create your own list of go-to recipes and have them at your fingertips,
whether shopping on the way home or looking for recipe ideas during a weekend away.

TO UNLOCK YOUR ACCESS VISIT BOOKS.OTTOLENGHI.CO.UK
AND ENTER YOUR UNIQUE CODE:  JETA-EB76-NBHQ-SY47

# SHOP ONLINE

We selected some of our favourite Palestinian ingredients and sourced as many as we could through Zaytoun, an organic, community-based supplier.

Go to ottolenghi.co.uk/falastin-favourites

Medjoul Dates, Rose Water, Pomegranate Molasses, Maftoul, Aleppo Chilli Flakes, Sumac, Palestinian Za'atar, Baharat, Palestinian Olive Oil, Fish Spice Mix, Tahini.

OTTOLENGHI